"All human history attests

That happiness for man—the hungry sinner!—

Since Eve ate apples, much depends on dinner."

—Lord Byron, *Don Juan*

A Literary Feast

A Literary Feast

AN ANTHOLOGY

Edited by Lilly Golden

THE ATLANTIC MONTHLY PRESS
NEW YORK

Published simultaneously in Canada
Printed in the United States of America

Library of Congress Cataloging-in-Publication Data

A Literary feast: an anthology / edited by Lilly Golden.
ISBN 0-87113-558-2
1. Gastronomy—Literary collections. 2. Dinners and dining—
Literary collections. 3. Food habits—Literary collections.
I. Golden, Lilly.
PN6071.G3L58   1993   641'.01'3—dc20   93-22856

DESIGN BY LAURA HOUGH

The Atlantic Monthly Press
841 Broadway
New York, NY 10003

FIRST PRINTING

"When the talk turns to eating, a subject of the greatest importance, only fools and sick men don't give it the attention it deserves."
                    —from *Like Water for Chocolate* by Laura Esquivel

"One of the delights of life is eating with friends; second to that is talking about eating. And, for an unsurpassed double whammy, there is talking about eating while you are eating with friends."
                    —from *Home Cooking: A Writer in the Kitchen* by Laurie Colwin

Contents

CONTENTS

CONTENTS

CONTENTS

A Literary Feast

LILLY GOLDEN

Introduction

A *Literary Feast* does not pretend to be a definitive anthology of food writing. Though some of the finest writers of gastronomy appear in these pages, they are flanked and somewhat out-numbered by writers of fiction. Each of these twenty-seven stories, essays, and excerpts from novels was chosen for its narrative excellence as well as for its culinary subject. You won't find recipes or hints on how to success-fully roast lamb. But you will read of characters ordering meals, conversing over well-laden tables, and even in a few cases preparing food—but mostly simply eating it. Although each piece can be defined by the food it features, none neglects the more profound exploration of our relationship with our repasts, shedding light beyond our gullets and into our hearts. And, best of all, these gustatory romps are recounted by extraordinary twentieth-century literary writers.

A truly splendid meal can be a multicourse epicurean extravaganza, or it can be as elemental as a peanut butter and jelly sandwich. Ingredients alone do not make a meal memorable. Much more is involved: care and fore-thought, atmosphere, company and communion, and, of course, appetite. The same is true of a good food story: a simple recounting of a meal will not suffice. All these stories, some fictional, some real, will delight and tantalize, provoke and reveal, as would any finely told tale. Food in literature is the sensual celebration of both the description and the described. To read about pleasure—and few can deny that eating is one of life's great pleasures—is not merely a vicarious thrill but a pure and direct source of joy itself.

3

Scenes of remarkable meals in the French countryside, as told by M. F. K. Fisher and Peter Mayle—stunning in both culinary accomplishment and sheer abundance—here share the same spine with stories of meals of the thoroughly American variety, including John Hersey's Thanksgiving story, "The Announcement," and Robin Hemley's pancake orgy, "All You Can Eat."

Human hungers beyond the need for food are expressed as well. Tobias Wolff's "Smorgasbord" depicts the perpetual physical, existential, and sexual hunger suffered by teenage boys. Two stories that exquisitely intertwine spiritual and physical hunger are Isak Dinesen's "Babette's Feast" and "Short Friday" by Isaac Bashevis Singer. These are mystical tales in which a meal is a gateway to transcendence, in one by the magic of the artist, in the other by humble piety, and in both by love.

Some stories are satires of our culinary preoccupations, like "An Abstract Art" by Jorge Luis Borges and Adolfo Bioy-Casares and "Something à la Carte?" by Lawrence Durrell. There is even a story in which the meal itself is never actually described. So rich is the subject of Hortense Calisher's "Mrs. Fay Dines on Zebra" that the food will not be missed at all.

From Hemingway's Paris to V. S. Pritchett's Spain, from Thomas Pynchon's banana breakfast to Virginia Woolf's Bœuf en Daube, the writers in this collection defy the often asked question of whether we eat to live or live to eat; instead they revel in the notion of eating well as a form of self-expression and a celebration of being alive.

These stories speak simultaneously to both our primal and our intellectual selves. They will delight the palate of the imagination and satisfy a hearty appetite for good literature as well as for good food. Read them straight through, like a twenty-seven-course meal—heavy courses are interspersed with ethereal palate cleansers—or in morsels, savored one piece at a time.

V. S. PRITCHETT

The Evils of Spain

We took our seats at the table. There were seven of us.

It was at one of those taverns in Madrid. The moment we sat down Juliano, the little, hen-headed, red-lipped consumptive who was paying for the dinner and who laughed not with his mouth but by crinkling the skin round his eyes into scores of scratchy lines and showing his bony teeth— Juliano got up and said, "We are all badly placed." Fernando and Felix said, "No, we are not badly placed." And this started another argument shouting between the lot of us. We had been arguing all the way to the restaurant. The proprietor then offered a new table in a different way. Unanimously we said, "No," to settle the row; and when he brought the table and put it into place and laid a red and white check tablecloth on it, we sat down, stretched our legs and said, "Yes. This table is much better."

Before this we had called for Angel at his hotel. We shook his hand or slapped him on the back or embraced him and two hung on his arm as we walked down the street. "Ah, Angel, the rogue!" we said, giving him a squeeze. Our smooth Mediterranean Angel! "The uncle!" we said. "The old scoundrel." Angel smiled, lowering his black lashes in appreciation. Juliano gave him a prod in the ribs and asked him if he remembered, after all these years, that summer at Biarritz? When we had all been together? The only time we had all been together before? Juliano laughed by making his eyes wicked and expectant, like one Andalusian reminding another of the great joke they had had the day poor So-and-So fell down the stairs and broke his neck.

5

"The day you were nearly drowned," Juliano said.

Angel's complexion was the color of white coffee; his hair, crinkled like a black fern, was parted in the middle, he was rich, soft-palmed and patient. He was the only well-dressed man among us, the suavest shouter. Now he sat next door but one to Juliano. Fernando was between them, Juan next to me and, at the end, Felix. They had put Caesar at the head of the table, because he was the oldest and the largest. Indeed at his age he found his weight tiring to the feet.

Caesar did not speak much. He gave his silent weight to the dinner, letting his head drop like someone falling asleep, and listening. To the noise we made his silence was a balance and he nodded all the time slowly, making everything true. Sometimes someone told some story about him and he listened to that, nodding and not disputing it.

But we were talking chiefly of that summer, the one when Angel (the old uncle!) had nearly been drowned. Then Juan, the stout, swarthy one, banged the table with his hairy hands and put on his horn-rimmed glasses. He was the smallest and most vehement of us, the one with the thickest neck and the deepest voice, his words like barrels rumbling in a cellar.

"Come on! Come on! Let's make up our minds! What are we going to eat? Eat! Eat!" he roared.

"Yes," we cried. "Drink! What are we going to drink?"

The proprietor, who was in his shirt sleeves and braces, said it was for us to decide. We could have anything we wanted. This started another argument. He stepped back a pace and put himself in an attitude of self-defense.

"Soup! Soup? Make up your minds about soup! Who wants soup?" bawled Juan.

"Red wine," some of us answered. And others, "Not red, white."

"Soup I said," shouted Juan. "Yes," we all shouted. "Soup."

"Ah," said Juan, shaking his head, in his slow miserable disappointed voice. "Nobody have any soup. I want some soup. Nobody soup," he said sadly to the proprietor.

Juliano was bouncing in his chair and saying, God he would never forget that summer when Angel was nearly drowned! When we had all been together. But Juan said Felix had not been there and we had to straighten that matter out. Juliano said:

"They carried him on to the beach, our little Angel on to the beach. And the beach superintendent came through the crowd and said, 'What's happening?' 'Nothing,' we said. 'A man knocked out.' 'Knocked out?' said the beach superintendent. 'Nothing,' we said. 'Drowned!' A lot of people left

the crowd and ran about over the beach saying, 'A man has been drowned.'
'Drowned,' said the beach superintendent. Angel was lying in the middle of
them all, unconscious, with water pouring out of his mouth."

"No! No!" shouted Fernando. "No. It wasn't like that."

"How do you mean, it wasn't like that?" cried Juliano. "I was there."
He appealed to us, "I was there."

"Yes, you were there," we said.

"I *was* there. I was there bringing him in. You say it wasn't like that,
but it was like that. We were all there." Juliano jumped protesting to his feet,
flung back his coat from his defying chest. His waistcoat was very loose over
his stomach, drafty.

"What happened was better than that," Fernando said.

"Ah," said Juliano, suddenly sitting down and grinning with his eyes
at everyone, very pleased at his show.

"It was better," he said. "How better?"

Fernando was a man who waited for silence and his hour. Once getting
possession of the conversation he never let it go, but held it in the long,
soothing ecstasy of a pliable embrace. All day long he lay in bed in his room
in Fuencarral with the shutters closed, recovering from the bout of the day
before. He was preparing himself to appear in the evening, spruce, grey-
haired and meaty under the deep black crescents of his eyebrows, his cheeks
ripening like plums as the evening advanced, his blue eyes, which got bloodshot early, becoming mistier. He was a man who ripened and moistened. He
talked his way through dinner into the night, his voice loosening, his eyes
misting, his walk becoming slower and stealthier, acting every sentence, as if
he were swaying through the exalted phase of inebriation. But it was an
inebriation purely verbal; an exaltation of dramatic moments, refinements
upon situations; and hour after hour passed until the dawn found him
sodden in his own anecdotes, like a fruit in rum.

"What happened was," Fernando said, "that I was in the sea. And after
a while I discovered Angel was in the sea. As you know there is nothing more
perilous than the sea, but with Angel in it the peril is tripled; and when I saw
him I was preparing to get as far away as possible. But he was making faces
in the water and soon he made such a face, so inhuman, so unnatural, I saw
he was drowning. This did not surprise me for Angel is one of those men
who, when he is in the sea, he drowns. There is some psychological antipa-
thy. Now when I see a man drowning my instinct is to get away quickly. A
man drowning is not a man. He is a lunatic. But a lunatic like Angel! But
unfortunately he got me before I could get away. There he was," Fernando
stood up and raised his arm, confronting the proprietor of the restaurant,

but staring right through that defensive man, "beating the water, diving, spluttering, choking, spitting, and, seeing he was drowning, for the man *was* drowning, caught hold of me, and we both went under. Angel was like a beast. He clung to me like seaweed. I, seeing this, awarded him a knockout— zum—but as the tenacity of man increases with unconsciousness, Angel stuck to me like a limpet, and in saving myself there was no escape from saving him."

"That's true," said Angel, admiring his fingernails. And Caesar nodded his head up and down twice, which made it true.

Juan then swung round and called out, "Eat! Food! Let us order. Let us eat. We haven't ordered. We do nothing but talk, not eat. I want to eat."

"Yes, come on," said Felix. "Eat. What's the fish?"

"The fish," said the proprietor, "is bacalao."

"Yes," everyone cried. "Bacalao, a good bacalao, a very good one. No, it must be good. No. I can't eat it unless it's good, very good *and* very good."

"No," we said. "Not fish. We don't want it."

"Seven bacalaos then?" said the proprietor.

But Fernando was still on his feet.

"And the beach inspector said, 'What's his name and address and has he any identity papers?' 'Man,' I said, 'he's in his bathing dress. Where could he keep his papers?' And Juan said, 'Get a doctor. Don't stand there asking questions. Get a doctor.' "

"That's true," said Juan gloomily. "He wasn't dead."

"Get a doctor, that was it," Angel said.

"And they got a doctor and brought him round and got half the Bay of Biscay out of him, gallons of it. It astonished me that so much water could come out of a man."

"And then in the evening," Juliano leaped up and clipped the story out of Fernando's mouth, "Angel says to the proprietor of the hotel . . ."

Juan's head had sunk to his chest. His hands were over his ears.

"Eat," he bawled in a voice of despair so final that we all stopped talking and gazed at him with astonishment for a few moments. Then in sadness he turned to me appealing. "Can't we eat? I am empty."

". . . said to the proprietor of the hotel," Fernando grabbed the tale back from Juliano, "who was rushing down the corridor with a face like a fish, 'I am the man who was drowned this morning.' And the proprietor who looked at Angel like a prawn, the proprietor said, 'M'sieu, whether you were drowned or not drowned this morning you are about to be roast. The hotel is on fire.' "

"That's right," we said. "The hotel was on fire."

"I remember," said Felix. "It began in the kitchen."

"How in the kitchen?"

This then became the argument.

"The first time ever I heard it was in the kitchen."

"But no," said Angel, softly rising to claim his life story for himself. Juliano clapped his hands and bounced with joy. "It was not like that."

"But we were all there, Angel," Fernando said, but Angel who spoke very rapidly said:

"No and no! And the proof of it is: What was I wearing?" He challenged all of us. We paused.

"Tripe," said Juan to me hopelessly wagging his head. "You like tripe? They do it well. Here! Phist!" he called the proprietor through the din. "Have you tripe, a good Basque tripe? No? What a pity! Can you get me some? Here! Listen," he shouted to the rest of the table. "Tripe," he shouted, but they were engrossed in Angel.

"Pajamas," Fernando said. "When you are in bed you wear your pajamas."

"Exactly, and they were not my pajamas."

"You say the fire was not in the kitchen," shouted Fernando, "because the pajamas you were wearing were not yours!" And we shouted back at Angel.

"They belonged to the Italian ambassador," said Angel, "the one who was with that beautiful Mexican girl."

Then Caesar, who, as I have said, was the oldest of us and sat at the head of the table, Caesar leaned his old big pale face forward and said in a hushed voice, putting out his hands like a blind man remembering:

"My God—but what a very beautiful woman she was," he said. "I remember her. I have never in my life," he said speaking all his words slowly and with grave concern, "seen such a beautiful woman."

Fernando and Angel, who had been standing, sat down. We all looked in awe at the huge, old-shouldered Caesar with his big pale face and the pockets under his little grey eyes, who was speaking of the most beautiful woman he had ever seen.

"She was there all that summer," Caesar said. "She was no longer young." He leaned forward with his hands on the table. "What must she have been when she was young?"

A beach, the green sea dancing down white upon it, that Mexican woman walking over the floor of a restaurant, the warm white houses, the night glossy black like the toe of a patent shoe, her hair black. We tried to think how many years ago this was. Brought by his voice to silence us, she was already fading.

The proprietor took his opportunity in our silence. "The bacalao is done in the Basque fashion with peppers and potatoes. Bring a bacalao," he snapped to a youth in the kitchen.

Suddenly Juan brought his fists on the table, pushed back his chair and beat his chest with one fist and then the other. He swore in his enormous voice by his private parts.

"It's eleven o'clock. Eat! For God's sake. Fernando stands there talking and talking and no one listens to anybody. It is one of the evils of Spain. Someone stop him. Eat."

We all woke up and glared with the defiance of the bewildered, rejecting everything he said. Then what he said to us penetrated. A wave roared over us and we were with him. We agreed with what he said. We all stood up and, by our private parts, swore that he was right. It was one of the evils of Spain.

The soup arrived. White wine arrived.

"I didn't order soup," some shouted.

"I said 'Red wine,'" others said.

"It is a mistake," the proprietor said. "I'll take it away." An argument started about this.

"No," we said. "Leave it. We want it." And then we said the soup was bad, and the wine was bad and everything he brought was bad, but the proprietor said the soup was good and the wine was good and we said in the end it was good. We told the proprietor the restaurant was good, but he said not very good, indeed bad. And then we asked Angel to explain about the pajamas.

PETER MAYLE

January

The effect of the weather on the in-
habitants of Provence is immediate and obvious. They expect every day to
be sunny, and their disposition suffers when it isn't. Rain they take as a
personal affront, shaking their heads and commiserating with each other in
the cafés, looking with profound suspicion at the sky as though a plague of
locusts is about to descend, and picking their way with distaste through the
puddles on the pavement. If anything worse than a rainy day should come
along, such as this sub-zero snap, the result is startling: most of the population disappears.

As the cold began to bite into the middle of January, the towns and
villages became quiet. The weekly markets, normally jammed and boister-
ous, were reduced to a skeleton crew of intrepid stallholders who were
prepared to risk frostbite for a living, stamping their feet and nipping from
hip flasks. Customers moved briskly, bought and went, barely pausing to
count their change. Bars closed their doors and windows tight and conducted
their business in a pungent fog. There was none of the usual dawdling on the
streets.

Our valley hibernated, and I missed the sounds that marked the passing
of each day almost as precisely as a clock: Faustin's rooster having his
morning cough; the demented clatter—like nuts and bolts trying to escape
from a biscuit tin—of the small Citroën van that every farmer drives home
at lunchtime; the hopeful fusillade of a hunter on afternoon patrol in the
vines on the opposite hillside; the distant whine of a chainsaw in the forest;

11

the twilight serenade of farm dogs. Now there was silence. For hours on end the valley would be completely still and empty, and we became curious. What was everybody doing?

Faustin, we knew, traveled around the neighboring farms as a visiting slaughterer, slitting the throats and breaking the necks of rabbits and ducks and pigs and geese so that they could be turned into terrines and hams and *confits*. We thought it an uncharacteristic occupation for a softhearted man who spoiled his dogs, but he was evidently skilled and quick and, like any true countryman, he wasn't distracted by sentiment. We might treat a rabbit as a pet or become emotionally attached to a goose, but we had come from cities and supermarkets, where flesh was hygienically distanced from any resemblance to living creatures. A shrink-wrapped pork chop has a sanitized, abstract appearance that has nothing whatever to do with the warm, mucky bulk of a pig. Out here in the country there was no avoiding the direct link between death and dinner, and there would be many occasions in the future when we would be grateful for Faustin's winter work.

But what did everyone else do? The earth was frozen, the vines were clipped and dormant, it was too cold to hunt. Had they all gone on holiday? No, surely not. These were not the kind of gentlemen farmers who spent their winters on the ski slopes or yachting in the Caribbean. Holidays here were taken at home during August, eating too much, enjoying siestas and resting up before the long days of the *vendange*. It was a puzzle, until we realized how many of the local people had their birthdays in September or October, and then a possible but unverifiable answer suggested itself: they were busy indoors making babies. There is a season for everything in Provence, and the first two months of the year must be devoted to procreation. We have never dared ask.

The cold weather brought less private pleasures. Apart from the peace and emptiness of the landscape, there is a special smell about winter in Provence which is accentuated by the wind and the clean, dry air. Walking in the hills, I was often able to smell a house before I could see it, because of the scent of woodsmoke coming from an invisible chimney. It is one of the most primitive smells in life, and consequently extinct in most cities, where fire regulations and interior decorators have combined to turn fireplaces into blocked-up holes or self-consciously lit "architectural features." The fireplace in Provence is still used—to cook on, to sit around, to warm the toes, and to please the eye—and fires are laid in the early morning and fed throughout the day with scrub oak from the Lubéron or beech from the foothills of Mont Ventoux. Coming home with the dogs as dusk fell, I always stopped to look from the top of the valley at the long zigzag of smoke ribbons drifting up from the farms that are scattered along the Bonnieux road. It was a sight that made me think of warm kitchens and well-seasoned stews, and it never failed to make me ravenous.

The well-known food of Provence is summer food—the melons and peaches and asparagus, the courgettes and aubergines, the peppers and tomatoes, the *aioli* and bouillabaisse and monumental salads of olives and anchovies and tuna and hard-boiled eggs and sliced, earthy potatoes on beds of multicolored lettuce glistening with oil, the fresh goat's cheeses—these had been the memories that came back to torment us every time we looked at the limp and shriveled selection on offer in English shops. It had never occurred to us that there was a winter menu, totally different but equally delicious.

The cold-weather cuisine of Provence is peasant food. It is made to stick to your ribs, keep you warm, give you strength, and send you off to bed with a full belly. It is not pretty, in the way that the tiny and artistically garnished portions served in fashionable restaurants are pretty, but on a freezing night with the Mistral coming at you like a razor there is nothing to beat it. And on the night one of our neighbors invited us to dinner it was cold enough to turn the short walk to their house into a short run.

We came through the door and my glasses steamed up in the heat from the fireplace that occupied most of the far wall of the room. As the mist cleared, I saw that the big table, covered in checked oilcloth, was laid for ten; friends and relations were coming to examine us. A television set chattered in the corner, the radio chattered back from the kitchen, and assorted dogs and cats were shooed out of the door as one guest arrived, only to sidle back in with the next. A tray of drinks was brought out, with pasties for the men and chilled, sweet muscat wine for the women, and we were caught in a crossfire of noisy complaints about the weather. Was it as bad as this in England? Only in the summer, I said. For a moment they took me seriously before someone saved me from embarrassment by laughing. With a great deal of jockeying for position—whether to sit next to us or as far away as possible, I wasn't sure—we settled ourselves at the table.

It was a meal that we shall never forget; more accurately, it was several meals that we shall never forget, because it went beyond the gastronomic frontiers of anything we had ever experienced, both in quantity and length.

It started with homemade pizza—not one, but three: anchovy, mushroom, and cheese, and it was obligatory to have a slice of each. Plates were then wiped with pieces torn from the two-foot loaves in the middle of the table, and the next course came out. There were pâtés of rabbit, boar, and thrush. There was a chunky, pork-based terrine laced with *marc*. There were *saucissons* spotted with peppercorns. There were tiny sweet onions marinated in a fresh tomato sauce. Plates were wiped once more and duck was brought in. The slivers of *magret* that appear, arranged in fan formation and lapped by an elegant smear of sauce on the refined tables of nouvelle cuisine—these were nowhere to be seen. We had entire breasts, entire legs, covered in a dark, savory gravy and surrounded by wild mushrooms.

We sat back, thankful that we had been able to finish, and watched with something close to panic as plates were wiped yet again and a huge, steaming casserole was placed on the table. This was the speciality of Madame our hostess—a rabbit *civet* of the richest, deepest brown—and our feeble requests for small portions were smilingly ignored. We ate it. We ate the green salad with knuckles of bread fried in garlic and olive oil, we ate the plump round *crottins* of goat's cheese, we ate the almond and cream gâteau that the daughter of the house had prepared. That night, we ate for England.

With the coffee, a number of deformed bottles were produced which contained a selection of locally made *digestifs*. My heart would have sunk had there been any space left for it to sink to, but there was no denying my host's insistence. I must try one particular concoction, made from an eleventh-century recipe by an alcoholic order of monks in the Basses-Alpes. I was asked to close my eyes while it was poured, and when I opened them a tumbler of viscous yellow fluid had been put in front of me. I looked in despair around the table. Everyone was watching me; there was no chance of giving whatever it was to the dog or letting it dribble discreetly into one of my shoes. Clutching the table for support with one hand, I took the tumbler with the other, closed my eyes, prayed to the patron saint of indigestion, and threw it back.

Nothing came out. I had been expecting at best a scalded tongue, at worst permanently cauterized taste buds, but I took in nothing but air. It was a trick glass, and for the first time in my adult life I was deeply relieved not to have a drink. As the laughter of the other guests died away, genuine drinks were threatened, but we were saved by the cat. From her headquarters on top of a large *armoire*, she took a flying leap in pursuit of a moth and crash-landed among the coffee cups and bottles on the table. It seemed like an appropriate moment to leave. We walked home pushing our stomachs before us, oblivious to the cold, incapable of speech, and slept like the dead.

ZELDA FITZGERALD

The Continental Angle

Gastronomic delight and sartorial pleasure radiated from the two people. They sat at a table on a polished dais under a canopy of horse-chestnuts eating of the fresh noon sunlight which turned the long, yellow bars of their asparagus to a chromatic xylophone. The hot, acrid sauce and the spring air disputed and wept together, Tweedledum and Tweedledee, over the June down that floated here and there before their vision like frayed places in a tapestry.

"Do you remember," she said, "the Ducoed chairs of Southern tearooms and the left-over look of the Sunday gingerbread that goes with a dollar dinner, the mustardy linen and the waiters' spotted dinner coats of a Broadway chophouse, the smell of mayonnaise you get with a meal in the shopping district, the pools of blue milk like artificial opals on a drugstore counter, the safe, plebeian intimacy of chocolate on the air, and the greasy smell of whipped cream in a sandwich emporium? There's the sterility of upper Broadway with the pancakes at Childs drowned in the pale hospital light, and Swiss restaurants with walls like a merry-go-round backdrop, and Italian restaurants latticed like the lacing of a small and pompous Balkan officer, and green peppers curling like garter snakes in marshy hors-d'oeuvre compartments, and piles of spaghetti like the sweepings from a dance hall under the red lights and paper flowers."

"Yes," he said, but with nostalgia, "and there are strips of bacon curling over the country sausage in the luminous filterings from the princely windows of the Plaza, and honeydew melon with just a whiff of lemon from narrow red benches that balustrade Park Avenue restaurants, and there's the impersonal masculinity of lunch at the Chatham, the diplomacy of dinner at the St. Regis; there are strawberries in winter on buffets that rise like fountains in places named Versailles and Trianon and Fontainebleau, and caviar in blocks of ice."

"If you eat late on Sunday at the Lafayette," she continued blandly, "the tables are covered with coffee cups and the deep windows let in the wheezing asphalt and you look over boxes of faded artificial flowers onto the tables where people have eaten conversation and dumped their ashes in their saucers while they talked, and at the Brevoort men with much to think about have eaten steak, thick, chewing like a person's footfalls in a heavily padded corridor. In all the basements where old English signs hang over the stairs, years ago they buried puddings, whereas if you have the energy to climb a flight of stairs, there are motherly nests of salad and perhaps something Hawaiian."

"Ah, and at Delmonicos there were meals with the flavor of a transatlantic liner," he said; "at Hicks there are illustration salads, gleaming, tumbling over the plate like a rajah's jewels, cream cheese and alligator pear and cherries floating about like balls on a Christmas tree. And *filet de sole* paves the Fifties, and shrimp cobbles Broadway, and grapefruits roll about the roof and turn roof gardens to celestial bowling alleys. There is cold salmon with the elegance of a lady's boudoir in the infinity of big hotel dining-rooms, and Mephistophelean crab cocktails that give you the sweat of a long horseback ride and pastry that spurts like summer showers in restaurants famed for their chef."

"And there are waffles spongy under syrups as aromatic as the heat that rises in a hedged lane after a July rain, and chicken in the red brick of Madison Avenue," she pursued. "And I have eaten in old places under stained-glass windows where the palm fronds reflected in my cream-of-tomato soup reminded me of embalming parlors, and I've gulped sweet potatoes in the Pennsylvania Station, ice-tea and pineapple salad under the spinning fans blowing travellers to a standstill, tomato skins in a club sandwich and the smell of pickles in the Forties."

"Yes," he said, "and raspberries trickling down the fountain at the Ritz, bubbling up and falling like the ball in a shooting-gallery spray, and eggs in a baked potato for ladies and—"

"*Pardon, est-ce que Madame a bien déjeuné?*"

"*C'était exquis, merci bien.*"

"*Et Monsieur, il se plaît chez vous?*"

"What the hell did he say, my dear? I learned my French in America and it doesn't seem to be completely adequate."

"Ah, sir, I understand perfectly. I be so bold as to ask if Monsieur like our restaurant, perhaps?" answered the waiter.

JOHN HERSEY

The Announcement

"Mother's a bit old-fashioned," Gordon said. In spite of his confidence in Beverly, he couldn't help feeling apprehensive about this first meeting. "Still wears hairpins, you know. I think they're made of deer horn. She winds a braid around on top like a crown."

"You don't have to . . . p-paint her," Bev said. "I'm going to see her with my own eyes, right? How much f-farther?"

"We're not far now. Just the other side of Pleasantville."

He left the exact distance hanging. In a moderate hurry, he kept the rented Skylark ticking along at sixty. Beverly looked just right to him. She was all in black, in an off-the-shoulder taffeta cocktail dress, with a triangular black silk shawl, knotted in front, so that there were only glimpses of skin. Bev's instincts were so unerring: his mother often chose black herself for cheerful occasions. Beverly's curly dark hair was blowing in the breeze from her half-opened window. She had understated her makeup that morning— how much she understood!

Gordon was especially nervous because his mother's Thanksgiving dinner had had to be postponed by a day. As usual, brother Peter, coming from Minneapolis with his family, had made a mess of things; there had been some kind of slipup with their train reservations. Gordon knew that his mother, with her great gift of denial, would sit through the meal in style and wouldn't show a single outward sign of distress. But Thanksgiving dinner on the day after!

Thanksgiving meant everything to his mother. The resilience of the New England settlers was in her arteries—the grit and bend of those fore-bears, who could survive a first blizzardy winter, scrape at hardscrabble soil in a thin spring, plant a fish head in every corn hill, pray away drought and the crashing down of hailstones, and, at last, stack the surviving stalks and roll in the huge pumpkins and shoot a wild turkey, and then feast, and murmur in gratitude to a jealous God. That Puritan side was only a part of her, though. She was, as well, a sensuous family woman, and Thanksgiving dinners were her joy and her victory. As children, Gordon and his brother Peter had basked in the sunlight of her nurture: strange to think of that hot motherly effulgence, because she so liked shadowy places and somber clothes. She had devoted herself to her husband—dead now ten years—with a quirky tenderness that had some cold spots in it. She had quarreled with him often, perhaps to starch up a certain rumpled softness in him, and Gordon had come to see that she had always lost the arguments but had somehow won by losing.

This mysterious femininity, yielding yet powerful, Victorian yet Emer-sonian too, had been what Gordon had looked for in a wife the first time, when he came back from the war in the South Pacific; but marrying an apparent clone of his mother hadn't worked. Sue hadn't turned out to fit the mold, and Gordon and she had had a rough parting, four years ago, in the autumn when Eisenhower beat Stevenson for the second time. No kids, thank goodness. Badly burned, he had gone it alone for three and a half years, and then had fallen in love with this complicated Beverly, who was not in the least like his mother. He and Bev had long since decided to marry, but for some reason—perhaps it was because Bev was fourteen years younger than he—he had postponed bringing her to meet his mother until now, on the special occasion of a Thanksgiving dinner, when, he thought, his mother's euphoria, as well as the sweet condiments in little bowls on her table (Beverly had a sugar-tooth), might ease the way on both sides. "Bev has a funny little stammer," he had said to his mother on the phone after accepting for both of them, as if that would explain all about Beverly in advance.

As they approached Chappaqua, Gordon's familiarity since childhood with the shapes of the hills thereabouts, his memory of each rough-cut stone bridge on the parkway, his long acquaintance even with certain noble trees along the road, especially some of the huge willows in the low places—first of all flora to put out yellow growth in the spring, last of all to trail their drying yellow feathers in the fall—these mnemonics of homing stirred up in his senses a rush of remembered small pleasures: the sight of his mother unwrapping a stick of butter and leaning down to let Barabbas, the old Lab, lick the traces off the wax paper; the taste of cinnamon toast; diving into huge piles of leaves when his father raked them up on Saturday afternoons in the fall; deep sounds, of cello and bassoon, on the Capehart; the gentle sidling of Whitefoot, the only cat he'd ever liked, snaking against his calf with a flirtatious aftertouch of her tail. All the years. He drove with care.

Then they were there. "Good God," Beverly said when they drove up under the darkness of the porte cochere. Gordon laughed. Yes, the house was a beast. Heavy-timbered, mouse-colored, surrounded by huge red maples which even with bared limbs fought off most of the afternoon's hazy light, the house loomed as a reminder of an era of aspiration and complacency that was, thank heavens, long gone. This monument to Daddy—Gordon called his father that—was planted in that purportedly tranquil zone, discovered by self-made men in the nineteen-twenties, of the one-hour commute to town on the Harlem Division of the New York Central. Never mind. To Gordon, at thirty-eight, it was still home.

Gordon gave one rap on the cast-iron knocker—a head, was it Samson's or a human-looking lion's?—and opened up the heavy door, which squealed its welcome on its long black strap hinges. He waved Bev in ahead of him. Here came Uncle Solbert and his wife, hurrying in good manners out of the living room to greet the newcomers.

"Gordie boy!" Uncle Solbert roared with a second-drink cordiality. Did Gordon remember that Uncle Bert was partial to old-fashioneds?

"Happy Thanksgiving," Aunt Beth cried, already all too happy herself. She, too. Apparently everyone was going to pretend that they had gathered on the right day.

"This is Beverly Zimmer," Gordon said. Bev was blinking. Gordon saw that she had forgotten to straighten her blown hair. She looked wild. The delicate wrinkles in her forehead showed up as she stood right under the down-pouring light of the hall ceiling fixture.

Now all the others, except for Gordon's mother, came rushing into the hall in a stampede of curiosity. Here were brother Peter and his Molly, not the least bit shamefaced. Introductions kept Gordon busy. Here were his mother's ancient dear friends, Miss Rankin and Miss Alderhoff. And here was Mr. Cannahan. Mr. Cannahan's eyes did a little dance when he saw Beverly's shawl slip to one side as she shook hands. "How beautiful," he murmured. And here was awful Freddie, Peter and Molly's son; was he still at Lawrenceville, or had he been kicked out? And sullen little niece Caroline, who, Gordon noticed, had remarkable breasts for—what was she?—a thirteen-year-old?

"Where's Mom?"

"K-k-k-Katy, in the k-kitchen," sang Uncle Solbert, off-key. Gordon felt a hot blush rise up his neck to his cheeks. His mother obviously hadn't passed on the little secret about Bev.

But there she came. His mother was wearing a charcoal-gray dress, which was almost entirely hidden by a wraparound blue apron. She had something in a dish in her hand. Her piercing dark eyes were looking not at him but at Beverly, and he was astonished by the sharp pang of joy and pride he felt when he saw the genuine warmth in the gathers of crow's feet—the smile lines—around his mother's eyes. She went straight to Beverly and, holding the dish out to one side, leaned forward and kissed her, but really kissed her, not just the air beside her cheek, and spoke a single word, "Beverly."

Beverly took a step backward and said, "I'm so . . . t-tickled to meet you." At once she had offered Gordon's mother the tiny hesitation and catch that he found so entrancing: a pause, as verbal choices came to her, and then a little splutter of emotion, tripping over a plosive consonant, as she settled on a word that sounded a bit odd but must have been, as usual, exactly what she meant.

Gordon's mother greeted him with a tight one-armed hug and then turned at once and hurried back to the kitchen, holding the dish high in her right hand to show the company why she was in such haste. Everyone drifted back to the living room. As they walked in, Gordon heard music coming from the old Capehart. Sibelius's Seventh. Ah, yes, one of his mother's favorites, that swooping deep-toned utterance, sad as whale song, from a country where for months the sun never came up over the horizon. Yet the sound was part of what made Gordon's spirits rise; it belonged, as he did, in this room, with its dark mahogany wainscoting and twisted black iron-work fireplace tools and mock-candle sconces holding tiny, dim, flame-shaped light bulbs; all those things were embedded in, and had somehow failed to darken, his makeup. Bev's face, as he quickly checked it now, reinforced his pleasure. Her eyes were twinkling at the sights in the room—that the look might contain elements of ambiguity: delight yet at the same time something like disbelief?

He saw that a bar had been set up on the old tea wagon in the corner of the room. "Have a Thanksgiving libation?" he quietly asked Bev.

"You can bet your . . . b-bottom dollar I will," she said. She surprised him by asking for gin and bitters. She usually sipped Dubonnet or Cinzano.

"Did you see that Macy's had a huge toy elephant in their parade?" he heard Miss Rankin say as he crossed to the tea wagon. The Persian rug he walked over was worn down to the warp in the trafficway from the hall and in front of several chairs.

"I wonder if those gigantic balloons in the parade aren't dangerous," Miss Alderhoff said. "I mean, if it's windy."

"There wasn't a breath of air yesterday," Aunt Beth said, and then she laughed hard, having given a little too much emphasis, Gordon thought, to "yesterday."

Leaning over the bar, looking for the gin, Gordon saw a bottle of amontillado with a little cardboard tag hung around its neck on a slip of ribbon. Looking more closely, he read the words written in his mother's hand on the tag:

BEST SHERRY
DO NOT USE

He would wait and see whether to tell Bev about that. He mixed her drink—he found bitters in a tiny square cruet—and shook up a manhattan for himself.

With his arrival in his mother's house he felt it proper that he should take over from Peter, two years his junior, the duties of a host, and when he had given Beverly her drink, he turned and said, "Anyone else? Mr. Cannahan?"

"Oh, *no*, thank you," Mr. Cannahan said, tearing his eyes away from the tantalizing knot that held Beverly's shawl in place, and rubbing his stomach to remind Gordon of the ulcer he had harbored there for so many, many years.

"Of course," Gordon said, remembering. "Forgive me. Beth? Pete? You ready?"

"I can get our own," Peter said.

Gordon sat down. He heard a thunking sound as the Capehart turned a record over. Then the dark Finnish keening resumed.

"And what do you do, Miss Swimmer?" Mr. Cannahan asked.

"Zimmer," Bev said sharply.

"Ah, Miss Zimmer," Mr. Cannahan said. "Lovely name."

"I do . . . n-nothing," Beverly said.

"Best occupation in the world!" Uncle Solbert shouted.

Gordon was trying to think of something sensible to say when his mother came into the room and took a chair. She had removed her apron. "Dear me," she said. "Such confusion. Flo says she'll be ready to serve in five minutes."

"What nice earrings," Beverly said, to Gordon's delight. She was going to be wonderful.

Gordon's mother put her hands over the amber pendants at her ears. "They hurt," she said. "But do you know? I had a brainstorm. I put Dr. Scholl's corn plasters on the screw pads. Perfect!"

"Perfect" was a word his mother often used, with an ever-so-slight Englishy softening of the r. She posted many little signs and notices around the house, like the tag on the sherry bottle, and Gordon thought of the one that used to be stuck beside the shower handle in the guest bathroom: FOR BEST SHOWERBATH, TURN TO TEN O'CLOCK. WAIT 45 SECONDS. PERFECT! But she was far from being a perfectionist; nor, Gordon had long since acknowledged, was she herself perfect. He sometimes thought that she considered one's manner of speaking more important than what one said. A person's emotional tone, a person's feeling toward her, toward the world, was what counted with her. Sometimes she nattered, rattled on without hearing herself. She was kind and warm, though, and always wanted to boost other people's morale. He remembered how, when Daddy was alive, she used to sound off about his being the big man around the place. "The eye of the owner is good for the land," she would say. Her George was "the only man on the island." Yet she had that appetite for quarrels. She often accused her husband, in front of the boys—absurdly, Gordon thought—of letting other women flirt with him. Not of his having flirted himself. She asked friends what was troubling them, really dug out the dirt; she wanted to sympathize, wanted to help, wanted to be loved for being loving. This last craving had sometimes struck Gordon, especially when he had troubles of his own, as a need for something much less adorable than it might seem—a need for some kind of firm grip on your arm. The miracle, though, was her persistent cheerfulness since Daddy's death. She seemed not to have a trouble in the world. Thinking of her now, Gordon had a sudden vivid and very happy memory of hot chocolate, French bread, honey.

He looked at Bev. She was smiling. She had loved that thing of the earlobe remedy. Her hair was still a mess. It didn't matter. The emotional tone was what mattered.

Flo, the cook, appeared in the archway from the hall and shouted, "All right, Mrs. Bronson!" Flo was a New England woman; she had her ways.

Brother Peter was the first to stand up. All his life, Peter had been hungry. "Come on, folks," he said. "Get your trotters in the trough."

Gordon went over and turned the Capehart off, and then he offered the crook of his arm to his mother. Taking it, she smiled at him and said, "I want you to carve, Son."

Everyone exclaimed at the sight of the table. Glass and silver winked in the afternoon light. Between two newly polished silver candelabra, each bearing five lighted candles of a garish red, stood a display, looking like fireworks bursting in air, of odd varieties of late autumn's greatest pride, the chrysanthemum. Pairs of bottles of red and white wine and two carafes of sweet cider stood on silver circlets on a tablecloth with beautiful doilies of Devonshire lace scattered about. At each place, next to a pale blue napkin folded to stand up, lay one of those crepe-paper tubes for children's parties with tabs to pull from the ends which make a little firecracker sound—each doubtless containing a colored paper hat and a favor of some kind. Strewn here and there were gravy boats and bowls brimming with all the things that Gordon had known Bev would love: watermelon-rind pickles, tomato mar-malade, peach chutney, quince jelly, spiced Jerusalem artichokes, green-tomato mincemeat, and, of course, loads of cranberry sauce.

Gordon's mother seated everyone. Gordon at the head of the table, herself at the other end. She put Peter at her right, and Mr. Cannahan at her left. Beverly was between Mr. Cannahan and Uncle Solbert; both men beamed at their luck. The others were scattered around. Gordon had Aunt Beth on his right and Molly on his left.

When they were all seated, Gordon's mother tinkled her wineglass with a knife, and after she had complete silence she said, "Peter, dear, would you say grace, please?" This was evenhanded: Gordon would carve, Peter would pray—a special privilege at Thanksgiving dinner.

"God in heaven," Peter said, with his head down and his eyes squeezed tight shut, "we thank you for this wonderful American tradition, we are grateful for prosperity and our mother's good health, we thank you for family values"—Gordon thought he heard awful little Freddie give a tiny grunt at that—"and the heritage of freedom you have granted our nation. And thanks, by the way, for the turkey-lurkey."

During this performance, Gordon had not bowed his head; he had watched Beverly. She had not lowered her head either but had stared at Peter with a look that gave Gordon a little twinge of concern. But then she laughed with everyone else at Peter's nonsense at the end, and when Uncle Bert started clapping, she joined in with the rest. Peter, acknowledging the ap-plause, clasped his hands above his head, like the winner of a gold medal.

Flo came in, her face pink, her hair flying every which way, and her apron splashed with gravy, carrying a huge, glistening turkey up at a level with her head, and now everyone both clapped and cheered. She put the bird down in front of Gordon and stood there gloating at it.

"What's in the stuffing, Flo?" Uncle Solbert called out when the hub-bub died down.

"Well, now, there's chestnuts, and country sausage—that's the thing!—onions, celery, let's see, thyme, sage, bread crumbs, of course, stale bread crumbs. And," she added, with a little lurch in her stance, "perhaps I shouldn't say, folks, but there's Madeira wine in there!" And she went off to the kitchen, cackling.

Picking up the carving knife, Gordon glanced at Beverly. She was looking at him. Her face was glowing. He stood up, took some passes, which he hoped looked skillful, with the knife-edge at the sharpening rod. He leaned forward to start his work.

While he carved, Flo brought in one dish after another, setting each down with a decisive little bang on a doily on the tablecloth, alongside serving spoons that were already dispersed there, and announcing each as she put it in place: mashed potatoes, both white and sweet, in separate casseroles, with browned marshmallows on top of the latter; oysters in cornmeal hasty pudding; cut green beans with rosemary; creamed onions; mushrooms braised with sorrel leaves; baked turnips flavored with maple syrup.

Waiting to be served, people pulled favor-crackers with their neighbors, and exclaimed cheerfully at the cheap things they found inside. Mr. Cannahan and Uncle Bert had a brief tiff about who would get to pull Beverly's cracker; Uncle Bert won by sheer force of the bourbon in his veins. He let Beverly pull Mr. Cannahan's cracker, though. Uncle Bert was the only one at the table to put on a crepe-paper hat. It was bright orange. Everyone was talking at once.

Flo brought in Mr. Cannahan's lunch: two bananas, mashed with a fork into a pulp on a plate. It was all his ulcer was going to allow him to eat. A general cry of commiseration went up, but Mr. Cannahan, looking right at Bev, called out, "I don't mind: it's the company that matters on holidays, isn't it?"

"You're a good sport," Gordon's mother said, patting Mr. Cannahan's hand.

There was great confusion while the plates went around and volunteers served things up in passing. "Light or dark?" Gordon kept calling out to various customers. The teenager Caroline couldn't make up her mind. She threw a beseeching glance at her mother, looking as if she might break into tears.

"You like white, honey," Molly said.

"I don't either," Caroline said.

"Suit yourself, kiddo," Molly said. "It's your funeral."

Gordon put a helping of both on Caroline's plate, and she flashed him an angry look.

At last things settled down. Gordon could sit. His back hurt a little from leaning over, but he felt important. He saw that Beverly had chosen red wine. People were tucking into their food, and for a while the room was quiet.

Then old Miss Rankin and old Miss Alderhoff started the ball rolling.

"Wasn't it sweet," Miss Rankin said, "that Jackie Kennedy had her baby on Thanksgiving night?"

"I was so offended," Miss Alderhoff said, "that AP fellow trying to take Mrs. Kennedy's picture on the way back from the delivery room. Is there no privacy in this world anymore? I mean to say, the President-elect's wife!"

"Another John Fitzgerald Kennedy, did you see what they're naming him?" Peter said with his mouth full. "Another Kennedy named for old Honey Fitz, the biggest crook in Boston history. How 'bout that?"

"The poor little thing's in a respirator," Miss Rankin said.

"Really?" said Gordon's mother, who never read the papers. "Why is that?"

"Premature," Miss Rankin said. "Six pounds three ounces. They say preemies are subject to, you know, breathing problems."

"Well!" Miss Alderhoff said. "It wasn't just *that*. They had to take it with a cesarean."

"Another Caesar in the Kennedy family," brother Peter said in triumph.

Beverly shook her forefinger sidewise at Peter. "Doesn't follow," she said, sounding testy. "The operation wasn't named for Caesar. Caesar was given the name that the operation already had, *sectio caesaria*, because he was born that way. That's the story that . . . P-Pliny the Elder tells, anyway."

Peter looked as though he'd been slapped. Gordon suddenly felt breathless, as if he had been jogging a little too fast.

"Actually," Beverly good-humoredly went on, "that doesn't make too much sense, because in those days they used cesareans only to save the baby when the mother died in ch-childbirth, and we know that Caesar's mother lived for more than f-fifty years after he was born. The f-first recorded cesarean on a living woman was about f-fifteen hundred. It was done by a Swiss . . . p-pig-gelder on his own wife."

The whole table was in silence. Only Uncle Bert, still wearing his orange hat, went on chewing. Gordon got up the courage to look at his mother, and he saw that she was beaming at Beverly. She had a look of amazement and delight on her face. "Mr. Cannahan," she said, "give Beverly a little more wine." Gordon, vibrating with pleasure, saw that the day was going to be a total success after all. The one thing he had been nervous about was Bev's unpredictable spurts of contrariness. He had been afraid of an inadvertent collision of some sort. Bev didn't mean anything by these little bumpy moments; they were for fun, though sometimes others didn't look at them that way. She had an octopus of a memory, and she knew a great deal (some of what she "knew" wasn't exactly so, but never mind), and it would have been hard to say whether she loved best sparring with brilliant people or straightening stupid people out. It was a secret of the constant peacefulness between her and Gordon that she seemed to consider Gordon neither brilliant nor stupid but just comfortably sensible. At this moment he felt a surge in his appetite. He loved Flo's oyster dish.

Miss Rankin piped up. "I wonder if they're going to have the Kennedy family nurse to take care of the baby," she said. "I imagine she took care of Jack himself and all his siblings when they were little. Think of the continuity of it! Miss Hennessy's her name."

"I doubt if they use the 'Miss,' " Miss Alderhoff said. "They'd just call her by her last name. 'Hennessy, would you change the baby's didies, please?' "

"You better believe no Kennedy would have anything to do with dirty diapers," Peter said with some spirit, looking right at Bev.

But Beverly seemed to have lost interest in Peter. Gordon saw that she had picked up one of the highly polished silver serving spoons that had not been used and was looking at her reflection on the back of it. What a long balloon face she would have in such a mirror! Yet she apparently saw the mess her hair was in, because she began patting it into place. Gordon thought with pleasure, She wants to leave herself in this house—for Bev had a theory that faces printed themselves on mirrors and stayed there forever. She had given herself to one of his mother's spoons.

Peter apparently didn't like Bev's not paying attention to him, and he said, still looking at her, "He's not President yet, thank God. I should have put that in my prayer."

Gordon rose to this. "A little more time for your fatuous Ike to play golf—right? Or like this week, taking care of shop on a quail shoot on some guy's estate in Georgia?"

"Now, boys," Mrs. Bronson said, "act your age. How many times have we seen this, Amos?" she said, smiling at Mr. Cannahan. "Every time these two grown men come home and sit down at the table, it only takes them half an hour to slip back and be ten and eight years old. Isn't that so?"

Mr. Cannahan obviously wanted to agree with his old friend the hostess, but you could also see that he didn't want to offend Gordon and Peter—not at their mother's table—and especially not the lovely young thing on his left, around whom these family breezes seemed in some mysterious way to be swirling. He held his tongue.

Miss Alderhoff, in tune with all pains and sorrows, both at this table and elsewhere, said, "Mr. Eisenhower shouldn't have gone out shooting in the rain, poor man. He has bursitis, you know."

Gordon could see his mother sagging somewhat in her chair. This, he knew, meant that she was groping with her foot under the table for the bulge of the bell button under the rug down there. Then she must have found it; he heard the buzzer in the kitchen, and Flo burst in. "We'll need another bottle of red wine up here, Flo," his mother said. "How's the supply down at that end, Beth?"

"We could use another bottle," Aunt Beth said.

"White or red, Beth?"

"It's all the same to *me*," Aunt Beth said. She laughed her tinkling laugh.

"I think red here, too, Mother," Gordon said.

"Two red," Flo said, giving the swinging door a little whack with the flat of her hand as she left the room.

"You were playing Sibelius before," Beverly said to Gordon's mother. "Do you specially like his music?"

"Oh, yes. Do you know 'The Swan of Tuonela'?"

"Then you must also like Brahms," Beverly said. "And probably Rachmaninoff. I was th-thinking, why is it that really good pianists and conductors seem to live forever? When I was a little girl, my mother took me to hear Rachmaninoff, he was an old, old man, playing two of his concertos with the Philharmonic. Two concertos in one evening. I think I fell asleep, but I've never forgotten—that old man's f-frightening . . . p-power."

"Ah, Beverly," Gordon's mother said, her face winy and soft, "I can't wait to be really old. That regime! You wake up at five-thirty or so, and they give you a cup of hot milk. You snooze a bit until breakfast. Then you sit for a while under the dogwood tree and doze off. Later, you walk over to look at the strawberries, and then you go back to your chair and they bring you some hot consommé, but you're bored with consommé, so you don't take it, you just sit there: the spots of sun filtering through the tiny white saucers of the dogwood blossoms are so dazzling. Good heavens, you must have dropped off, it's lunchtime! After lunch you lie down on the sofa with a knitted throw over you. Then you get up and play some solitaire. A bath.

A highball. Supper. You fall asleep listening to the radio—only that's not your night-sleep—you'll need a toddy to insure your night-sleep. And then they put you to bed, and they actually tuck you in like a child. Think of it!"

Gordon felt a rush of gratitude. Beverly was so fine. Her face, like his mother's, was rosy and melted and a tiny bit swollen by the warmed blood of friendliness. Her scarf had slid down off to the left, and he stared at the curve of her bare pink neck down onto her pale bare shoulder. Suddenly, putting his fork down, he was overcome by a wish that he could get up and go around there and take Bev by the hand, and lead her upstairs to his old room, and receive her in his boyhood bed, and celebrate with her what there was to be most thankful for on this earth.

But Miss Rankin, who was perhaps not looking forward quite so eagerly as Gordon's mother to being "really old," broke his spell. She said in a cranky voice, "Did anyone see David Susskind interviewing Khrushchev in New York the other night?"

"Sure did," Uncle Solbert said, his orange hat askew. "He gave the old bugger what for, didn't he?"

"Did you notice," Miss Alderhoff said, "that Khrushchev drank mineral water instead of coffee during the program? He must have indigestion."

Little Freddie spoke up for the first time. "Susskind sucks," he said.

"I hope the big K does have a bad stomach," Peter said, speaking again straight to Bev. "God damn peasant."

"That's just it, Peter!" Beverly said. "Every clever Russian wants you to *think* he's a peasant. Did you ever read Gorky's reminiscence of . . . T-Tolstoy?" Gordon smiled at the thought of Peter reading even the morning paper. "Gorky read a story of his out loud to Tolstoy, and Tolstoy said he'd got his p-peasants all wrong. The old man said a Russian peasant will come up to you and talk in a silly and incoherent way. He does this on . . . p-purpose, so you'll think he's . . . st-stupid. He knows that people are open and direct with stupid people, and that's just what he wants, because you blurt out everything, you show all your c-cards, and right away he knows your . . . w-weaknesses."

"I think Beverly has a point there, Peter," Gordon's mother said, tapping Peter on the shoulder.

Peter colored violently. He started to say something, but Beverly had turned to Mr. Cannahan, who had finished his mashed bananas, and she was saying, "I like people with weak stomachs. It means that they . . . th-think about things. Maybe they think too m-much sometimes. But at least they think." As she said that last sentence she swerved her gaze back toward Peter.

Gordon saw that his mother was charmed by Beverly's kindness to Mr.

Cannahan, and Mr. Cannahan looked as if he might faint from pleasure. But Peter was still very red, and as he chewed, his lower jaw seemed to push out like a bulldozer blade. Gordon knew he must break in somehow, to change the drift of things.

He urgently pinged the back of his knife against his wineglass and then raised the glass and said, "Here's to the two women I love most in this world."

He knew on the instant that he had made a terrible mistake. He saw his mother, faced with the appalling idea of equivalence, suddenly looking at him as if she had no idea who he was. Bev, stricken pale, reached for her wineglass, presumably to raise it to his mother, or perhaps, Gordon thought in sudden panic, to throw it down the whole length of the table at him, but instead she clumsily knocked it over, and a flood of red, like guilty blood, soaked into one of the priceless lace doilies.

A dead silence followed, a pause in which a creaking of dry timbers could be heard, as if the whole house around them were heaving a deep sigh. Then came such a rush of exclamations that Gordon had a sensation of watching a speeded-up footage of film.

Peter cried out, "Ha!"

"Salt! Salt!" Aunt Beth shouted. "Put a lot of salt on it. I tell you, it's the only way to prevent a stain."

Beverly said, all too distinctly, "Sh-shit!" and then quickly added, "I'm s-so s-sorry, Mrs. Bronson."

"Jesus Christ," Peter said.

Uncle Solbert, absurd in his orange paper hat, said in a shocked voice, "Peter!"

Gordon's mother said to Peter, "Watch your tongue, Son. Have you forgotten what day this is?"—as if she herself had forgotten what day it actually was.

Old Miss Alderhoff pushed her chair back and stood up. "Well!" she said, "I am going to get a box of salt," and she marched around the table to the kitchen door.

Peter's wife, Molly, at Gordon's left, chose this moment to shout, "Mother Bronson, you've *always* favored Gordon over Petie. *Always.* You're not fair!"

Gordon's mother snapped out, "You stay out of this, Molly."

Little Caroline stood up, knocked her chair over backward, and ran sobbing into the living room. Awful Freddie's eyes were popping out with his first signs of pleasure all day. Miss Alderhoff appeared, with Flo right behind her holding high a blue cylindrical box as if it were the Statue of Liberty's torch, and they strode around the table in tandem. "Where is it? Where is it?" Flo kept asking. Uncle Solbert pointed; Flo leaned over his shoulder and poured a heap of salt on Beverly Zimmer's taint.

Gordon's first thought, scanning his mother's face for what might happen next, was that she suddenly looked a hundred. It was as if she'd got, all at once, her wish to be "really old." The caverns under her eyes had gone dark, her cheeks were bloodless, and the left side of her mouth sagged as if she'd had a stroke. He thought, Oh, God, I've ruined her Thanksgiving. And then, suddenly, with a forkful of maple-flavored turnip on his tongue and with his eyes abruptly peeled to truths for which there was no way of giving thanks, he saw the appalling emptiness, the bleakness, of his mother's life. Here she sat in a dark house with her best friends: two gossipy old maids and a man whose stomach burned year after year with the acidity of his enigmatic needs—three companions of her days and nights in empty prattle during endless bridge games. On top of that, she'd had to cope with her alcoholic brother Solbert and alcoholic sister-in-law Beth, who lived nearby. And then her raging son Peter; and his Molly, with a voice like the one you heard as a child on a tin-can telephone with a string stretched to the speaker's can; and their rotten children, her only grandchildren, affording her, too sadly, a hollow pride in her legacy. And then: what of the other son, at that moment swallowing turnip—what of him?

Gordon's mother turned to Beverly and asked in a kindly voice, "What do you like about my son?"

Gordon wondered what sort of trap his mother was setting.

"G-Gordon? Gordon?" Beverly asked twice, perhaps to stall for time. "What I like about G-Gordon is that he doesn't . . . sm-smoke cigars."

Mrs. Bronson laughed. "Good for you!" she said with generous admiration, as if Beverly had managed to drive a passing shot over the net that was stretched between them.

"Do you have any idea why he likes you?"

It was Beverly's turn to laugh. "He likes my being . . . di-di-di-disorderly. In my . . . th-thinking. You see, your son is very neat—very careful which dr-drawers he p-puts things in."

Gordon saw that the color was coming back into his mother's face. By God, she was a strong one, she had recovered, she was enjoying herself. He was tempted to ask his mother what it was in Beverly that *she* was beginning to like, but he was afraid to.

"How 'bout *your* drawers?" Peter said to Beverly. "Is he, like you say, c-careful?"

Little Freddie snickered.

"Shut *up*, Peter!" Uncle Solbert shouted.

"My heavens," Mr. Cannahan said.

"Molly," Gordon's mother said, projecting a hushed voice the length of the table, "sometimes your husband can be very annoying. But I'm sure you know that of your own knowledge." She turned back to Beverly and said, "Tell me more about my Gordon."

"Well," Bev said, "he's sort of muh-muh . . . m-*my* Gordon right now."

"Ah," Mrs. Bronson said. "You stake a claim. Do you believe his intentions are honorable, as they used to say?"

"Better ask him," Beverly said without a trace of a stammer.

"Gordon," his mother said, "serve some more turkey to whoever wants it, please."

Gordon felt a stab of anger. Having said that he and Peter reverted to being eight and ten years old at her table, his mother was now, for her purposes, treating him like a child. Staking *her* claim, he guessed. Careful to control his voice, he said, "Beverly and I are going to be married."

Uncle Solbert tore his paper hat off and waved it in circles over his head and shouted, "Hurray!"

"Congratulations," Mr. Cannahan said to Beverly, looking heart-broken.

"My God," Peter said.

"And you chose to tell me this at Thanksgiving dinner?" Gordon's mother said.

"I thought you'd be happy for me, Mother."

"Oh, but I am," she said, her voice trembling. "You have picked a winner. You've shown very good sense, Son." She turned to Beverly and said, her eyes brimming, "I have liked you, Miss Zimmer, from the moment you walked in the front door. My Gordon, if you will permit me to call him that once more, is a very lucky boy."

After a long pause Beverly said, "Your p-peach ch-chutney is the b-best I ever tasted."

"Thank you, my dear." Gordon saw his mother's face relax into a terrible smile of surrender, and he felt a rush of contrition and pity. She was amazing. She had caught her balance. "Marriage," she was saying to Bev, "isn't an easy estate. You'd better have a little chat with Molly down there about it. I was fairly lucky myself, but it wasn't easy, you know. My husband was an indecisive man, and—"

But Miss Alderhoff had raised her glass, and was calling out in a shrill voice, "Let's drink to the engagement. To Gordon and Miss Zimmer!"

"Yes! Yes!" cried Miss Rankin. "To the engagement!"

Uncle Solbert and Aunt Beth both cheered, but others at the table were quiet as they lifted their glasses and drank. Peter hesitated.

"Drink up, darling," Gordon's mother said to Peter. She seemed to be herself again. She caressed his arm. "Wish your brother luck, darling."

"Here's mud in your eye," Peter said to Gordon, before he gulped at his glass. He did not look at Beverly.

LUDWIG BEMELMANS

Grapes for Monsieur Cape

I was a commis de rang in Monsieur Victor's domain for several months, during which I met some remarkable people but none more remarkable than the maître d'hôtel whom the others sometimes called "Beau Maxime" because he was so ugly, and sometimes "Useless." Maxime was a bankrupt hotelkeeper from Paris. His ugliness was almost decorative; he had arthritis, and could hardly see out over the two cocoa-colored hammocks of wrinkles that hung under his smeary eyes. He had his station on the dining-room balcony where he could walk up and down with his cane and his beard and see himself reflected in the mirror.

He was a great trouble to the chefs de rang, the commis, and the kitchen because he took the guests' orders down wrong, forgot things, dictated orders upside down; his hand was too shaky to write, he held the menu up against his face and read it through a lorgnette.

When guests had eaten, smoked, and talked, and there was still no sign of a tip for him, a kind of hysteria would come over Beau Maxime. He became part of the table then. With heavy breath, he moved glasses about, took away a sugar bowl, dusted off a few breadcrumbs with the edge of his menu. Then he would leave for a while, but not for long, and the chicanery would start all over again. Again he moved the glasses back to where they were before; his eyelids twitched as he looked at the people; he brought a clean napkin to cover up a little coffee stain, he took away a vacant chair. If still nothing had happened, he bent to the guest's ear and asked if everything had been all right.

He mumbled as the guests started to leave, and watched them in the mirror and outside of it with a kind of despair in his face and hands, as if in a minute it would be too late to keep something terrible from happening. He kept behind them, pulled out their chairs, and bowed, and if again nothing happened, then he played his last card. He hung his stick on the banister, the service table, or over the back of a chair, and ran after them. He had a glove in his pocket, which he kept for just such purposes; he pulled this glove out and, in the center of the Jade Lounge, asked if they had forgotten it. Sometimes this worked; they would say no, but give him his dollar, and then he climbed back to the restaurant and up to his balcony.

He ate unbelievable amounts of food. The maîtres d'hôtel had luncheon and dinner before the guests, a very bad arrangement. They should be fed afterwards; a man who has just filled himself cannot recommend things well, he is asleep on his feet and makes unpleasant noises. But, as a matter of fact, they did also eat afterwards.

On the stations where the chefs and commis had their service tables, which contained extra plates, silver, napkins, vinegar, oil, ketchup bottles, and mustard pots, there were also electric heaters. On these heaters the commis put all the food that was left over after his chef had served the guests. After the guests had left, the commis took the food down to the employees' dining-room, where the chef de rang and his commis, sitting across from each other, shared it. With these meals they usually had a bottle of wine, bought underhand, and since the portions were liberal, and the food excellent, and too much of everything was ordered, the men ate very well and of the best, that is all of them did except the chefs and commis on Beau Maxime's station.

For after each serving he visited all the service tables on his station, of which there were three, and carefully lifted the covers of the casseroles, stirred around in them with a fork, fished out wings of capons, little tender foie gras dumplings, pieces of truffle, cocks' combs. Then he sent a commis for soup plates and, while the poor chef and the commis stared at him, he filled one of the plates with the very best of their leftovers. He grunted while he did this, his eyes shone and almost fell into the pots. For his second soup plate he would take a lobster claw, tilt the casserole to get the fine sauce for it, add some rice. In the third plate might go a little curry. When he had enough, one of the commis whom he had robbed, a pale little French boy, had to take the plate upstairs to the captains' dining-room. (On the stairway, when no one could see him, the commis carefully spat into all three plates.) Beau Maxime followed, a long French bread under his arm as if it were an umbrella.

Up there, he ate slowly, then moved his chair over to the window. From this third-floor window one could see over the curtains and into the fitting-room of a corsetière on the second floor of the building across the street, where, in the afternoon, fat women undressed to try on corsets. Beau Maxime took off his shoes and put his feet on a pile of used napkins that were put there to be counted later. He watched the scene for an hour and then fell asleep. A busboy cleared away the dishes and reset the table for the dinner of the maître d'hôtel, which was served at five-thirty. Maxime woke up in time for that, put on his shoes, and turned around, to eat.

He was the worst, this Beau Maxime, but all maîtres d'hôtel love to eat. They lean over sideboards, behind high screens, to stuff something quickly away. They are especially fond of little fried things which they can pick up from hot dishes as the commis bring them up from the kitchen, such easily disposed of things as whitebait, oyster crabs, fried scallops, frogs' legs, and fried potatoes. They have learned to eat so that their cheeks and jaws do not move; they can eat in the middle of the dining-room and no one know it.

One of the maîtres d'hôtel in the Splendide, a very good-looking one, had a front tooth missing, it was being repaired. At one very busy luncheon he took a green olive from a tray behind the screen on one of his service tables. Just then he was called to a table; the publisher Frank Munsey wanted to order the rest of his luncheon while he waited for his soup to cool. Mr. Munsey looked over the card that was handed him and decided on some *tête de veau en tortue*. As the maître d'hôtel repeated this, with its many T's, the olive pit shot out through the hole in his teeth and landed in Mr. Munsey's soup.

Fortunately the publisher was bent over talking to someone at the next table and saw nothing. The maître d'hôtel nervously asked if he could not take the soup back and get something hotter, but Mr. Munsey, a very much feared guest, said he had been waiting for it to cool, it was just about right now.

But there is a way out of such difficulties, a technique of upset and confusion, often employed in dangerous situations with hard clients. The maître d'hôtel first instructs the chef de rang and the commis; there is a small quick meeting—then excitement, noise, shouting, a waving in the face of bills of fare, some pushing, and one, two, three, the soup is gone. All this happens while the maître d'hôtel is a few tables away, so that the client can call him to complain. He comes, is surprised, and calls the waiter names: "Specimen of an idiot, where is the soup of Monsieur Munsey?" "Ah, pardon—I thought—" "You should not think, stupid one! Ah, Monsieur Munsey, pardon, pardon." The soup is back on the table after the commis, behind the screen, has fished the olive pit out with his fingers. For the rest of the meal the guest has perfect service, and when he leaves, the maître d'hôtel says once more: "So sorry about the soup," and for this he gets sometimes one, two, or five dollars, but never from Mr. Munsey.

But then, this maître d'hôtel was luckier than the one who had his station on the balcony diagonally across from Maxime's. He was a restless, hoppy Frenchman whose body was forever bending into the shape of compliments. He walked mostly backwards, like a crab, pulling customers from the door to his station. When he had nothing else to do, he made little pirouettes, looked at himself in a corner of the mirror, quickly, birdlike in gesture, tugged at his sleeves, pushed a handkerchief into his cuff. Old guests whom he knew from the Paris Splendide he greeted with both arms up in the air, wiggling to the door with dancing paces, with smiles of joy on his face. He had been in America only three weeks when I met him.

He had a trick of showing the anatomy of the kitchen on his own body. With his palm held flat as the blade of a carving knife, he traced the shape of a breast of guinea hen from under his arm to the lapel of his dress coat and down to his ribs. Lifting his leg up to the level of the table, he showed on it the cut of meat that was used for an *ossi bughi à la milanaise*. When speaking of fish, he again used his palm, laying it flat if the talk was of sole, and with the other hand he cut filets therefrom. He made a good deal of money, for many people love this theater.

One did not. She was the wife of a steel man, who was also a judge. She was old and ugly; her dresses were like the robes of a stout priest, they fell flat from a plateau of flesh under her chin and covered a tub filled with fat. Stomach, legs, and breasts were pressed together in this volume so one could not see where they began and ended. Out of the shoulders came two arms, red and thick, coarse-skinned, with common hands. The feet were in tight shoes.

From her hat there usually hung a veil; when the veil was lifted, it revealed a face that had the texture of an old pocketbook; on its worn-out corners rested the ends of a mouth, that was closed to with a snap. Gray, carmine, and purple veins covered her face, and patches of its skin would jump as does the skin on the flanks of horses when flies come near them. Her ears were thick bunches on one disorderly shape that included face, neck, and shoulders.

She had to stop for breath at every step when she came up the short, decorative stairway of the restaurant. She would stop to hold onto the banister, to groan and take hold of herself, and she would look around as if for help, as if angry, yet not what the word helpless means.

Behind her, baldheaded and quiet, walked the Steel Judge, mostly in light gray clothes and with a face that was old, Japanese, and cigar-colored. Madame always referred to him as "The Judge."

Large compliments went to them from the man who opened the door of their car on the sidewalk, from Monsieur Victor on the stairway, from all the maîtres d'hôtel, the chefs de rang, the commis, the musicians, from the last coatroom girl. For they were very liberal, and gave a small fortune away at Christmas time.

Madame also brought with her on every visit her own butler. He carried her own wine cooler and at large parties arrived with a second man to supplement his supply of the champagne she liked. The judge and his wife were invited to the very best parties, but no matter at whose table she sat, Madame insisted on her own champagne.

She laughed with the sound of a wild bird, a screech, that filled the large oval dining-room with its "Kwaaa, kaaa, kwaaaaa," and she laughed most in the company of her friends, two women who were always with her when she came alone—one who was equally fearful and dressed with the same costly despair, the wife of some streetcar magnate; and the second intimate, a woman with traces of gentility, a face that once must have been nice, who could not see, squinted, and had an Italian villa in Long Island, but a political husband with a red nose. They called themselves, when speaking of anything they would do together, "We Girls."

These three arrived one day when the only free table good enough, at which they could be seated immediately and without trouble, was on the edge of the balcony, in front of the mirror, on the station of the hoppy Frenchman. He bowed and scraped, danced and pirouetted, and pulled out their chairs. They sat down, and Madame complained, as she often did, about the fact that the menu was printed in French.

"What is," she asked the maître d'hôtel, "what is an *escalope de veau à l'ancienne?*"

He lifted his leg and with a flat hand showed her from what part of the animal the cutlet came. That was easy, but *veau* was difficult. He thought about the problem for a minute with many grimaces, and then smiled. He bent down, made a cute figure, and put his face close to the hat to say that he did not know the *américain* word for *veau*, but that he would try to explain.

"You have a son, Madame?"

"No," she said.

"Well, we assume you have a son, Madame."

"So what?"

"You, Madame, are *vache*, your son is *veau*. *Escalope de veau* is a cutlet of son of cow."

She laughed her terrible laugh again, called for Monsieur Victor and said:

"Fire that son of a bitch."

Everyone in the hotel was saying: "Monsieur Cape is coming, Monsieur Cape is coming from England." There was much cleaning up and shining, and everybody seemed to be afraid of Monsieur Cape. For Monsieur Cape was the president of our company. His offices were in London, and from there he always went on his rounds first to Paris, where the company had another big hotel, then across to Rio de Janeiro and Havana, where the company also had restaurants, and finally to the Splendide.

Serafini told me that from Thursday on I would be on duty every morning at seven, with clean collar, brushed hair, shined shoes, and fingernails in shape, to serve Monsieur Cape's breakfast; and that, he added, was "a great honor."

At last the great man arrived, was received with much bowing and scraping, and was installed in the Adam Suite, one of the private apartments, our most palatial accommodations. It was a completely isolated duplex home with its own salon, dining-room, staircase, and back service-entrance. Up the latter, every morning, I brought breakfast to him and his niece. For he had brought a very beautiful niece with him, a girl with blue eyes and ash-blond hair. He had many nieces, the chambermaid told me; this was the fifth one, and always a different one came with him from England, and the maid closed one eye when she said that.

In bed Mr. Cape was very small and not much bigger when he got up. He had a red face with a small beard at the bottom, which made it look like a radish upside down. He talked very little and walked back and forth, playing with the keys in his pocket and looking at the floor, like Uncle Hans. One of the first things he did whenever he came from England was to go to the coatroom of the restaurant, where there was a beautiful Irish girl, take her arm, go behind a sea-green drapery with her, and there whisper a joke into her ear. Unlike the nieces, it was always the same joke.

For his breakfast I had to go down into the kitchen and first of all order a basket of fruit from an old Frenchman in charge of them. The fruit was kept in the innermost and coldest refrigerator of a series of three, one inside the other. I gave the old Frenchman a slip on which I had written: "*Un Panier de Fruit,"* and under this, underscored with two thick lines: *"Pour Monsieur Cape."*

It always took a lot of time. The old man searched for the keys, unlocked each refrigerator in turn, skewered the slip on a long bent needle that hung over his desk, and said to himself several times: *"Un panier de fruit, pour Monsieur Cape."* When we were inside, he held the fruit up to his eyes, placed it in the basket, and rearranged it several times to get the right Fruit Basket feeling.

When all was built up to his satisfaction, he placed a bunch of grapes on top, a big beautiful Belgian hothouse bunch with fat grapes that were so closely pressed together that some of them had square sides. These grapes came six bunches to a box, in a bed of ground cork and soft tissue paper. Then, in the open spaces around the grapes, the old Frenchman put a few more figs and plums, and finally he straightened out and said: *"Voilà, mon petit, un panier de fruit pour Monsieur Cape."*

I carried the basket of fruit carefully upstairs. In the warm air outside of the icebox a film of water in tiny beads set on all the fruit; the plums were most beautiful that way. Fruit should always be served so, from out of the cold.

On my first trip up, I also took with me a fingerbowl, a pair of silver shears for the grapes, and the linen. Then I went down again, by the private staircase, through the reception room of the apartment, out the door to the hotel corridor, down with the service elevator, across the pantry, and down into the kitchen. On the second trip up, I brought the orange juice for the niece, the porridge, and the tea. For everything I had to write slips with *"Pour Monsieur Cape"* underlined.

After I had carried all this upstairs, I sat in the salon and waited until Monsieur Cape rang. The little alcohol flames burned under the silver kettle—he made his own tea—and under the porridge which stood in a dish of hot water. For the toast I had to run down a third time while Monsieur Cape ate his fruit. It was a job nobody liked.

It took a long time for him to wake up. I started with the basket of fruit at seven-thirty and busied myself with this breakfast until about nine-thirty, because, while I was there, no one could call me away for any other duty. On the desk in the salon were the accounts of the hotel. I read them every morning; much was in red ink; it did not seem to be a very profitable hotel. Uncle Hans's hotels were much better paying. After I had read the accounts and the English funny papers, there was nothing to do.

I started on the first day to eat a few of the grapes on the Belgian hothouse bunch. The bunch got to look bad on one side, so I turned it around. But still Monsieur Cape did not ring, and I ate more on the good side. Then the bunch was altogether bad-looking; it was impossible to serve it to anyone and so I finished it and put some figs in its place. From then on I ate a bunch of grapes every morning.

Soon after I had eaten the grapes, a door would open and I would hear a little swish of nightgown and soft steps. That was the niece going to her own bedroom. Then another door would open and close and soon the little bell would ring and Monsieur Cape got his breakfast. The niece would come in and say "Good morning" to me and to the uncle, and then she would sit on the side of the bed and help him prepare his tea. When I bent over, I could smell her hair and see that she was very young and firm and beautiful.

When I took the dishes down and brought the basket back to the icebox, it was about nine-thirty and the first chef was in his office, through the window of which he could see me pass and hand the basket back to the old man.

The first chef was, of course, also a Frenchman, but he was tall and, unlike most cooks and most Frenchmen, very quiet and self-controlled. One had to stand close to him to hear what he said, for he never raised his voice, not even in the greatest luncheon rush, when dishes clattered and the cooks were red in the face and excited and everybody ran and shouted. He was very saving for the hotel and he knew the contents of all his iceboxes. He also knew about the fruit and the basket for Mr. Cape and, of course, about the grapes.

When I came back with the basket, he always stepped to the door and looked at it, and said quietly: "They are costly, these grapes of Belgium." I wrote out a slip then, for *"Une grappe de raisin de Belgique,"* and for whatever other fruit had been used up, and the old man took it in exchange for the slip I had given him before for the whole basket. The first slip was torn up, and the slip for the grapes was collected by the accounting department with all the others and billed, but of course the president of the company had everything free and never received a bill.

All this went along very nicely for weeks. In the morning I served Monsieur Cape and in the evening worked in the wind-swept roof garden, overlooking the city from the thirty-second floor. There was a foyer on it with little tables and a large buffet that was made of tin containers filled with ice and with a little fountain in its center.

About six o'clock I had to be up there and help arrange cold dishes on the ice: large salmons in parsley and lemons, glacéd pheasants, poussins in aspic, cold boeuf à la mode, galantines of capon, hors d'oeuvres, saucissons d'Arles, sauce verte, mayonnaise, beautifully decorated salads, strawberry tarts with whipped cream, compotes—many fine, good things. The first chef supervised all this and watched out that nothing disappeared.

On a very hot evening Monsieur Cape and his niece came and waited for their dinner guests in the chairs in front of the buffet. In a little while Monsieur Cape was walking back and forth, with his hands in his pockets playing with his keys. The chef had not seen Monsieur Cape since his arrival and he bowed and smiled. The guests were arriving now and engaging Monsieur Cape in conversation as they walked away from the buffet, and I thought everything was going to turn out all right. But the chef walked in front of them, and Monsieur Cape shook hands with him and introduced him to his guests. The air became thick, and though the chef spoke so quietly, I could hear him say: "Monsieur Cape loves the Belgian hothouse grapes I send up every morning, yes?"

"What Belgian hothouse grapes?" asked Monsieur Cape.

I did not hear any more because I went out quickly with some plates.

The chef sent for me, he held my arm so tight it hurt, and he said quietly: "*Sacré voleur!* It is shameful, such a young man of good family as you are! You will never be allowed to serve Monsieur Cape again."

A. J. LIEBLING

A Good Appetite

In the heroic age before the First World War, there were men and women who ate, in addition to a whacking lunch and a glorious dinner, a voluminous *souper* after the theater or the other amusements of the evening. I have known some of the survivors, octogenarians of unblemished appetite and unfailing good humor—spry, wry, and free of the ulcers that come from worrying about a balanced diet—but they have had no emulators in France since the doctors there discovered the existence of the human liver. From that time on, French life has been built to an increasing extent around that organ, and a niggling caution has replaced the old recklessness; the liver was the seat of the Maginot mentality. One of the last of the great around-the-clock gastronomes of France was Yves Mirande, a small, merry author of farces and musical-comedy books. In 1955, Mirande celebrated his eightieth birthday with a speech before the curtain of the Théâtre Antoine, in the management of which he was associated with Mme. B., a protégée of his, forty years younger than himself. But the theater was only half of his life. In addition, M. Mirande was an unofficial director of a restaurant on the Rue Saint-Augustin, which he had founded for another protégée, also forty years younger than himself; this was Mme. G., a Gasconne and a magnificent cook. In the restaurant on the Rue Saint-Augustin, M. Mirande would dazzle his juniors, French and American, by dispatching a lunch of raw Bayonne ham and fresh figs, a hot sausage in crust, spindles of filleted pike in a rich rose *sauce Nantua*, a leg of lamb larded with anchovies, artichokes on a pedestal

43

of foie gras, and four or five kinds of cheese, with a good bottle of Bordeaux and one of champagne, after which he would call for the Armagnac and remind Madame to have ready for dinner the larks and ortolans she had promised him, with a few *langoustes* and a turbot—and, of course, a fine *civet* made from the *marcassin*, or young wild boar, that the lover of the leading lady in his current production had sent up from his estate in the Sologne. "And while I think of it," I once heard him say, "we haven't had any woodcock for days, or truffles baked in the ashes, and the cellar is becoming a disgrace—no more '34s and hardly any '37s. Last week, I had to offer my publisher a bottle that was far too good for him, simply because there was nothing between the insulting and the superlative."

M. Mirande had to his credit a hundred produced plays, including a number of great Paris hits, but he had just written his first book for print, so he said "my publisher" in a special mock-impressive tone. "An informal sketch for my definitive autobiography," he would say of this production. The informal sketch, which I cherish, begins with the most important decision in Mirande's life. He was almost seventeen and living in the small Breton port of Lannion—his offstage family name was Le Querrec—when his father, a retired naval officer, said to him, "It is time to decide your future career. Which will it be, the Navy or the Church?" No other choice was conceivable in Lannion. At dawn, Yves ran away to Paris.

There, he had read a thousand times, all the famous wits and cocottes frequented the tables in front of the Café Napolitain, on the Boulevard des Capucines. He presented himself at the café at nine the next morning—late in the day for Lannion—and found that the place had not yet opened. Soon he became a newspaperman. It was a newspaper era as cynically animated as the corresponding period of the Bennett-Pulitzer-Hearst competition in New York, and in his second or third job he worked for a press lord who was as notional and niggardly as most press lords are; the publisher insisted that his reporters be well turned out, but did not pay them salaries that permitted cab fares when it rained. Mirande lived near the fashionable Montmartre cemetery and solved his rainy-day pants-crease problem by crashing funeral parties as they broke up and riding, gratis, in the carriages returning to the center of town. Early in his career, he became personal secretary to Clemenceau and then to Briand, but the gay theater attracted him more than politics, and he made the second great decision of his life after one of his political patrons had caused him to be appointed *sous-préfet* in a provincial city. A *sous-préfet* is the administrator of one of the districts into which each of the ninety *départements* of France is divided, and a young *sous-préfet* is often headed for a precocious rise to high positions of state. Mirande, attired in the magnificent uniform that was then de rigueur, went to his "capital," spent one night there, and then ran off to Paris again to direct a one-act farce. Nevertheless, his connections with the serious world remained cordial. In the restaurant on the Rue Saint-Augustin, he introduced me to Colette, by that time a national glory of letters.

The regimen fabricated by Mirande's culinary protégée, Mme. G., maintained him *en pleine forme*. When I first met him, in the restaurant during the summer of the Liberation, he was a sprightly sixty-nine. In the spring of 1955, when we renewed a friendship that had begun in admiration of each other's appetite, he was as good as ever. On the occasion of our reunion, we began with a *truite au bleu*—a live trout simply done to death in hot water, like a Roman emperor in his bath. It was served up doused with enough melted butter to thrombose a regiment of Paul Dudley Whites, and accompanied, as was right, by an Alsatian wine—a Lacrimae Sanctae Odiliae, which once contributed slightly to my education. Long ago, when I was very young, I took out a woman in Strasbourg and, wishing to impress her with my knowledge of local customs, ordered a bottle of Ste. Odile. I was making the same mistake as if I had taken out a girl in Boston and offered her baked beans. "How quaint!" the woman in Strasbourg said. "I haven't drunk that for years." She excused herself to go to the telephone, and never came back.

After the trout, Mirande and I had two meat courses, since we could not decide in advance which we preferred. We had a magnificent *daube provençale*, because we were faithful to *la cuisine bourgeoise*, and then *pintadous*—young guinea hens, simply and tenderly roasted—with the first asparagus of the year, to show our fidelity to *la cuisine classique*. We had clarets with both courses—a Pétrus with the *daube*, a Cheval Blanc with the guineas. Mirande said that his doctor had discounseled Burgundies. It was the first time in our acquaintance that I had heard him admit he had a doctor, but I was reassured when he drank a bottle and a half of Krug after luncheon. We had three bottles between us—one to our loves, one to our countries, and one for symmetry, the last being on the house.

Mirande was a small, alert man with the face of a Celtic terrier—salient eyebrows and an upturned nose. He looked like an intelligent Lloyd George. That summer, in association with Mme. B., his theatrical protégée, he planned to produce a new play of Sartre's. His mind kept young by the theater of Mme. B., his metabolism protected by the restaurant of Mme. G., Mirande seemed fortified against all eventualities for at least another twenty years. Then, perhaps, he would have to recruit new protégées. The Sunday following our reunion, I encountered him at Longchamp, a racecourse where the restaurant does not face the horses, and diners can keep first things first.

There he sat, radiant, surrounded by celebrities and champagne buckets, sending out a relay team of commissionaires to bet for him on the successive tips that the proprietors of stables were ravished to furnish him between races. He was the embodiment of a happy man. (I myself had a nice thing at 27-1.)

The first alteration in Mirande's fortunes affected me so directly that I did not at once sense its gravity for him. Six weeks later, I was again in Paris. (That year, I was shuttling frequently between there and London.) I was alone on the evening I arrived, and looked forward to a pleasant dinner at Mme. G.'s, which was within two hundred meters of the hotel, in the Square Louvois, where I always stop. Madame's was more than a place to eat, although one ate superbly there. Arriving, I would have a bit of talk with the proprietress, then with the waitresses—Germaine and Lucienne—who had composed the original staff. Waiters had been added as the house prospered, but they were of less marked personality. Madame was a bosomy woman—voluble, tawny, with a big nose and lank black hair—who made one think of a Saracen. (The Saracens reached Gascony in the eighth century.) Her conversation was a chronicle of letters and the theater—as good as a subscription to *Figaro Littéraire*, but more advanced. It was somewhere between the avant-garde and the main body, but within hailing distance of both and enriched with the names of the great people who had been in recently—M. Cocteau, Gene Kelly, la Comtesse de Vogüé. It was always well to give an appearance of listening, lest she someday fail to save for you the last order of larks *en brochette* and bestow them on a more attentive customer. With Germaine and Lucienne, whom I had known when we were all younger, in 1939, the year of the *drôle de guerre*, flirtation was now perfunctory, but the *carte du jour* was still the serious topic—for example, how the fat Belgian industrialist from Tournai had reacted to the *caille vendangeuse*, or quail potted with fresh grapes. "You know the man," Germaine would say. "If it isn't dazzling, he takes only two portions. But when he has three, then you can say to yourself . . ." She and Lucienne looked alike—compact little women, with high foreheads and cheekbones and solid, muscular legs, who walked like *chasseurs à pied*, a hundred and thirty steps to the minute. In 1939, and again in 1944, Germaine had been a brunette and Lucienne a blonde, but in 1955 Germaine had become a blonde, too, and I found it hard to tell them apart.

Among my fellow customers at Mme. G.'s I was always likely to see some friend out of the past. It is a risk to make an engagement for an entire evening with somebody you haven't seen for years. This is particularly true in France now. The almost embarrassingly pro-American acquaintance of the Liberation may be by now a Communist Party-line hack; the idealistic young Resistance journalist may have become an editorial writer for the reactionary newspaper of a textile magnate. The Vichy apologist you met in Washington in 1941, who called de Gaulle a traitor and the creation of the British Intelligence Service, may now tell you that the General is the best thing ever, while the fellow you knew as a de Gaulle aide in London may now compare him to Sulla destroying the Roman Republic. As for the women, who is to say which of them has resisted the years? But in a good restaurant that all have frequented, you are likely to meet any of them again, for good restaurants are not so many nowadays that a Frenchman will permanently desert one—unless, of course, he is broke, and in that case it would depress you to learn of his misfortunes. If you happen to encounter your old friends when they are already established at their tables, you have the opportunity to greet them cordially and to size them up. If you still like them, you can make a further engagement.

On the ghastly evening I speak of—a beautiful one in June—I perceived no change in the undistinguished exterior of Mme. G.'s restaurant. The name—something like Prospéria—was the same, and since the plate-glass windows were backed with scrim, it was impossible to see inside. Nor, indeed, did I notice any difference when I first entered. The bar, the tables, the banquettes covered with leatherette, the simple décor of mirrors and pink marble slabs were the same. The premises had been a business employees' bar-and-café before Mme. G., succeeding a long string of obscure proprietors, made it illustrious. She had changed the fare and the clientele but not the cadre. There are hundreds of identical fronts and interiors in Paris, turned out by some mass producer in the late twenties. I might have been warned by the fact that the room was empty, but it was only eight o'clock and still light outdoors. I had come unusually early because I was so hungry. A man whom I did not recognize came to meet me, rubbing his hands and hailing me as an old acquaintance. I thought he might be a waiter who had served me. (The waiters, as I have said, were not the marked personalities of the place.) He had me at a table before I sensed the trap.

"Madame goes well?" I asked politely.

"No, Madame is lightly ill," he said, with what I now realize was a guilty air.

He presented me with a *carte du jour* written in the familiar purple ink on the familiar wide sheet of paper with the name and telephone number of the restaurant at the top. The content of the menu, however, had become Italianized, the spelling had deteriorated, and the prices had diminished to a point where it would be a miracle if the food continued distinguished.

"Madame still conducts the restaurant?" I asked sharply.

I could now see that he was a Piedmontese of the most evasive description. From rubbing his hands he had switched to twisting them.

"Not exactly," he said, "but we make the same cuisine."

I could not descry anything in the smudged ink but misspelled noodles and unorthographical *"escaloppinis"*; Italians writing French by ear produce a regression to an unknown ancestor of both languages.

"Try us," my man pleaded, and, like a fool, I did. I was hungry. Forty minutes later, I stamped out into the street as purple as an *aubergine* with rage. The minestrone had been cabbage scraps in greasy water. I had chosen *côtes d'agneau* as the safest item in the mediocre catalogue that the Prospéria's prospectus of bliss had turned into overnight. They had been cut from a tired Alpine billy goat and seared in machine oil, and the *haricots verts* with which they were served resembled decomposed whiskers from a theatrical costume beard.

"The same cuisine?" I thundered as I flung my money on the falsified *addition* that I was too angry to verify. "You take me for a jackass!"

I am sure that as soon as I turned my back the scoundrel nodded. The restaurant has changed hands at least once since then.

In the morning, I telephoned Mirande. He confirmed the disaster. Mme. G., ill, had closed the restaurant. Worse, she had sold the lease and the good will, and had definitely retired.

"What is the matter with her?" I asked in a tone appropriate to fatal disease.

"I think it was trying to read Simone de Beauvoir," he said. "A syncope."

Mme. G. still lives, but Mirande is dead. When I met him in Paris the following November, his appearance gave no hint of decline. It was the season for his sable-lined overcoat *à l'impresario*, and a hat that was a furry cross between a porkpie and a homburg. Since the restaurant on the Rue Saint-Augustin no longer existed, I had invited him to lunch with me at a very small place called the Gratin Dauphinois, on the Rue Chabanais, directly across from the building that once housed the most celebrated sporting house in Paris. The Rue Chabanais is a short street that runs from the Square Louvois to the Rue des Petits Champs—perhaps a hundred yards— but before the reform wave stimulated by a Municipal Councilor named Marthe Richard at the end of the Second World War, the name Chabanais had a cachet all its own. Mme. Richard will go down in history as the Carry Nation of sex. Now the house is closed, and the premises are devoted to some low commercial purpose. The walls of the midget Gratin Dauphinois are hung with cartoons that have a nostalgic reference to the past glories of the street.

Mirande, when he arrived, crackled with jokes about the locale. He taunted me with being a criminal who haunts the scene of his misdeeds. The fare at the Gratin is robust, as it is in Dauphiné, but it did not daunt Mirande. The wine card, similarly, is limited to the strong, rough wines of Arbois and the like, with a couple of Burgundies for clients who want to show off. There are no clarets; the proprietor hasn't heard of them. There are, of course, a few champagnes, for wedding parties or anniversaries, so Mirande, with Burgundies discounseled by his doctor, decided on champagne throughout the meal. This was a *drôle* combination with the mountain food, but I had forgotten about the lack of claret when I invited him.

We ordered a couple of dozen *escargots en pots de chambre* to begin with. These are snails baked and served, for the client's convenience, in individual earthenware crocks, instead of being forced back into shells. The snail, of course, has to be taken out of his shell to be prepared for cooking. The shell he is forced back into may not be his own. There is thus not even a sentimental justification for his reincarceration. The frankness of the service *en pot* does not improve the preparation of the snail, nor does it detract from it, but it does facilitate and accelerate his consumption. (The notion that the shell proves the snail's authenticity, like the head left on a woodcock, is invalid, as even a suburban housewife knows nowadays; you can buy a tin of snail shells in a supermarket and fill them with a mixture of nutted cream cheese and chopped olives.)

Mirande finished his dozen first, meticulously swabbing out the garlicky butter in each *pot* with a bit of bread that was fitted to the bore of the crock as precisely as a bullet to a rifle barrel. Tearing bread like that takes practice. We had emptied the first bottle of champagne when he placed his right hand delicately on the point of his waistcoat farthest removed from his spinal column.

"Liebling," he said, "I am not well."

It was like the moment when I first saw Joe Louis draped on the ropes. A great pity filled my heart. "*Maître*," I said, "I will take you home."

The dismayed *patronne* waved to her husband in the kitchen (he could see her through the opening he pushed the dishes through) to suspend the preparation of the *gendarme de Morteau*—the great smoked sausage in its tough skin—that we had proposed to follow the snails with. ("Short and broad in shape, it is made of pure pork and . . . is likely to be accompanied . . . by hot potato salad."—Waverly Root, page 217.) We had decided to substitute for the *pommes à l'huile* the *gratin dauphinois* itself. ("Thinly sliced potatoes are moistened with boiled milk and beaten egg, seasoned with salt, pepper, and nutmeg, and mixed with grated cheese, of the Gruyère type. The potatoes are then put into an earthenware dish which has been rubbed with garlic and then buttered, spotted with little dabs of butter, and sprinkled with more grated cheese. It is then cooked slowly in not too hot an oven."—Root, page 228.) After that, we were going to have a fowl in cream with *morilles*—wild black mushrooms of the mountains. We abandoned all.

I led Mirande into the street and hailed a taxi.

"I am not well, Liebling," he said. "I grow old."

He lived far from the restaurant, beyond the Place de l'Etoile, in the Paris of the successful. From time to time on our way, he would say, "It is nothing. You must excuse me. I am not well."

The apartment house in which he and Mme. B. lived resembled one of the chic modern museums of the quarter, with entrance gained through a maze of garden patches sheathed in glass. Successive metal grilles swung open before us as I pushed buttons that Mirande indicated—in these modern palaces there are no visible flunkies—until we reached an elevator that smoothly shot us upward to his apartment, which was rather larger in area than the Square Louvois. The décor, with basalt columns and floors covered with the skin of jumbo Siberian tigers—a special strain force-fed to supply old-style movie stars—reminded me of the sets for *Belphégor*, a French serial of silent days that I enjoyed when I was a student at the Sorbonne in 1926. (It was, I think, about an ancient Egyptian high priest who came to life and set up bachelor quarters in Paris in the style of the Temple of Karnak.) Three or four maids rushed to relieve Mirande of his sable-lined coat, his hat, and his cane topped with the horn of an albino chamois. I helped him to a divan on which two Theda Baras could have defended their honor simultaneously against two villains of the silents without either couple's getting in the other's way. Most of the horizontal surfaces in the room were covered with sculpture and most of the vertical ones with large paintings. In pain though he was, Mirande called my attention to these works of art.

"All the sculptures are by Renoir," he said. "It was his hobby. And all the paintings are by Maillol. It was *his* hobby. If it were the other way around, I would be one of the richest chaps in France. Both men were my friends. But then, one doesn't give one's friends one's bread and butter. And, after all, it's less banal as it is."

After a minute, he asked me to help him to his bedroom, which was in a wing of the apartment all his own. When we got there, one of the maids came in and took his shoes off.

"I am in good hands now, Liebling," he said. "Farewell until next time. It is nothing."

I telephoned the next noon, and he said that his doctor, who was a fool, insisted that he was ill.

Again I left Paris, and when I returned, late the following January, I neglected Mirande. A Father William is a comforting companion for the middle-aged—he reminds you that the best is yet to be and that there's a dance in the old dame yet—but a sick old man is discouraging. My conscience stirred when I read in a gossip column in *France-Dimanche* that Toto Mirande was convalescing nicely and was devouring caviar at a great rate—with champagne, of course. (I had never thought of Mirande as Toto, which is baby slang for "little kid," but from then on I never referred to him in any other way; I didn't want anybody to think I wasn't in the know.) So the next day I sent him a pound of fresh caviar from Kaspia, in the Place de la Madeleine. It was the kind of medication I approved of.

I received a note from Mirande by tube next morning, reproaching me for spoiling him. He was going better, he wrote, and would telephone in a day or two to make an appointment for a return bout. When he called, he said that the idiotic doctor would not yet permit him to go out to a restaurant, and he invited me, instead, to a family dinner at Mme. B.'s. "Only a few old friends, and not the cuisine I hope to give you at Maxim's next time," he said. "But one makes out."

On the appointed evening, I arrived early—or on time, which amounts to the same thing—*chez* Mme. B.; you take taxis when you can get them in Paris at the rush hours. The handsome quarter overlooking the Seine above the Trocadéro is so dull that when my taxi deposited me before my host's door, I had no inclination to stroll to kill time. It is like Park Avenue or the near North Side of Chicago. So I was the first or second guest to arrive, and Mme. B.'s fourteen-year-old daughter, by a past marriage, received me in the Belphégor room, apologizing because her mother was still with Toto—she called him that. She need not have told me, for at that moment I heard Madame, who is famous for her determined voice, storming at an unmistakable someone: "You go too far, Toto. It's disgusting. People all over Paris are kind enough to send you caviar, and because you call it monotonous, you throw it at the maid! If you think servants are easy to come by . . ."

When they entered the room a few minutes later, my old friend was all smiles. "How did you know I adore caviar to such a point?" he asked me. But I was worried because of what I had heard; the Mirande I remembered would never have been irritated by the obligation to eat a few extra kilos of fresh caviar. The little girl, who hoped I had not heard, embraced Toto. "Don't be angry with *Maman!*" she implored him.

My fellow guests included the youngish new wife of an old former Premier, who was unavoidably detained in Lille at a congress of the party he now headed; it mustered four deputies, of whom two formed a Left Wing and two a Right Wing. ("If they had elected a fifth at the last election, or if, by good luck, one had been defeated, they could afford the luxury of a Center," Mirande told me in identifying the lady. "*C'est malheureux*, a party without a Center. It limits the possibilities of maneuver.") There was also an amiable couple in their advanced sixties or beginning seventies, of whom the husband was the grand manitou of Veuve Clicquot champagne. Mirande introduced them by their right name, which I forget, and during the rest of the evening addressed them as M. and Mme. Clicquot. There was a forceful, black-haired man from the Midi, in the youth of middle age—square-shouldered, stocky, decisive, blatantly virile—who, I was told, managed Mme. B.'s vinicultural enterprises in Provence. There were two guests of less decided individuality, whom I barely remember, and filling out the party were the young girl—shy, carefully unsophisticated and unadorned—Mme. B., Mirande, and me. Mme. B. had a strong triangular face on a strong triangular base—a strong chin, high cheekbones, and a wide, strong jaw, but full of stormy good nature. She was a woman who, if she had been a man, would have wanted to be called Honest John. She had a high color and an iron handgrip, and repeatedly affirmed that there was no affectation about her, that she was *sans façon*, that she called her shots as she saw them. "I won't apologize," she said to me. "I know you're a great feeder, like Toto here, but I won't offer you the sort of menu he used to get in that restaurant you know of, where he ruined his plumbing. Oh, that woman! I used to be so jealous. I can offer only a simple home dinner." And she waved us toward a marble table about twenty-two feet long. Unfortunately for me, she meant it. The dinner began with a kidney-and-mushroom mince served in a giant popover—the kind of thing you might get at a literary hotel in New York. The inner side of the pastry had the feeling of a baby's palm, in the true tearoom tradition.

"It is savory but healthy," Madame said firmly, setting an example by taking a large second helping before starting the dish on its second round. Mirande regarded the untouched doughy fabric on his plate with diaphanously veiled horror, but he had an excuse in the state of his health. "It's still a little rich for me, darling," he murmured. The others, including me, delivered salvos of compliments. I do not squander my moral courage on minor crises. M. Clicquot said, "Impossible to obtain anything like this *chez* Lapérouse!" Mme. Clicquot said, "Not even at the Tour d'Argent!"

"And what do you think of my little wine?" Mme. B. asked M. Clicquot. "I'm so anxious for your professional opinion—as a rival producer, you know."

The wine was a thin *rosé* in an Art Nouveau bottle with a label that was a triumph of lithography; it had spires and monks and troubadours and blondes in wimples on it, and the name of the *cru* was spelled out in letters with Gothic curlicues and pennons. The name was something like Château Guillaume d'Aquitaine, *grand vin.*

"What a madly gay little wine, my dear!" M. Clicquot said, repressing, but not soon enough, a grimace of pain.

"One would say a Tavel of a good year," I cried, "if one were a complete bloody fool." I did not say the second clause aloud.

My old friend looked at me with new respect. He was discovering in me a capacity for hypocrisy that he had never credited me with before.

The main course was a shoulder of mutton with white beans—the poor relation of a gigot, and an excellent dish in its way, when not too dry. This was.

For the second wine, the man from the Midi proudly produced a red, in a bottle without a label, which he offered to M. Clicquot with the air of a tomcat bringing a field mouse to its master's feet. "Tell me what you think of this," he said as he filled the champagne man's glass.

M. Clicquot—a veteran of such challenges, I could well imagine—held the glass against the light, dramatically inhaled the bouquet, and then drank, after a slight stiffening of the features that indicated to me that he knew what he was in for. Having emptied half the glass, he deliberated.

"It has a lovely color," he said.

"But what is it? What is it?" the man from the Midi insisted.

"There are things about it that remind me of a Beaujolais," M. Clicquot said (he must have meant that it was wet), "but on the whole I should compare it to a Bordeaux" (without doubt unfavorably).

Mme. B.'s agent was beside himself with triumph. "Not one or the other!" he crowed. "It's from the *domaine*—the Château Guillaume d'Aquitaine!"

The admirable M. Clicquot professed astonishment, and I, when I had emptied a glass, said that there would be a vast market for the wine in America if it could be properly presented. "Unfortunately," I said, "the cost of advertising . . . ." and I rolled my eyes skyward.

"Ah, yes," Mme. B. cried sadly. "The cost of advertising!"

I caught Mirande looking at me again, and thought of the Pétrus and the Cheval Blanc of our last meal together *chez* Mme. G. He drank a glass of the red. After all, he wasn't going to die of thirst.

For dessert, we had a simple fruit tart with milk—just the thing for an invalid's stomach, although Mirande didn't eat it.

M. Clicquot retrieved the evening, oenologically, by producing two bottles of a wine "impossible to find in the cellars of any restaurant in France"—Veuve Clicquot '19. There is at present a great to-do among wine merchants in France and the United States about young wines, and an accompanying tendency to cry down the "legend" of the old. For that matter, hardware clerks, when you ask for a can opener with a wooden handle that is thick enough to give a grip and long enough for leverage, try to sell you complicated mechanical folderols. The motivation in both cases is the same—simple greed. To deal in wines of varied ages requires judgment, the sum of experience and flair. It involves the risk of money, because every lot of wine, like every human being, has a life span, and it is this that the good vintner must estimate. His object should be to sell his wine at its moment of maximum value—to the drinker as well as the merchant. The vintner who handles only young wines is like an insurance company that will write policies only on children; the unqualified dealer wants to risk nothing and at the same time to avoid tying up his money. The client misled by brochures warning him off clarets and champagnes that are over ten years old and assuring him that Beaujolais should be drunk green will miss the major pleasures of wine drinking. To deal wisely in wines and merely to sell them are things as different as being an expert in ancient coins and selling Indian-head pennies over a souvenir counter.

Despite these convictions of mine about wine, I should never have tried a thirty-seven-year-old champagne on the recommendation of a lesser authority than the blessed M. Clicquot. It is the oldest by far that I have ever drunk. (H. Warner Allen, in *The Wines of France*, published circa 1924, which is my personal wine bible, says, "In the matter of age, champagne is a capricious wine. As a general rule, it has passed its best between fifteen and twenty, yet a bottle thirty years old may prove excellent, though all its fellows may be quite undrinkable." He cites Saintsbury's note that "a Perrier Jouet of 1857 was still majestical in 1884," adding, "And all wine-drinkers know of such amazing discoveries." Mr. Root, whose book is not a foolish panegyric of everything French, is hard on champagne, in my opinion. He falls into a critical error more common among writers less intelligent: he attacks it for not being something else. Because its excellences are not those of Burgundy or Bordeaux, he underrates the peculiar qualities it does not share with them, as one who would chide Dickens for not being Stendhal, or Marciano for not being Benny Leonard.)

The Veuve Clicquot '19 was tart without brashness—a refined but effective understatement of younger champagnes, which run too much to rhetoric, at best. Even so, the force was all there, to judge from the two glasses that were a shade more than my share. The wine still had a discreet *cordon*—the ring of bubbles that forms inside the glass—and it had developed the color known as "partridge eye." I have never seen a partridge's eye, because the bird, unlike woodcock, is served without the head, but the color the term indicates is that of serious blood or a maple leaf on the turn.

"How nice it was, life in 1919, eh, M. Clicquot?" Mirande said as he sipped his second glass.

After we had finished M. Clicquot's offering, we played a game called lying poker for table stakes, each player being allowed a capital of five hundred francs, not to be replenished under any circumstances. When Mme. B. had won everybody's five hundred francs, the party broke up. Mirande promised me that he would be up and about soon, and would show me how men reveled in the heroic days of *la belle époque*, but I had a feeling that the bell was cracked.

I left Paris and came back to it seven times during the next year, but never saw him. Once, being in his quarter in the company of a remarkably pretty woman, I called him up, simply because I knew he would like to look at her, but he was too tired. I forget when I last talked to him on the telephone. During the next winter, while I was away in Egypt or Jordan or someplace where French papers don't circulate, he died, and I did not learn of it until I returned to Europe.

When Mirande first faltered, in the Rue Chabanais, I had failed to correlate cause and effect. I had even felt a certain selfish alarm. If eating well was beginning to affect Mirande at eighty, I thought, I had better begin taking in sail. After all, I was only thirty years his junior. But after the dinner at Mme. B.'s, and in the light of subsequent reflection, I saw that what had undermined his constitution was Mme. G.'s defection from the restaurant business. For years, he had been able to escape Mme. B.'s solicitude for his health by lunching and dining in the restaurant of Mme. G., the sight of whom Mme. B. could not support. Entranced by Mme. G.'s magnificent food, he had continued to live "like a cock in a pie"—eating as well, and very nearly as much, as when he was thirty. The organs of the interior—never very intelligent, in spite of what the psychosomatic quacks say—received each day the amount of pleasure to which they were accustomed, and never marked the passage of time; it was the indispensable roadwork of the prize-fighter. When Mme. G., good soul, retired, moderation began its fatal inroads on his resistance. My old friend's appetite, insufficiently stimulated, started to loaf—the insidious result, no doubt, of the advice of the doctor whose existence he had revealed to me by that slip of the tongue about why he no longer drank Burgundy. Mirande commenced, perhaps, by omitting the fish course after the oysters, or the oysters before the fish, then began neglecting his cheeses and skipping the second bottle of wine on odd Wednesdays. What he called his pipes (*"ma tuyauterie"*), being insufficiently exercised, lost their tone, like the leg muscles of a retired champion. When, in his kindly effort to please me, he challenged the *escargots en pots de chambre*, he was like an old fighter who tries a comeback without training for it. That, however, was only the revelation of the rot that had already taken place. What always happens happened. The damage was done, but it could so easily have been averted had he been warned against the fatal trap of abstinence.

W. SOMERSET MAUGHAM

The Three Fat Women of Antibes

One was called Mrs. Richman and she was a widow. The second was called Mrs. Sutcliffe; she was American and she had divorced two husbands. The third was called Miss Hickson and she was a spinster. They were all in the comfortable forties and they were all well off. Mrs. Sutcliffe had the odd first name of Arrow. When she was young and slender she had liked it well enough. It suited her and the jests it occasioned though too often repeated were very flattering; she was not disinclined to believe that it suited her character too: it suggested directness, speed and purpose. She liked it less now that her delicate features had grown muzzy with fat, that her arms and shoulders were so substantial and her hips so massive. It was increasingly difficult to find dresses to make her look as she liked to look. The jests her name gave rise to now were made behind her back and she very well knew that they were far from obliging. But she was by no means resigned to middle age. She still wore blue to bring out the color of her eyes and, with the help of art, her fair hair had kept its lustre. What she liked about Beatrice Richman and Frances Hickson was that they were both so much fatter than she, it made her look quite slim; they were both of them older and much inclined to treat her as a little young thing. It was not disagreeable. They were good-natured women and they chaffed her pleasantly about her beaux; they had both given up the thought of that kind of nonsense, indeed Miss Hickson had never given it a moment's consideration, but they were sympathetic to her flirtations. It was understood that one of these days Arrow would make a third man happy.

"Only you mustn't get any heavier, darling," said Mrs. Richman.

"And for goodness' sake make certain of his bridge," said Miss Hickson.

They saw for her a man of about fifty, but well-preserved and of distinguished carriage, an admiral on the retired list and a good golfer, or a widower without encumbrances, but in any case with a substantial income. Arrow listened to them amiably, and kept to herself that fact that this was not at all her idea. It was true that she would have liked to marry again, but her fancy turned to a dark slim Italian with flashing eyes and a sonorous title or to a Spanish don of noble lineage; and not a day more than thirty. There were times when, looking at herself in her mirror, she was certain she did not look any more than that herself.

They were great friends, Miss Hickson, Mrs. Richman and Arrow Sutcliffe. It was their fat that had brought them together and bridge that had cemented their alliance. They had met first at Carlsbad, where they were staying at the same hotel and were treated by the same doctor who used them with the same ruthlessness. Beatrice Richman was enormous. She was a handsome woman, with fine eyes, rouged cheeks and painted lips. She was very well content to be a widow with a handsome fortune. She adored her food. She liked bread and butter, cream, potatoes and suet puddings, and for eleven months of the year ate pretty well everything she had a mind to, and for one month went to Carlsbad to reduce. But every year she grew fatter. She upbraided the doctor, but got no sympathy from him. He pointed out to her various plain and simple facts.

"But if I'm never to eat a thing I like, life isn't worth living," she expostulated.

He shrugged his disapproving shoulders. Afterwards she told Miss Hickson that she was beginning to suspect he wasn't so clever as she had thought. Miss Hickson gave a great guffaw. She was that sort of woman. She had a deep bass voice, a large flat sallow face from which twinkled little bright eyes; she walked with a slouch, her hands in her pockets, and when she could do so without exciting attention smoked a long cigar. She dressed as like a man as she could.

"What the deuce should I look like in frills and furbelows?" she said. "When you're as fat as I am you may just as well be comfortable."

She wore tweeds and heavy boots and whenever she could went about bareheaded. But she was as strong as an ox and boasted that few men could drive a longer ball than she. She was plain of speech, and she could swear more variously than a stevedore. Though her name was Frances she preferred to be called Frank. Masterful, but with tact, it was her jovial strength of character that held the three together. They drank their waters together, had their baths at the same hour, they took their strenuous walks together, pounded about the tennis court with a professional to make them run, and ate at the same table their sparse and regulated meals. Nothing impaired their good humor but the scales, and when one or other of them weighed as much on one day as she had the day before neither Frank's coarse jokes, the *bonhomie* of Beatrice nor Arrow's pretty kittenish ways sufficed to dispel the gloom. Then drastic measures were resorted to, the culprit went to bed for twenty-four hours and nothing passed her lips but the doctor's famous vegetable soup which tasted like hot water in which a cabbage had been well rinsed.

Never were three women greater friends. They would have been independent of anyone else if they had not needed a fourth at bridge. They were fierce, enthusiastic players and the moment the day's cure was over they sat down at the bridge table. Arrow, feminine as she was, played the best game of the three, a hard, brilliant game, in which she showed no mercy and never conceded a point or failed to take advantage of a mistake. Beatrice was solid and reliable. Frank was dashing; she was a great theorist, and had all the authorities at the tip of her tongue. They had long arguments over the rival systems. They bombarded one another with Culbertson and Sims. It was obvious that not one of them ever played a card without fifteen good reasons, but it was also obvious from the subsequent conversation that there were fifteen equally good reasons why she should not have played it. Life would have been perfect, even with the prospect of twenty-four hours of that filthy soup when the doctor's rotten (Beatrice) bloody (Frank) lousy (Arrow) scales pretended one hadn't lost an ounce in two days, if only there had not been this constant difficulty of finding someone to play with them who was in their class.

It was for this reason that on the occasion with which this narrative deals Frank invited Lena Finch to come and stay with them at Antibes. They were spending some weeks there on Frank's suggestion. It seemed absurd to her, with her common sense, that immediately the cure was over Beatrice who always lost twenty pounds should by giving way to her ungovernable appetite put it all on again. Beatrice was weak. She needed a person of strong will to watch her diet. She proposed then that on leaving Carlsbad they should take a house at Antibes, where they could get plenty of exercise—everyone knew that nothing slimmed you like swimming—and as far as possible could go on with the cure. With a cook of their own they could at least avoid things that were obviously fattening. There was no reason why they should not all lose several pounds more. It seemed a very good idea.

Beatrice knew what was good for her, and she could resist temptation well enough if temptation was not put right under her nose. Besides, she liked gambling, and a flutter at the Casino two or three times a week would pass the time very pleasantly. Arrow adored Antibes, and she would be looking her best after a month at Carlsbad. She could just pick and choose among the young Italians, the passionate Spaniards, the gallant Frenchmen, and the long-limbed English who sauntered about all day in bathing trunks and gay-colored dressing-gowns. The plan worked very well. They had a grand time. Two days a week they ate nothing but hard-boiled eggs and raw tomatoes and they mounted the scales every morning with light hearts. Arrow got down to eleven stone and felt just like a girl; Beatrice and Frank by standing in a certain way just avoided the thirteen. The machine they had bought registered kilograms, and they got extraordinarily clever at translating these in the twinkling of an eye to pounds and ounces.

But the fourth at bridge continued to be the difficulty. This person played like a foot, the other was so slow that it drove you frantic, one was quarrelsome, another was a bad loser, a third was next door to a crook. It was strange how hard it was to find exactly the player you wanted.

One morning when they were sitting in pajamas on the terrace overlooking the sea, drinking their tea (without milk or sugar) and eating a rusk prepared by Dr. Hudebert and guaranteed not to be fattening, Frank looked up from her letters.

"Lena Finch is coming down to the Riviera," she said.

"Who's she?" asked Arrow.

"She married a cousin of mine. He died a couple of months ago and she's just recovering from a nervous breakdown. What about asking her to come here for a fortnight?"

"Does she play bridge?" asked Beatrice.

"You bet your life she does," boomed Frank in her deep voice. "And a damned good game too. We should be absolutely independent of outsiders."

"How old is she?" asked Arrow.

"Same age as I am."

"That sounds all right."

It was settled. Frank, with her usual decisiveness, stalked out as soon as she had finished her breakfast to send a wire, and three days later Lena Finch arrived. Frank met her at the station. She was in deep but not obtrusive mourning for the recent death of her husband. Frank had not seen her for two years. She kissed her warmly and took a good look at her.

"You're very thin, darling," she said.

Lena smiled bravely.

"I've been through a good deal lately. I've lost a lot of weight."

Frank sighed, but whether from sympathy with her cousin's sad loss, or from envy, was not obvious.

Lena was not, however, unduly depressed, and after a quick bath was quite ready to accompany Frank to Eden Roc. Frank introduced the stranger to her two friends and they sat down in what was known as the Monkey House. It was an enclosure covered with glass overlooking the sea, with a bar at the back, and it was crowded with chattering people in bathing costumes, pajamas or dressing-gowns, who were seated at the tables having drinks. Beatrice's soft heart went out to the lorn widow, and Arrow, seeing that she was pale, quite ordinary to look at and probably forty-eight, was prepared to like her very much. A waiter approached them.

"What will you have, Lena dear?" Frank asked.

"Oh, I don't know, what you all have, a dry Martini or a White Lady."

Arrow and Beatrice gave her a quick look. Everyone knows how fattening cocktails are.

"I daresay you're tired after your journey," said Frank kindly.

She ordered a dry Martini for Lena and a mixed lemon and orange juice for herself and her two friends.

"We find alcohol isn't very good in all this heat," she explained.

"Oh, it never affects me at all," Lena answered airily. "I like cocktails."

Arrow went very slightly pale under her rouge (neither she nor Beatrice ever wet their faces when they bathed and they thought it absurd of Frank, a woman of her size, to pretend she liked diving) but she said nothing. The conversation was gay and easy, they all said the obvious things with gusto, and presently they strolled back to the villa for luncheon.

In each napkin were two little antifat rusks. Lena gave a bright smile as she put them by the side of her plate.

"May I have some bread?" she asked.

The grossest indecency would not have fallen on the ears of those three women with such a shock. Not one of them had eaten bread for ten years. Even Beatrice, greedy as she was, drew the line there. Frank, the good hostess, recovered herself first.

"Of course, darling," she said and turning to the butler asked him to bring some.

"And some butter," said Lena in that pleasant easy way of hers.

There was a moment's embarrassed silence.

"I don't know if there's any in the house," said Frank, "but I'll inquire. There may be some in the kitchen."

"I adore bread and butter, don't you?" said Lena, turning to Beatrice.

Beatrice gave a sickly smile and an evasive reply. The butler brought a long crisp roll of French bread. Lena slit it in two and plastered it with the butter which was miraculously produced. A grilled sole was served.

"We eat very simply here," said Frank. "I hope you won't mind."

"Oh, no, I like my food very plain," said Lena as she took some butter and spread it over her fish. "As long as I can have bread and butter and potatoes and cream I'm quite happy."

The three friends exchanged a glance. Frank's great sallow face sagged a little and she looked with distaste at the dry, insipid sole on her plate. Beatrice came to the rescue.

"It's such a bore, we can't get cream here," she said. "It's one of the things one has to do without on the Riviera."

"What a pity," said Lena.

The rest of the luncheon consisted of lamb cutlets, with the fat carefully removed so that Beatrice should not be led astray, and spinach boiled in water, with stewed pears to end up with. Lena tasted her pears and gave the butler a look of inquiry. That resourceful man understood her at once and though powdered sugar had never been served at that table before handed her without a moment's hesitation a bowl of it. She helped herself liberally. The other three pretended not to notice. Coffee was served and Lena took three lumps of sugar in hers.

"You have a very sweet tooth," said Arrow in a tone which she struggled to keep friendly.

"We think saccharine so much more sweetening," said Frank, as she put a tiny tablet of it into her coffee.

"Disgusting stuff," said Lena.

Beatrice's mouth drooped at the corners, and she gave the lump sugar a yearning look.

"Beatrice," boomed Frank sternly.

Beatrice stifled a sigh, and reached for the saccharine.

Frank was relieved when they could sit down to the bridge table. It was plain to her that Arrow and Beatrice were upset. She wanted them to like Lena and she was anxious that Lena should enjoy her fortnight with them. For the first rubber Arrow cut with the newcomer.

"Do you play Vanderbilt or Culbertson?" she asked her.

"I have no conventions," Lena answered in a happy-go-lucky way, "I play by the light of nature."

"I play strict Culbertson," said Arrow acidly.

The three fat women braced themselves to the fray. No conventions indeed! They'd learn her. When it came to bridge even Frank's family feeling was forgotten and she settled down with the same determination as the others to trim the stranger in their midst. But the light of nature served Lena very well. She had a natural gift for the game and great experience. She played with imagination, quickly, boldly, and with assurance. The other players were in too high a class not to realize very soon that Lena knew what she was about, and since they were all thoroughly good-natured, generous women, they were gradually mollified. This was real bridge. They all enjoyed themselves. Arrow and Beatrice began to feel more kindly towards Lena, and Frank, noticing this, heaved a fat sigh of relief. It was going to be a success.

After a couple of hours they parted, Frank and Beatrice to have a round of golf, and Arrow to take a brisk walk with a young Prince Roccamare whose acquaintance she had lately made. He was very sweet and young and good-looking. Lena said she would rest.

They met again just before dinner.

"I hope you've been all right, Lena dear," said Frank. "I was rather conscience-stricken at leaving you with nothing to do all this time."

"Oh, don't apologize. I had a lovely sleep and then I went down to Juan and had a cocktail. And d'you know what I discovered? You'll be so pleased. I found a dear little tea-shop where they've got the most beautiful thick fresh cream. I've ordered half a pint to be sent every day. I thought it would be my little contribution to the household."

Her eyes were shining. She was evidently expecting them to be delighted.

"How very kind of you," said Frank, with a look that sought to quell the indignation that she saw on the faces of her two friends. "But we never eat cream. In this climate it makes one so bilious."

"I shall have to eat it all myself then," said Lena cheerfully.

"Don't you ever think of your figure?" Arrow asked with icy deliberation.

"The doctor said I must eat."

"Did he say you must eat bread and butter and potatoes and cream?"

"Yes. That's what I thought you meant when you said you had simple food."

"You'll get simply enormous," said Beatrice.

Lena laughed gaily.

"No, I shan't. You see, nothing ever makes me fat. I've always eaten everything I wanted to and it's never had the slightest effect on me."

The stony silence that followed this speech was only broken by the entrance of the butler.

"*Mademoiselle est servie,*" he announced.

They talked the matter over late that night, after Lena had gone to bed, in Frank's room. During the evening they had been furiously cheerful, and they had chaffed one another with a friendliness that would have taken in the keenest observer. But now they dropped the mask. Beatrice was sullen, Arrow was spiteful and Frank was unmanned.

"It's not very nice for me to sit there and see her eat all the things I particularly like," said Beatrice plaintively.

"It's not very nice for any of us," Frank snapped back.

"You should never have asked her here," said Arrow.

"How was I to know?" cried Frank.

"I can't help thinking that if she really cared for her husband she would hardly eat so much," said Beatrice. "He's only been buried two months. I mean, I think you ought to show some respect for the dead."

"Why can't she eat the same as we do?" asked Arrow viciously. "She's a guest."

"Well, you heard what she said. The doctor told her she must eat."

"Then she ought to go to a sanatorium."

"It's more than flesh and blood can stand, Frank," moaned Beatrice.

"If I can stand it you can stand it."

"She's your cousin, she's not our cousin," said Arrow. "I'm not going to sit there for fourteen days and watch that woman make a hog of herself."

"It's so vulgar to attach all this importance to food," Frank boomed, and her voice was deeper than ever. "After all the only thing that counts really is spirit."

"Are you calling *me* vulgar, Frank?" asked Arrow with flashing eyes.

"No, of course she isn't," interrupted Beatrice.

"I wouldn't put it past you to go down in the kitchen when we're all in bed and have a good square meal on the sly."

Frank sprang to her feet.

"How dare you say that, Arrow! I'd never ask anybody to do what I'm not prepared to do myself. Have you known me all these years and do you think me capable of such a mean thing?"

"How is it you never take off any weight then?"

Frank gave a gasp and burst into a flood of tears.

"What a cruel thing to say! I've lost pounds and pounds."

She wept like a child. Her vast body shook and great tears splashed on her mountainous bosom.

"Darling, I didn't mean it," cried Arrow.

She threw herself on her knees and enveloped what she could of Frank in her own plump arms. She wept and the mascara ran down her cheeks.

"D'you mean to say I don't look thinner?" Frank sobbed. "After all I've gone through."

"Yes, dear, of course you do," cried Arrow through her tears. "Everybody's noticed it."

Beatrice, though naturally of a placid disposition, began to cry gently. It was very pathetic. Indeed, it would have been a hard heart that failed to be moved by the sight of Frank, that lion-hearted woman, crying her eyes out. Presently, however, they dried their tears and had a little brandy and water, which every doctor had told them was the least fattening thing they could drink, and then they felt much better. They decided that Lena should have the nourishing food that had been ordered her and they made a solemn resolution not to let it disturb their equanimity. She was certainly a first-rate bridge player and after all it was only for a fortnight. They would do whatever they could to make her stay enjoyable. They kissed one another warmly and separated for the night feeling strangely uplifted. Nothing should interfere with the wonderful friendship that had brought so much happiness into their three lives.

But human nature is weak. You must not ask too much of it. They ate grilled fish while Lena ate macaroni sizzling with cheese and butter; they ate grilled cutlets and boiled spinach while Lena ate *pâté de foie gras*; twice a week they ate hard-boiled eggs and raw tomatoes, while Lena ate peas swimming in cream and potatoes cooked in all sorts of delicious ways. The chef was a good chef and he leapt at the opportunity afforded him to send up one dish more rich, tasty and succulent than the other.

"Poor Jim," sighed Lena, thinking of her husband, "he loved French cooking."

The butler disclosed the fact that he could make half a dozen kinds of cocktail and Lena informed them that the doctor had recommended her to drink burgundy at luncheon and champagne at dinner. The three fat women persevered. They were gay, chatty and even hilarious (such is the natural gift that women have for deception) but Beatrice grew limp and forlorn, and Arrow's tender blue eyes acquired a steely glint. Frank's deep voice grew more raucous. It was when they played bridge that the strain showed itself. They had always been fond of talking over their hands, but their discussions had been friendly. Now a distinct bitterness crept in and sometimes one pointed out a mistake to another with quite unnecessary frankness. Discussion turned to argument and argument to altercation. Sometimes the session ended in angry silence. Once Frank accused Arrow of deliberately letting her down. Two or three times Beatrice, the softest of the three, was reduced to tears. On another occasion Arrow flung down her cards and swept out of the room in a pet. Their tempers were getting frayed. Lena was the peacemaker.

"I think it's such a pity to quarrel over bridge," she said. "After all, it's only a game."

It was all very well for her. She had had a square meal and half a bottle of champagne. Besides, she had phenomenal luck. She was winning all their money. The score was put down in a book after each session, and hers mounted up day after day with unfailing regularity. Was there no justice in the world? They began to hate one another. And though they hated her too they could not resist confiding in her. Each of them went to her separately and told her how detestable the others were. Arrow said she was sure it was bad for her to see so much of women so much older than herself. She had a good mind to sacrifice her share of the lease and go to Venice for the rest of the summer. Frank told Lena that with her masculine mind it was too much to expect that she could be satisfied with anyone so frivolous as Arrow and so frankly stupid as Beatrice.

"I must have intellectual conversation," she boomed. "When you have a brain like mine you've got to consort with your intellectual equals."

Beatrice only wanted peace and quiet.

"Really I hate women," she said. "They're so unreliable; they're so malicious."

By the time Lena's fortnight drew to its close the three fat women were barely on speaking terms. They kept up appearances before Lena, but when she was not there made no pretenses. They had got past quarrelling. They ignored one another, and when this was not possible treated each other with icy politeness.

Lena was going to stay with friends on the Italian Riviera and Frank saw her off by the same train as that by which she had arrived. She was taking away with her a lot of their money.

"I don't know how to thank you," she said, as she got into the carriage. "I've had a wonderful visit."

If there was one thing that Frank Hickson prided herself on more than on being a match for any man it was that she was a gentlewoman, and her reply was perfect in its combination of majesty and graciousness.

"We've all enjoyed having you here, Lena," she said. "It's been a real treat."

But when she turned away from the departing train she heaved such a vast sigh of relief that the platform shook beneath her. She flung back her massive shoulders and strode home to the villa.

"Ouf!" she roared at intervals. "Ouf!"

She changed into her one-piece bathing-suit, put on her espadrilles and a man's dressing-gown (no nonsense about it) and went to Eden Roc. There was still time for a bathe before luncheon. She passed through the Monkey House, looking about her to say good morning to anyone she knew, for she felt on a sudden at peace with mankind, and then stopped dead still. She could not believe her eyes. Beatrice was sitting at one of the tables, by herself; she wore the pajamas she had bought at Molyneux's a day or two before, she had a string of pearls round her neck, and Frank's quick eyes saw that she had just had her hair waved; her cheeks, her eyes, her lips were made up. Fat, nay vast, as she was, none could deny that she was an extremely handsome woman. But what was she doing? With the slouching gait of the Neanderthal man which was Frank's characteristic walk she went up to Beatrice. In her back bathing-dress Frank looked like the huge cetacean which the Japanese catch in the Torres Straits and which the vulgar call a sea-cow.

"Beatrice, what are you doing?" she cried in her deep voice.

It was like the roll of thunder in the distant mountains. Beatrice looked at her coolly.

"Eating," she answered.

"Damn it, I can see you're eating."

In front of Beatrice was a plate of *croissants* and a plate of butter, a pot of strawberry jam, coffee and a jug of cream. Beatrice was spreading butter thick on the delicious hot bread, covering this with jam, and then pouring the thick cream over all.

"You'll kill yourself," said Frank.

"I don't care," mumbled Beatrice with her mouth full.

"You'll put on pounds and pounds."

"Go to hell!"

She actually laughed in Frank's face. My God, how good those *croissants* smelled!

"I'm disappointed in you, Beatrice. I thought you had more character."

"It's your fault. That blasted woman. You would have her down. For a fortnight I've watched her gorge like a hog. It's more than flesh and blood can stand. I'm going to have one square meal if I bust."

The tears welled up to Frank's eyes. Suddenly she felt very weak and womanly. She would have liked a strong man to take her on his knee and pet her and cuddle her and call her little baby names. Speechless she sank down on a chair by Beatrice's side. A waiter came up. With a pathetic gesture she waved towards the coffee and *croissants*.

"I'll have the same," she sighed.

She listlessly reached out her hand to take a roll, but Beatrice snatched away the plate.

"No, you don't," she said. "You wait till you get your own."

Frank called her a name which ladies seldom apply to one another in affection. In a moment the waiter brought her *croissants*, butter, jam and coffee.

"Where's the cream, you fool?" she roared like a lioness at bay.

She began to eat. She ate gluttonously. The place was beginning to fill up with bathers coming to enjoy a cocktail or two after having done their duty by the sun and the sea. Presently Arrow strolled along with Prince Roccamare. She had on a beautiful silk wrap which she held tightly round her with one hand in order to look as slim as possible and she bore her head high so that he should not see her double chin. She was laughing gaily. She felt like a girl. He had just told her (in Italian) that her eyes made the blue of the Mediterranean look like pea-soup. He left her to go into the men's room to brush his sleek black hair and they arranged to meet in five minutes for a drink. Arrow walked on to the women's room to put a little more rouge on her cheeks and a little more red on her lips. On her way she caught sight of Frank and Beatrice. She stopped. She could hardly believe her eyes.

"My God!" she cried. "You beasts. You hogs." She seized a chair. "Waiter."

Her appointment went clean out of her head. In the twinkling of an eye the waiter was at her side.

"Bring me what these ladies are having," she ordered.

Frank lifted her great heavy head from her plate.

"Bring me some *pâté de foie gras*," she boomed.

"Frank!" cried Beatrice.

"Shut up."

"All right. I'll have some too."

The coffee was brought and the hot rolls and cream and the *pâté de foie gras* and they set to. They spread the cream on the *pâté* and they ate it. They devoured great spoonfuls of jam. They crunched the delicious crisp bread voluptuously. What was love to Arrow then? Let the Prince keep his palace in Rome and his castle in the Apennines. They did not speak. What they were about was much too serious. They ate with solemn, ecstatic fervor.

"I haven't eaten potatoes for twenty-five years," said Frank in a far-off brooding tone.

"Waiter," cried Beatrice, "bring fried potatoes for three."

"*Très bien, Madame.*"

The potatoes were brought. Not all the perfumes of Arabia smelled so sweet. They ate them with their fingers.

"Bring me a dry Martini," said Arrow.

"You can't have a dry Martini in the middle of a meal, Arrow," said Frank.

"Can't I? You wait and see."

"All right then. Bring me a double dry Martini," said Frank.

"Bring three double dry Martinis," said Beatrice.

They were brought and drunk at a gulp. The women looked at one another and sighed. The misunderstandings of the last fortnight dissolved and the sincere affection each had for the other welled up again in their hearts. They could hardly believe that they had ever contemplated the possibility of severing a friendship that had brought them so much solid satisfaction. They finished the potatoes.

"I wonder if they've got any chocolate éclairs," said Beatrice.

"Of course they have."

And of course they had. Frank thrust one whole into her huge mouth, swallowed it and seized another, but before she ate it she looked at the other two and plunged a vindictive dagger into the heart of the monstrous Lena.

"You can say what you like, but the truth is she played a damned rotten game of bridge, really."

"Lousy," agreed Arrow.

But Beatrice suddenly thought she would like a meringue.

JORGE LUIS BORGES AND ADOLFO BIOY-CASARES

An Abstract Art

At the risk of wounding the noble sensibilities of all Argentines (whatever their particular or political persuasion), the fact must be faced that at this late date a tourist Mecca of the modern New World like Buenos Aires boasts but a single *tenebrarium*—located, at that, in a backwater of the city some several blocks from the nearest subway station. All things considered, however, the establishment stands for an effort worthy of the highest praise, for a real breakthrough in the Chinese wall of our general unfashionableness. More than one acute and far-ranging observer has dropped us the hint *ad nauseum* that the aforementioned *tenebrarium* is still far from holding its own with counterparts in Amsterdam or Basel or Paris or Denver, Colorado, or Bruges la Morte.

Without entangling ourselves in so ticklish a problem, we wish for the time being to pay homage to Ubalde Morpurgo, whose voice cries out in the wilderness from eight to eleven P.M. nightly except Mondays, backed—we must be frank—by a handful of cognoscenti who dutifully take turns at attendance. On two occasions, we ourselves have partaken of those symposia and, both times, save for Morpurgo himself, the half-glimpsed faces of the dinner crowd were never quite the same. Not so, of course, the contagious enthusiasm. Our memory shall never forget either the metallic music of the cutlery or the occasional crash of a breaking tumbler.

Delving into prehistory, it should be mentioned that this *petite histoire* began, like so many others—in Paris! The forerunner, as every knows, the beacon who got the ball rolling, was none other than the Flemish (or Dutch)

Frans Praetorius. Long ago, Praetorius' lucky star drew him to a certain Symbolist café which was frequented, off and on, by the now justly forgotten Vielé-Griffin. Those were the good old days of the third or fourth of January, 1884! The ink-begrimed hands of the entire upcoming literary generation clamored over each issue of the magazine *Étape* as it came rolling hot off the press.

Let us go back in time to the Café Procope. Someone sporting a bohemian beret waves aloft an article buried at the back of the aforesaid publication; another, all petulance and military moustache, swears over and over again that he will not rest until he finds out who the author is; a third points with his meerschaum pipe to a person of timid smile and hairless head who, absorbed in his great blond beard, sits silent in a corner. Let light be shed on the mystery. The man upon whom astonished faces, pointing fingers, and gaping eyes focus is the Flemish (or Dutch) Frans Praetorius already alluded to.

The article is brief, and its dry-as-dust style smacks of test tube and alembic, but its authoritative tone soon musters a following. In its half page, not a single simile from Greco-Roman mythology is to be found, not a word is wasted. The writer sticks to his thesis—that the basic tastes are four: sour, salty, insipid, and bitter. This creed stirs discussion, provokes disagreement, but in the end for each unbeliever there are now a thousand devoted hearts. In 1891, Praetorius publishes the today classical *Les Saveurs*; let us not forget, by the way, that the Grand Man, yielding with unimpeachable good will to a host of unknown correspondents, adds to his previous catalogue a fifth taste, that of sweetness, which, for reasons it would be impertinent to go into here, had hitherto eluded his perspicacity.

Then, in 1892, an inveterate haunter of the Procope named Ishmael Querido throws open the portals of the almost legendary establishment Les Cinq Saveurs in a location just around the corner from the Panthéon des Invalides itself. The place is friendly and unassuming. For the payment of a small fee upon entrance, the eventual customer is entitled to one of five alternative choices: a lump of sugar, a cube of aloes, a cotton wafer, a grapefruit rind, or a *granum salis*. These items figure prominently in an early menu that it was recently our privilege to peruse in a certain *cabinet bibliographique* in the port city of Bordeaux.

In the beginning, to choose one of the five was to deny yourself acquaintance with the other four, but in time Querido was to give the nod to succession, to rotation, and, finally, to mixing. He hardly reckoned, however, with the justified scruples of Praetorius, who argued that sugar besides being sweet tastes like sugar (who could refute this?) and that the admission of the grapefruit rind clearly constituted an infraction. It was a manufacturing pharmacist, the druggist Payot, who sliced the Gordian knot; he began furnishing Querido each week with twelve hundred identical pyramids, each an inch high and each affording the palate one of the now celebrated five tastes—sour, insipid, salty, sweet, and bitter. A veteran of these early campaigns has assured us that at first the pyramids were grayish and translucent and that later on, to make things easier, they were endowed with the five well-known colors, white, black, yellow, red, and blue.

Lured on, perhaps by the prospect of gain, perhaps by the word "bittersweet," Querido fell into the dangerous error of trying combinations. Even today purists accuse him of having pandered to public gluttony with his hundred and twenty pyramids of different shades of color. But such promiscuity led to Querido's rapid downfall; that self-same year he was forced to sell his establishment to another chef, a nobody who desecrated the temple of tastes by selling, for Christmas purposes, stuffed turkeys. Praetorius commented philosophically, "*C'est la fin du monde.*"*

In a certain sense this utterance was to prove prophetic to both forerunners. Querido, who spent his tottering years in the streets specializing in the sale of gumdrops, in the full summertide of 1904 finally paid his fare to Charon. Completely heartbroken, Praetorius managed to survive him by some fourteen years. The project of erecting a commemorative monument to each had the full backing of high government officials, the press, public opinion, the military-industrial complex, the turf club, the clergy, and the mostly highly reputed artistic and gastronomic circles. The funds allocated, however, did not permit the erection of two figures and so the sculptor's chisel had to limit itself to a single likeness that would synthesize the one's unkempt beard, the flat noses of the two, and the other's laconic stance. One hundred and twenty miniature pyramids worked in relief in the pedestal strike a note of freshness in the monument.

Both ideologists dispatched, we stand now before pure cookery's high priest, Pierre Moulonguet. His first manifesto dates from 1915; the *Manuel Raisonné* (three volumes in large octavo) from 1929. Moulonguet's theoretical tenets are so well known that we may safely limit ourselves here, God willing, to no more than the barest lifeless outline of them. The Abbot Brémond foresaw the possibilities of a poetry purely poetical; abstract and concrete artists—both words are obviously synonyms—strive

---

*The French meaning is: " 'Tis the end of the world." [Joint note of the French Academy, the Argentine Academy of Letters, and the American Academy of Arts and Letters.]

after pictorial painting which condescends neither to anecdote nor to the slavish imitation of nature. In a like way, using weighty arguments, Pierre Moulonguet plumped for what he daringly called "culinary cooking." Its aim, as the words imply, was a cuisine owing nothing to the plastic arts or to the object of nourishment. Vivid colors, elegant serving platters, and what common prejudice calls a well-presented dish—all these were banned; and banned was the crassly pragmatic orchestration of protein, vitamins, and the carbohydrates.

The age-old and ancestral tastes of veal, salmon, fish, pork, venison, mutton, parsley, *omelette surprise*, and tapioca—all dismissed by that cruel tyrant Praetorius—were now returned to astonished palates in the form (no compromising with the plastic arts) of a runny, grayish, mucilaginous mush. The diner, at last freed from the bonds of the much-touted five tastes, was again able to order himself fried chicken southern-style or coq au vin—but everything, as we know, took on the standard amorphous texture. Today as yesterday, tomorrow as today, and ever the same. A single nonconformist cast his shadow on the scene: we speak of Praetorius, who, like so many precursors, cannot tolerate the slightest deviation. He could not tolerate the slightest deviation from the path he had blazed thirty-three years earlier.

Victory, however, did not lack her Achilles' heel. A hand, any half-dozen fingers, are more than enough on which to count the now classic chefs—Dupont de Montpellier, Julio Cejador—unmatched in the art of turning the whole rich gamut of comestibles into the one runny mush demanded by the code.

But then in 1932 the miracle took place, worked by a cipher out of the crowd. Every reader knows his name: Jean-Françoise Darracq. J.-F.D. opened in Geneva a restaurant exactly like all others, serving dishes in no way different from those of the past: the mayonnaise was yellow, the greens green, the cassata a rainbow, the roast beef red. He was at the point of being dubbed a reactionary when then and there he laid the golden egg. One evening, in perfect calm, with a smile about to flicker across his lips and with that sureness of hand that genius alone commands, Darracq carried out the simple act destined to place him forever at the top-most point of the pinnacle in the entire annals of cookery. He snapped out the lights. There, in that instant, the first *tenebrarium* was launched.

JAY JACOBS

A Feeder in France

If you've ever driven through southern Provence, taking the most direct route from Arles to Marseille, you've passed unaware through St.-Hippolyte. Arles, the major Gallic outpost of the early Roman Empire and the nearest city of any size, lies some nine miles to the west, and the nearest village, Raphèle, is obscure enough to have long ago adopted the coattail designation Raphèle-les-Arles to facilitate mail delivery from other parts of France. St.-Hippolyte itself, a couple of miles east of Raphèle, is a mere flyspeck on the most detailed maps of the region, a fork in the road whose dozen or so inhabitants incorporate into *their* mail address the locator "*par* Raphèle-les-Arles." According to Juliette Treillard, the place is properly called Croix-St.-Hippolyte after its single distinguishing feature: a rusted wrought-iron roadside cross, half-hidden by foliage, unnoticed by passing motorists (except the few who stop to pee beside its pedestal), and in truth not worth noticing.

Such as it is, St.-Hippolyte, with its half-dozen small buildings hunkered down against the southward sweep of the mistral, straddles route nationale 113, which divides the fragrant hay-rich plain of La Petite Crau from the rock-strewn barrens of La Grande Crau. The little Crau is unmistakably van Gogh country, just as the environs of Aix-en-Provence, some thirty-five miles to the southeast, unmistakably belong to Cézanne. (The transition between the two is startlingly abrupt, and, on their respective turfs, both painters turn out to be surprisingly naturalistic.)

Le Diable Vert, a superb restaurant, is within reasonable walking distance of St.-Hippolyte, and L'Oustau de Baumanière, a world-famous one, is a fifteen-minute drive away. At the time of which I write, however, neither establishment was any better known to lifelong residents of St.-Hippolyte than was the dark side of the moon.

During the year and a half we spent there, the population of St.-Hippolyte totaled fewer than twenty-five, including the three of us, our cat Jeoffry, and the half-dozen goats kept by our landlady Juliette Treillard and her sister Marie-Antoinette, both maiden ladies of a certain age. (More accurately, of an *uncertain* age: they looked to be sixtyish but appearances can be deceiving on the Crau, where women work hard and weather fast.) Although the demoiselles Treillard made what they considered adequate meals of a shared brace of small mackerel or a thin slice apiece of cold ham, thereby contributing nothing of statistical significance to the community's general penchant for unrestrained gluttony, the per capita food intake was staggering, and our immediate neighbor, Pierre du Bellon, was the hamlet's undisputed champion gourmand, his whip-lean physique notwithstanding.

Du Bellon subjected us to a rude awakening on our first morning in residence by firing off both barrels of a shotgun right underneath our bedroom window: BLAM! and BLAM! again. After scrambling through the two upstairs rooms and satisfying myself that none of us had been murdered in our beds, I threw open the shutters to see what the hell was going on. My first glimpse of du Bellon was of a reedlike figure with gingery receding hair, gun cradled in the crook of one arm as he extended the other toward a diminutive grounded ruffle of bloody feathers. Dangling from a large plane tree in our communal front yard, a caged Judas bird frantically tried to explain away its betrayal of the victim.

M. and Mme. Pierre du Bellon, as it soon transpired, were prosperous forgers of Spanish antiques and, respectively, a Norman transplanted to the Midi for reasons of health and a Swiss-Corsican blonde who would have been some punkins on the Champs-Elysées, let alone a rutted quagmire in rural Provence. Du Bellon, an indefatigable hunter and insatiable eater of larks, thrushes, warblers, buntings, and the other songbirds collectively known as *petits oiseaux* or ortolans, didn't often bag anything in his own dooryard, having long since annihilated the edible avian population of St.-Hippolyte and the proximate fields. He owned what was then reputed to be the only home freezer in the region, which he stocked with birds he shot one at a time over an area of a hundred-odd square miles. (Artillery in hand, he'd leap into his car at the merest rumor of a chirp having emanated from a cypress or fig tree ten miles distant.) Periodically, when he had accumulated quarry he deemed sufficient to a proper tuck-in, he'd sit down for an evening of open-ended gourmandise, while Mme. du Bellon served the spit-roasted delicacies in relays of four. He would bag just one more bird at St.-Hippolyte, and—thanks to Jeoffry the cat, who happened to be standing nearby and gazing aloft open-mouthed as it fell—wouldn't get to eat it. Until that moment, he had found *très amusant* the idea of an American family bringing a Persian cat to that part of the world. At that moment, the cat might well have been blown to kingdom come had du Bellon not expended the last of his ammunition.

Du Bellon was routinely affable during our first discouragingly bleak winter in sunny Provence; his daughter Marie-France, a woman of an interesting age (going on seven), became our three-year-old Roger's inseparable inamorata, and the prospective in-laws necessarily established an entente cordiale. With onset of warmer weather, however, his cordiality toward his expatriate neighbors increased apace as Roger and I began to return from our explorations of the neighborhood's irrigation ditches bearing dozens of dozens of fennel-fattened snails. Although free for the taking, the gastropods cost me dear: I'd come home with a face swollen to pumpkin convexity by the monster mosquitoes that populated the ditches, while Roger invaded their haunts with impunity.

"I can eat more escargots than you can," du Bellon announced one morning, slapping me across my swollen face with a nonexistent glove. "The hell you can," I replied. Ground rules were set forth: I would supply the escargots; Gwynne would do the initial preparatory work; du Bellon's wife would stuff and broil the buggers and serve them two dozen at a time; du Bellon and I would eat them in unison until one of us cried *oncle*. Informed that his arrangement wasn't altogether fair to the ladies, du Bellon grudgingly allowed Gwynne to participate as a contestant but explained that *his* wife would necessarily be *hors de combat*. "She can't cook *and* eat," he reasoned. "Anyway, she's not too fond of snails."

According to *Larousse Gastronomique*, "To avoid the risk of poisoning, snails must be deprived of food for some time before they are eaten, for they may have fed on plants harmless to themselves but poisonous to humans. Furthermore, it is advisable only to eat operculated snails, that is to say snails which have sealed themselves into their shells to hibernate." In my own reasonably extensive experience, snails will retreat behind their opercula as soon as they're convinced that nothing is to be gained by continued public exposure. With several hundred operculated snails on hand, I borrowed a couple of ancient burlap sacks from Juliette Treillard, filled them with operculated escargots, and hung them in an upstairs closet. The idea was to deprive them of nutrients until any potentially toxic substances had been expunged from their digestive systems. As a final step in the process,

Gwynne would immerse the snails in heavily acidulated water, which impels the critters to barf up whatever residual matter may remain in their innards.

Somewhere in her writings, if memory serves, M. F. K. Fisher describes an experience of her own that ours duplicated in every particular. In short, operculated snails are merely playing possum: if a single captive snail among the multitudes finds a way out of its predicament, every last one of its fellows will follow suit. (This, as I would learn some time later, is a talent snails share with lobsters. I once lost three dozen specimens of *Homarus americanus* when one of their number found an escape hatch in a storm-damaged lobster pot and led a freedom march from riverine imprisonment on the Maine coast to open water somewhere this side of Cherbourg. For a couple of summers thereafter, any local lobsterman I ran into made a point of informing me that "something real peculiah" had happened to him that very morning; that he had "pulled up a lobstah" whose claws were already pegged. By the end of the second summah the process of genetic mutation set in motion by the first escapee had engendered something like four hundred pre-pegged lobstahs.)

To get back to the snails, the sacks I borrowed from Juliette were so threadbare that the captives' weight apparently split the burlap within minutes of their incarceration. An ill-fitting closet door in no way impeded their travel plans.

Now, when the poet Theodore Roethke wrote "Snail, snail, glister me forward," he may have been in a bigger hurry to get home than he realized. As a speedster, the snail has been given bad press throughout history. In English, the term "snail's pace" goes back at least to the fifteenth century, and English writers have been denigrating the snail's footwork since, with John Heywood, Will Shakespeare, Fanny Burney, George Borrow, and others using the gastropod mollusk as a metaphor for sluggish locomotion. (The word "sluggish" itself is of course an aspersion on the snail's close kinsfellow, the common garden slug, which moves at about the same rate of speed and is simply a snail without a roof over its head.)

According to statistics randomly gathered by *Playboy* magazine, which usually concerns itself with racier matters, a snail's pace is 0.00758 mph. Unfortunately, *Playboy* neglected to specify which of the twenty-four-thousand-odd species of terrestrial snails it had clocked, or whether the figure represents the average speed of snails in general. Whatever it represents, 0.00758 mph works out to a little better than ten feet per hour. My own impression, based on altogether unscientific observation, is that a Provençal escargot of the *petits gris* variety can cover a good deal more ground than that, but even ten feet amounts to a significant distance in a very small two-bedroom house.

In any event, my own escargots glistered themselves forward with astonishing alacrity, leaving mucoid contrails to mark their passage over floors, walls, ceilings, and freestanding objects. Within hours, every pocket of every garment in the house had become an operculated snail's sleeping bag. Snails invaded the wine cellar, gluing themselves to bottles and demijohns; the chimney, where they inadvertently converted themselves to smoked delicacies we didn't have the perspicacity to market commercially; the garden, where they fattened on day lilies and vine leaves; the beams, the pantry, and our infant son Mathieu's cradle. They attached themselves to the undersides of furniture, the top of the mantel, the insoles of boots. Attempts to corral the critters were something like trying to empty the Mediterranean with a bailing bucket. For every escargotcha, a dozen or more free spirits turned up where they shouldn't have been.

The evening of the showdown was approaching apace, and the inhabitants of St.-Hippolyte, naturally predisposed in favor of experienced local talent, took a dim view of my prospects, or so I was informed by Juliette Treillard. Juliette! Juliette of the shrewd, hooded liquid-brown eyes and long, probing bill-like nose: a nose perpetually adrip during the winter with a single crystalline droplet at its end; a nose beside which she would lay a bony forefinger in moments of reflection, slowly drawing one felt-slippered foot up from the wet earth and into her voluminous skirts like some great shawled stork.

Juliette was the owner, the historian, and the social arbiter of St.-Hippolyte, its grande dame and the most delightfully dotty woman I've known in a lifetime of consorting with mixed nuts. She and Marie-Antoinette maintained and lived above a murky monochromatic general store stocked for the most part with defunct ballpoint pens and empty cardboard cartons; the latter, piled higgledy-piggledy from floor to ceiling, periodically avalanched all over the premises, burying groceries, yard goods, cats, and cashbox with Pompeiian finality. With Marie-Antoinette's gentle acquiescence, Juliette leased St.-Hippolyte's meadow spring and fall to itinerant shepherds, and to hay balers during the summer. She rented the community's smithy and a few dwellings to an astonishing assortment of oddballs, kept her goats in a dilapidated barn, and, I devoutly believe, played the piano under water by the light of the full moon.

On a morning after one of Juliette's midnight recitals (which rendered Chopin and Debussy as *glong, glong, glong*), I entered her store, with Roger in tow, to pick up a few staples. Juliette was gutting some mackerel purchased a half-hour earlier from the fishmonger who visited St.-Hippolyte twice weekly. Today, Roger is no Adonis. At that time, though, he might have fluttered down from the frescoed ceiling of some rococo Bavarian chapel. With his full mop of spun-gold curls and saucer eyes of cornflower blue, he'd had a devastating effect on older women of Mediterranean derivation even before he got to the south of France. Riding my shoulders back in New York's Little Italy during the street festival of San Gennaro, he'd been mobbed by Neapolitan-born matrons who, apparently identifying him with the Christ child of countless chromolithographs, insisted on laying adoring hands on him. Perhaps as a result of the experience, he would spook when fussed over in foreign languages, and he remained adamant, after two weeks in France, in his refusal to learn so much as a single word of French. (He was quick, however, to mock the accent. "Ees eet expahnseeve?" he had asked of a toy cash register seen in an Arles Christmas display and sorely coveted.)

Roger's first encounters with Juliette Treillard had been brief and violent. "Oh, *il est tellement mignon!*" she would exclaim as he joined us in the dooryard, whereupon he would kick viciously at her single accessible shin. Picking herself up from the ground, the poor woman would lay a forefinger alongside her nose and again retract half her landing gear. "*Soyez sage, mon p'tit ange,*" she would coo, again to be unceremoniously dumped on her derriere. Then, with Juliette in full retreat, the little angel would be marched back into the house and given what-for.

The language barrier was soon broken through the agency of Marie-France du Bellon. Like her mother, Marie-France was a honey-haired looker. Normally, she would have passed our house only while running each day's single errand to and from the Treillard store, where she picked up such staples as milk, flour, soap, and *vin ordinaire*. Once aware of Roger's presence, though, she had begun to make individual trips for each of the needed items, parading endlessly past our yard with her pert nose in the air and with a brown eye cocked slyly in the direction of the *petit étranger*. Roger had observed her comings and goings with feigned indifference for four or five days before breaking down. At last, he had sidled up to me and, blushing scarlet, mumbled, "How do you ask someone to play with you in French?" I told him, and after whispering the talismanic phrase to himself a few times, he had raced across the yard, yelling, "Hey! My name's Roger. *Voulez-vous jouer avec moi?*" We seldom saw him between meals thereafter, and within two weeks he was speaking French like a native, rolling his *ars* exaggeratedly in the Provençal style.

Once he had mastered the language, Roger found Juliette's effusions much more to his liking. On the rare occasions when Marie-France was unavailable, he'd seek out the old spinster's company, clamber onto her lap, and revel in her embrace. On the morning in question, he launched himself at her as soon as we entered the store, but she shrank back, crying, "Not now, little angel, I'm covered with mess from these fish." Deprived of physical contact, Roger stood as close beside her as he could, while Juliette went on with the job at hand, of which she was making a royal bollix. After an uncharacteristically perfunctory recital of the usual pleasantries, she laid a finger beside her nose, fixed me with the sort of gaze ordinarily reserved for family scapegraces and terminally ill loved ones, and got down to business.

Du Bellon, she informed me, was a renowned eater from a race of renowned eaters. Although she admired me for rising to his challenge, discretion in this case would have been the far better part of valor. There was simply no way that I, an American through no fault of my own, with no tradition of grand gourmandise to sustain me, could possibly defeat a man of M. du Bellon's vast experience, innate savoir-faire, and heroic appetite. If the truth be told, I had been taken monumentally unfair advantage of by an unprincipled opportunist who had everything to gain and nothing to lose. Reflect, I was told: when had M. du Bellon ever challenged anyone to an ortolan-eating contest, an agon that would entail the sacrifice of any of his hoarded birds to any belly but his own? M. du Bellon, Juliette concluded, had merely devised a ploy whereby he could enjoy the limitless fruits of my labors at no cost to himself. Worse, he would add insult to injury by subjecting me to a humiliating trouncing that generations of St.-Hippolytans yet unborn would evoke and cackle over as long as Frenchmen felt the need to assert their God-given superiority to callow outlanders.

As she'd warmed to her subject, Juliette had forgotten her fish and absently fondled Roger's curls, smearing them thoroughly with blood and guts. I took the kid back to the house, stood him beneath the kitchen pump, and sluiced him clean. On reflection, Juliette's homily seemed predicated on some false suppositions. After all, I decided, *she* had no way of knowing that as a ten-year-old I'd eaten eighteen pancakes at breakfast one morning and nine years later had put away seven mountainous helpings of fried oysters in an air force mess hall.

What I'd overlooked, however, was that both feats had been accomplished spontaneously, whereas a couple of challenge situations had damned near hospitalized me. The first of these debacles had been set in motion by my innocent assertion, while I was still in my teens, that "I could eat these things all night." "These things" were ordinary commercial potato chips. The setting was a raffish tavern in Carthage, Missouri, where I was maladroitly attempting to romance an Ozark mountain girl over a few late-evening beers.

I should have known better when my inamorata bet me I couldn't finish two family-size sacks of chips in ten minutes. As an occasional ingester of glass and razor blades (talents she would display after a pleasant sufficiency of 3.2 brew), Kate had made herself privy to certain masticatory arcana of which I was altogether ignorant. (Another of her wee-hour specialties was traversing a lengthy railroad trestle in the seminude while hanging by her hands from its underside, a hundred feet or so above a boulder-strewn gulley.) Hell, I reasoned, two large sacks of chips don't add up to a pound of provender. How could I lose? "What do you bet?" I demanded. "You do it, and you can feel my tits," she replied. I don't remember what I'd have forfeited had I failed. Perhaps just the chance to fondle the flesh.

The upshot of the story is that I felt Kate's tits that night. I also felt as though a troupe of Cossacks had performed a saber dance in my mouth and rubbed the contents of a salt mine into my myriad wounds. What I'd failed to take into account was that potato chips snaffled up in inordinate quantity and inordinate haste have the same effect on human tissue as so many improperly masticated razor blades or drinking glasses. Exquisite as it might have been in other circumstances, the first real feel I'd ever copped didn't seem worth a week of painful convalescence.

The second of my great alimentary disasters had occurred a few months after the potato chip incident, in a scruffy café in the Mexican quarter of San Antonio, where a couple of other GIs and I were lacing our tacos with progressively more potent doses of Tabasco sauce. With steam hissing out of my ears, I affected a tolerance for the stuff that enabled me, or so I claimed, to chug down a six-ounce bottleful of the stuff in one gulp. Pelf was tabled ("One'll getcha two you can't"), and a fresh bottle was ordered and uncapped. Once again, I damned near died in the process of collecting on a bet. The last thing I remember seeing (in a john mirror before submerging my head in a sinkful of cold water) was a pumpkin-sized anthropomorphic tomato, its lips puffed like pillows, its eyes starting out of their sockets. As I passed out, the available options seemed death by strangulation or drowning, but one of my companions fished my head from the sink and flushed enough beer through my system to extinguish the inferno.

On the day of the confrontation with du Bellon, I made a serious tactical blunder. On the theory that the hungrier I was, the more I'd be able to eat, I skipped breakfast and dinner. As a reader of A. J. Liebling, I should have known better. It was Liebling's tested contention that serious quantitative eating entails constant conditioning; that an empty stomach is no arena for gastronomic heroics; and that the best warm-up for sustained gluttony is a respectably ample meal. Liebling's idea of a respectably ample meal was perhaps best articulated in his sorrowful analysis of Marcel Proust's effete approach to the responsibilities of his craft:

The Proust *madeleine* phenomenon is now as firmly established in folklore as Newton's apple or Watt's steam engine. The man ate a tea biscuit, the taste evoked memories, he wrote a book. . . . In the light of what Proust wrote with so mild a stimulus, it is the world's loss that he did not have a heartier appetite. On a dozen Gardiner's Island oysters, a bowl of clam chowder, a peck of steamers, some bay scallops, three sautéed soft-shelled crabs, a few ears of fresh-picked corn, a thin swordfish steak of generous area, a pair of lobsters, and a Long Island duck, he might have written a masterpiece.

Pierre du Bellon was no such malignerer as his more celebrated countryman. When I ran into him at the café in Raphèle, a bit past noon on the day of our scheduled match, he was sipping a preprandial pastis and holding forth on his two favorite subjects: what he had eaten at his last meal and what he'd be eating at his next. Kissing his bunched fingertips at appropriate intervals, he described the previous evening's repast and his impending lunch in meticulous detail, larding an extended inventory with *formidables*, *délicieuxes*, *magnifiques*, *superlatifs*, etc. He savored one meal as enthusiastically in anticipation as he did the other in retrospect. Even as he spoke, he informed his listeners, Mme. du Bellon was preparing a light midday collation that would begin with half a dozen of his precious ortolans and progress through *soupe de poisson*, a *friture* of whitebait, a brace of *rougets à la provençale*, assorted vegetables, a tossed salad, a small round of grapeseed-encrusted goat cheese, and *crème renversée*. In a transparent attempt to psyche me out, he refrained from any mention of the impending snail duel, tacitly dismissing it as a mere bagatelle.

The city of Arles has its own recipe for snails, but most Arlesians prefer the standard Burgundian treatment to their own *escargots à l'arlésienne*. Although a gentleman in all other respects, du Bellon, as the challenger, had violated the traditional code of honor by choosing the weapons: *escargots à la bourguignonne*, which are infinitely richer and more filling than the butterless local preparation. In themselves, snails pose no greater a challenge to anyone's capacity than so many small boiled shrimp or steamer clams. To eat *escargots à la bourguignonne*, however, is necessarily to eat far more bread than, and about as much butter as, snail meat. The sauce, of course, is the essence of the dish, and the only way the sauce can be eaten is with quantities of bread. Hence, to eat snails with anything like proper self-respect, the eater who takes them on en masse is obliged to ingest both inordinate amounts of bread and enough butter to bring his arterial traffic to a standstill.

Somehow, I'd neglected to take these factors into consideration when the gauntlet was flung down, and the magnitude of the task at hand didn't dawn on me until I arrived *chez* du Bellon, to find what appeared to be a small village bakery's daily output stacked like cordwood on the dining-room table. Wine was arrayed in proportionate abundance, and du Bellon sat beaming across this vista like a cat at a tethered mouse.

By the fourth and fifth round of a dozen snails apiece, a flushed Mme. du Bellon had worked herself into an uncharacteristic mucksweat racing to and from the kitchen, where she was assisted by Gwynne, who had dropped out of the contest early on. I was beginning to bloat like a dead Tanganyikan elephant in midsummer, but du Bellon jauntily moiled bits of bread around in his snail butter, scarfing them down with obvious relish as he held forth on a variety of subjects with quintessential Gallic urbanity, while I gagged, glassy-eyed, in my effort to keep pace. By dozen seven, several liters of wine-swollen bread and gut-lurching cholesterol overload, accentuated by massive overdoses of garlic, had me reeling along what's called Queer Street in pugilistic parlance. By round nine, never wanting to see food in any form again, I was ready to throw in the towel when Mme. du Bellon announced that the contest would be forthwith terminated and adjudged a draw so that the roast might not be overdone.

ERNEST HEMINGWAY

Hunger Was Good Discipline

You got very hungry when you did not eat enough in Paris because all the bakery shops had such good things in the windows and people ate outside at tables on the sidewalk so that you saw and smelled the food. When you had given up journalism and were writing nothing that anyone in America would buy, explaining at home that you were lunching out with someone, the best place to go was the Luxembourg Gardens where you saw and smelled nothing to eat all the way from the place de l'Observatoire to the rue de Vaugirard. There you could always go into the Luxembourg Museum and all the paintings were sharpened and clearer and more beautiful if you were belly-empty, hollow-hungry. I learned to understand Cézanne much better and to see truly how he made landscapes when I was hungry. I used to wonder if he were hungry too when he painted; but I thought possibly it was only that he had forgotten to eat. It was one of those unsound but illuminating thoughts you have when you have been sleepless or hungry. Later I thought Cézanne was probably hungry in a different way.

After you came out of the Luxembourg you could walk down the narrow rue Férou to the place St-Sulpice and there were still no restaurants, only the quiet square with its benches and trees. There was a fountain with lions, and pigeons walked on the pavement and perched on the statues of the bishops. There was the church and there were shops selling religious objects and vestments on the north side of the square.

From this square you could not go farther towards the river without passing shops selling fruits, vegetables, wines, or bakery and pastry shops. But by choosing your way carefully you could work to your right round the grey-and-white stone church and reach the rue de l'Odéon and turn up to your right towards Sylvia Beach's bookshop and on your way you did not pass too many places where things to eat were sold. The rue de l'Odéon was bare of eating places until you reached the square, where there were three restaurants.

By the time you reached 12 rue de l'Odéon your hunger was contained but all of your perceptions were heightened again. The photographs looked different and you saw books that you had never seen before.

"You're too thin, Hemingway," Sylvia would say. "Are you eating enough?"

"Sure."

"What did you eat for lunch?"

My stomach would turn over and I would say, "I'm going home for lunch now."

"At three o'clock?"

"I didn't know it was that late."

"Adrienne said the other night she wanted to have you and Hadley for dinner. We'd ask Fargue. You like Fargue, don't you? Or Larbaud. You like him. I know you like him. Or anyone you really like. Will you speak to Hadley?"

"I know she'd love to come."

"I'll send her a *pneu*. Don't you work so hard now that you don't eat properly."

"I won't."

"Get home now before it's too late for lunch."

"They'll save it."

"Don't eat cold food either. Eat a good hot lunch."

"Did I have any mail?"

"I don't think so. But let me look."

She looked and found a note and looked up happily and then opened a closed door in her desk.

"This came while I was out," she said. It was a letter and it felt as though it had money in it. "Wedderkop," Sylvia said.

"It must be from *Der Querschnitt*. Did you see Wedderkop?"

"No. But he was here with George. He'll see you. Don't worry. Perhaps he wanted to pay you first."

"It's six hundred francs. He says there will be more."

"I'm awfully glad you reminded me to look. Dear Mr. Awfully Nice."

"It's damned funny that Germany is the only place I can sell anything. To him and the *Frankfurter Zeitung.*"

"Isn't it? But don't you worry ever. You can sell stories to Ford," she teased me.

"Thirty francs a page. Say one story every three months in the *Transatlantic.* Story five pages long makes one hundred and fifty francs a quarter. Six hundred francs a year."

"But, Hemingway, don't worry about what they bring now. The point is that you can write them."

"I know. I can write them. But nobody will buy them. There is no money coming in since I quit journalism."

"They will sell. Look. You have the money for one right there."

"I'm sorry, Sylvia. Forgive me for speaking about it."

"Forgive you for what? Always talk about it or about anything. Don't you know all writers ever talk about is their troubles? But promise me you won't worry and that you'll eat enough."

"I promise."

"Then get home now and have lunch."

Outside on the rue de l'Odéon I was disgusted with myself for having complained about things. I was doing what I did of my own free will and I was doing it stupidly. I should have bought a large piece of bread and eaten it instead of skipping a meal. I could taste the brown lovely crust. But it is dry in your mouth without something to drink. You God-damn complainer. You dirty phony saint and martyr, I said to myself. You quit journalism of your own accord. You have credit and Sylvia would have loaned you money. She has, plenty of times. Sure. And then the next thing you would be compromising on something else. Hunger is healthy and the pictures do look better when you are hungry. Eating is wonderful too and do you know where you are going to eat right now?

Lipp's is where you are going to eat, and drink too.

It was a quick walk to Lipp's and every place I passed that my stomach noticed as quickly as my eyes or my nose made the walk an added pleasure. There were few people in the brasserie and when I sat down on the bench against the wall with the mirror in back and a table in front and the waiter asked if I wanted beer I asked for a *distingué*, the big glass mug that held a liter, and for potato salad.

The beer was very cold and wonderful to drink. The *pommes à l'huile* were firm and marinated and the olive oil delicious. I ground black pepper over the potatoes and moistened the bread in the olive oil. After the first heavy draught of beer I drank and ate very slowly. When the *pommes à l'huile* were gone I ordered another serving and a *cervelas*. This was a sausage like a heavy, wide frankfurter split in two and covered with a special mustard sauce.

I mopped up all the oil and all of the sauce with bread and drank the beer slowly until it began to lose its coldness and then I finished it and ordered a *demi* and watched it drawn. It seemed colder than the *distingué* and I drank half of it.

I had not been worrying, I thought. I knew the stories were good and someone would publish them finally at home. When I stopped doing news-paper work I was sure the stories were going to be published. But every one I sent out came back. What had made me so confident was Edward O'Brien's taking the *My Old Man* story for the *Best Short Stories* book and then dedicating the book for that year to me. Then I laughed and drank some more beer. The story had never been published in a magazine and he had broken all his rules to take it for the book. I laughed again and the waiter glanced at me. It was funny because, after all that, he had spelled the name wrong. It was one of two stories I had left when everything I had written was stolen in Hadley's suitcase that time at the Gare de Lyon when she was bringing the manuscripts down to me to Lausanne as a surprise, so I could work on them on our holidays in the mountains. She had put in the originals, the typescripts and the carbons, all in manila folders. The only reason I had the one story was that Lincoln Steffens had sent it out to some editor who sent it back. It was in the mail while everything else was stolen. The other story that I had was the one called *Up in Michigan*, written before Miss Stein had come to our flat. I had never had it copied because she said it was *inaccrochable*. It had been in a drawer somewhere.

So after we had left Lausanne and gone down to Italy I showed the racing story to O'Brien, a gentle, shy man, pale, with pale-blue eyes, and straight lanky hair he cut himself, who lived then as a boarder in a monastery up above Rapallo. It was a bad time and I did not think I could write any more then, and I showed the story to him as a curiosity, as you might show, stupidly, the binnacle of a ship you had lost in some incredible way, or as you might pick up your booted foot and make some joke about it if it had been amputated after a crash. Then, when he read the story, I saw he was hurt far more than I was. I had never seen anyone hurt by a thing other than death or unbearable suffering except Hadley when she told me about the things being gone. She had cried and cried and could not tell me. I told her that no matter what the dreadful thing was that had happened nothing could be that bad, and whatever it was, it was all right and not to worry. We could work it out. Then, finally, she told me. I was sure she could not have brought the carbons too, and I hired someone to cover for me on my newspaper job. I was making good money then at journalism, and took the train for Paris. It was true all right, and I remember what I did in the night after I let myself into the flat and found it was true. That was over now and Chink had taught me never to discuss casualties; so I told O'Brien not to feel so bad. It was probably good for me to lose early work and I told him all that stuff you feed the troops. I was going to start writing stories again I said and, as I said it, only trying to lie so that he would not feel so bad, I knew that it was true.

Then I started to think in Lipp's about when I had first been able to write a story after losing everything. It was up in Cortina d'Ampezzo when I had come back to join Hadley there after the spring skiing which I had to interrupt to go on assignment to the Rhineland and the Ruhr. It was a very simple story called *Out of Season* and I had omitted the real end of it which was that the old man hanged himself. This was omitted on my new theory that you could omit anything if you knew that you omitted, and the omitted part would strengthen the story and make people feel something more than they understood.

Well, I thought, now I have them so they do not understand them. There cannot be much doubt about that. There is most certainly no demand for them. But they will understand the same way that they always do in painting. It only takes time and it only needs confidence.

It is necessary to handle yourself better when you have to cut down on food so you will not get too much hunger-thinking. Hunger is good discipline and you learn from it. And as long as they do not understand it you are ahead of them. Oh sure, I thought, I'm so far ahead of them now that I can't afford to eat regularly. It would not be bad if they caught up a little.

I knew I must write a novel. But it seemed an impossible thing to do when I had been trying with great difficulty to write paragraphs that would be the distillation of what made a novel. It was necessary to write longer stories now as you would train for a longer race. When I had written a novel before, the one that had been lost in the bag stolen at the Gare de Lyon, I still had the lyric facility of boyhood that was as perishable and as deceptive as youth was. I knew it was probably a good thing that it was lost, but I knew too that I must write a novel. I would put it off, though, until I could not help doing it. I was damned if I would write one because it was what I should do if we were to eat regularly. When I had to write it, then it would be the only thing to do and there would be no choice. Let the pressure build. In the meantime I would write a long story about whatever I knew best.

By this time I had paid the check and gone out and turned to the right and crossed the rue de Rennes so that I would not go to the Deux Magots for coffee and was walking up the rue Bonaparte on the shortest way home.

What did I know best that I had not written about and lost? What did I know about truly and care for the most? There was no choice at all. There was only the choice of streets to take you back fastest to where you worked. It went up Bonaparte to Guynemer, then to the rue d'Assas, up the rue Notre-Dame-des-Champs to the Closerie des Lilas.

I sat in a corner with the afternoon light coming in over my shoulder and wrote in the notebook. The waiter brought me a café crème and I drank half of it when it cooled and left it on the table while I wrote. When I stopped writing I did not want to leave the river where I could see the trout in the pool, its surface pushing and swelling smooth against the resistance of the log-driven piles of the bridge. The story was about coming back from the war but there was no mention of the war in it.

But in the morning the river would be there and I must make it and the country and all that would happen. There were days ahead to be doing that each day. No other thing mattered. In my pocket was the money from Germany so there was no problem. When that was gone some other money would come in.

All I must do now was stay sound and good in my head until morning when I would start to work again.

M. F. K. FISHER

Define This Word

T hat early spring I met a young ser-
vant in northern Burgundy who was almost fanatical about food, like a
medieval woman possessed by the devil. Her obsession engulfed even my
appreciation of the dishes she served, until I grew uncomfortable.

It was the off season at the old mill which a Parisian chef had bought
and turned into one of France's most famous restaurants, and my mad
waitress was the only servant. In spite of that she was neatly uniformed, and
showed no surprise at my unannounced arrival and my hot dusty walking
clothes.

She smiled discreetly at me, said, "Oh, but certainly!" when I asked if
I could lunch there, and led me without more words to a dark bedroom
bulging with First Empire furniture, and a new white bathroom.

When I went into the dining room it was empty of humans . . . a
cheerful ugly room still showing traces of the *petit-bourgeois* parlor it had
been. There were aspidistras on the mantel; several small white tables were
laid with those imitation "peasant-ware" plates that one sees in Paris china
stores, and very good crystal glasses; a cat folded under some ferns by the
window ledge hardly looked at me; and the air was softly hurried with the
sound of high waters from the stream outside.

I waited for the maid to come back. I knew I should eat well and slowly,
and suddenly the idea of dry sherry, unknown in all the village *bistros* of the
last few days, stung my throat smoothly. I tried not to think of it; it would

be impossible to realize. Dubonnet would do. But not as well. I longed for sherry.

The little maid came into the silent room. I looked at her stocky young body, and her butter-colored hair, and noticed her odd pale voluptuous mouth before I said, "Mademoiselle, I shall drink an *apéritif*. Have you by any chance—"

"Let me suggest," she interrupted firmly, "our special dry sherry. It is chosen in Spain for Monsieur Paul."

And before I could agree she was gone, discreet and smooth.

She's a funny one, I thought, and waited in a pleasant warm tiredness for the wine.

It was good. I smiled approval at her, and she lowered her eyes, and then looked searchingly at me again. I realized suddenly that in this land of trained nonchalant waiters I was to be served by a small waitress who took her duties seriously. I felt much amused, and matched her solemn searching gaze.

"Today, Madame, you may eat shoulder of lamb in the English style, with baked potatoes, green beans, and a sweet."

My heart sank. I felt dismal, and hot and weary, and still grateful for the sherry.

But she was almost grinning at me, her lips curved triumphantly, and her eyes less palely blue.

"Oh, in *that* case a trout, of course—a *truite au bleu* as only Monsieur Paul can prepare it!"

She glanced hurriedly at my face, and hastened on. "With the trout, one or two young potatoes—oh, very delicately boiled," she added before I could protest, "very light."

I felt better. I agreed. "Perhaps a leaf or two of salad after the fish," I suggested. She almost snapped at me. "Of course, of course! And naturally our *hors d'oeuvres* to commence." She started away.

"No!" I called, feeling that I must assert myself now or be forever lost. "No!"

She turned back, and spoke to me very gently. "But Madame has never tasted our *hors d'oeuvres*. I am sure that Madame will be pleased. They are our specialty, made by Monsieur Paul himself. I am sure," and she looked reproachfully at me, her mouth tender and sad, "I am sure that Madame would be very much pleased."

I smiled weakly at her, and she left. A little cloud of hurt gentleness seemed to hang in the air where she had last stood.

I comforted myself with sherry, feeling increasing irritation with my own feeble self. Hell! I loathed *hors d'oeuvres!* I conjured disgusting visions of square glass plates of oily fish, of soggy vegetables glued together with cheap mayonnaise, or rank radishes and tasteless butter. No, Monsieur Paul or not, sad young pale-faced waitress or not, I hated *hors d'oeuvres.*

I glanced victoriously across the room at the cat, whose eyes seemed closed.

II

Several minutes passed. I was really very hungry.

The door banged open, and my girl came in again, less discreet this time. She hurried toward me.

"Madame, the wine! Before Monsieur Paul can go on—" Her eyes watched my face, which I perversely kept rather glum.

"I think," I said ponderously, daring her to interrupt me, "I think that today, since I am in Burgundy and about to eat a trout," and here I hoped she noticed that I did not mention *hors d'oeuvres*, "I think I shall drink a bottle of Chablis 1929—*not* Chablis Village 1929."

For a second her whole face blazed with joy, and then subsided into a trained mask. I knew that I had chosen well, had somehow satisfied her in a secret and incomprehensible way. She nodded politely and scuttled off, only for another second glancing impatiently at me as I called after her, "Well cooled, please, but not iced."

I'm a fool, I thought, to order a whole bottle. I'm a fool, here all alone and with more miles to walk before I reach Avallon and my fresh clothes and a bed. Then I smiled at myself and leaned back in my solid wide-seated chair, looking obliquely at the prints of Gibson girls, English tavern scenes, and hideous countrysides that hung on the papered walls. The room was warm; I could hear my companion cat purring under the ferns.

The girl rushed in, with flat baking dishes piled up her arms on napkins, like the plates of a Japanese juggler. She slid them off neatly in two rows on to the table, where they lay steaming up at me, darkly and infinitely appetizing.

"*Mon Dieu!* All for me?" I peered at her. She nodded, her discretion quite gone now and a look of ecstatic worry on her pale face and eyes and lips.

There were at least eight dishes. I felt almost embarrassed, and sat for a minute looking weakly at the fork and spoon in my hand.

"Perhaps Madame would care to start with the pickled herring? It is not like any other. Monsieur Paul prepares it himself, in his own vinegar and wines. It is very good."

I dug out two or three brown filets from the dish, and tasted. They were truly unlike any others, truly the best I had ever eaten, mild, pungent, meaty as fresh nuts.

I realized the maid had stopped breathing, and looked up at her. She was watching me, or rather a gastronomic X-ray of the herring inside me, with a hypnotized glaze in her eyes.

"Madame is pleased?" she whispered softly.

I said I was. She sighed, and pushed a sizzling plate of broiled endive toward me, and disappeared.

I had put a few dull green lentils on my plate, lentils scattered with minced fresh herbs and probably marinated in tarragon vinegar and walnut oil, when she came into the dining room again with the bottle of Chablis in a wine basket.

"Madame should be eating the little baked onions while they are hot," she remarked over her shoulder as she held the bottle in a napkin and uncorked it. I obeyed meekly, and while I watched her I ate several more than I had meant to. They were delicious, simmered first in strong meat broth, I think, and then drained and broiled with olive oil and new-ground pepper.

I was fascinated by her method of uncorking a vintage wine. Instead of the Burgundian procedure of infinite and often exaggerated precautions against touching or tipping or jarring the bottle, she handled it quite nonchalantly, and seemed to be careful only to keep her hands from the cool bottle itself, holding it sometimes by the basket and sometimes in a napkin. The cork was very tight, and I thought for a minute that she would break it. So did she; her face grew tense, and did not loosen until she had slowly worked out the cork and wiped the lip. Then she poured an inch of wine in a glass, turned her back to me like a priest taking Communion, and drank it down. Finally some was poured for me, and she stood with the bottle in her hand and her full lips drooping until I nodded a satisfied yes. Then she pushed another of the plates toward me, and almost rushed from the room.

I ate slowly, knowing that I should not be as hungry as I ought to be for the trout, but knowing too that I had never tasted such delicate savory morsels. Some were hot, some cold. The wine was light and cool. The room, warm and agreeably empty under the rushing sound of the stream, became smaller as I grew used to it.

My girl hurried in again, with another row of plates up one arm, and a large bucket dragging at the other. She slid the plates deftly on to the table, and drew a deep breath as she let the bucket down against the table leg.

"Your trout, Madame," she said excitedly. I looked down at the gleam of the fish curving through its limited water. "But first a good slice of Monsieur Paul's *pâté*. Oh yes, oh yes, you will be very sorry if you miss this. It is rich, but appetizing, and not at all too heavy. Just this one morsel!"

And willy-nilly I accepted the large gouge she dug from a terrine. I prayed for ten normal appetites and thought with amused nostalgia of my usual lunch of cold milk and fruit as I broke off a crust of bread and patted it smooth with the paste. Then I forgot everything but the exciting faint decadent flavor in my mouth.

I beamed up at the girl. She nodded, but from habit asked if I was satisfied. I beamed again, and asked, simply to please her, "Is there not a faint hint of *marc*, or perhaps cognac?"

"*Marc*, Madame!" And she awarded me the proud look of a teacher whose pupil has showed unexpected intelligence. "Monsieur Paul, after he has taken equal parts of goose breast and the finest pork, and broken a certain number of egg yolks into them, and ground them *very*, very fine, cooks all with seasoning for some three hours. *But*," she pushed her face nearer, and looked with ferocious gloating at the *pâté* inside me, her eyes like X-rays, "he never stops stirring it! Figure to yourself the work of it—stir, stir, never stopping!

"Then he grinds in a suspicion of nutmeg, and then adds, very thoroughly, a glass of *marc* for each hundred grams of *pâté*. And is Madame not pleased?"

Again I agreed, rather timidly, that Madame was much pleased, that Madame had never, indeed, tasted such an unctuous and exciting *pâté*. The girl wet her lips delicately, and then started as if she had been pin-struck.

"But the trout! My God, the trout!" She grabbed the bucket, and her voice grew higher and more rushed.

"Here is the trout, Madame. You are to eat it *au bleu*, and you should never do so if you had not seen it alive. For if the trout were dead when it was plunged into the *court bouillon* it would not turn blue. So, naturally, it must be living."

I knew all this, more or less, but I was fascinated by her absorption in the momentary problem. I felt quite ignorant, and asked her with sincerity, "What about the trout? Do you take out its guts before or after?"

"Oh, the trout!" She sounded scornful. "Any trout is glad, truly glad, to be prepared by Monsieur Paul. His little gills are pinched, with one flash of the knife he is empty, and then he curls in agony in the *bouillon* and all is over. And it is the curl you must judge, Madame. A false *truite au bleu* cannot curl.''

She panted triumph at me, and hurried out with the bucket.

III

She *is* a funny one, I thought, and for not more than two or three minutes I drank wine and mused over her. Then she darted in, with the trout correctly blue and agonizingly curled on a platter, and on her crooked arm a plate of tiny boiled potatoes and a bowl.

When I had been served and had cut off her anxious breathings with an assurance that the fish was the best I had ever tasted, she peered again at me and at the sauce in the bowl. I obediently put some of it on the potatoes: no fool I, to ruin *truite au bleu* with a hot concoction! There was more silence.

"Ah!" she sighed at last. "I knew Madame would feel thus! Is it not the most beautiful sauce in the world with the flesh of a trout?"

I nodded incredulous agreement.

"Would you like to know how it is done?"

I remembered all the legends of chefs who guarded favorite recipes with their very lives, and murmured yes.

She wore the exalted look of a believer describing a miracle at Lourdes as she told me, in a rush, how Monsieur Paul threw chopped chives into hot sweet butter and then poured the butter off, how he added another nut of butter and a tablespoonful of thick cream for each person, stirred the mixture for a few minutes over a slow fire, and then rushed it to the table.

"So simple?" I asked softly, watching her lighted eyes and the tender lustful lines of her strange mouth.

"So simple, Madame! But," she shrugged, "you know, with a master—"

I was relieved to see her go; such avid interest in my eating wore on me. I felt released when the door closed behind her, free for a minute or so from her victimization. What would she have done, I wondered, if I had been ignorant or unconscious of any fine flavors?

She was right, though, about Monsieur Paul. Only a master could live in this isolated mill and preserve his gastronomic dignity through loneliness and the sure financial loss of unused butter and addled eggs. Of course, there was the stream for his fish, and I knew his *pâtés* would grow even more edible with age; but how could he manage to have a thing like roasted lamb ready for any chance patron? Was the consuming interest of his one maid enough fuel for his flame?

I tasted the last sweet nugget of trout, the one nearest the blued tail, and poked somnolently at the minute white billiard balls that had been eyes. Fate could not harm me, I remembered winily, for I had indeed dined today, and dined well. Now for a leaf of crisp salad, and I'd be on my way.

The girl slid into the room. She asked me again, in a respectful but gossipy manner, how I had liked this and that and the other things, and then talked on as she mixed dressing for the endive.

"And now," she announced, after I had eaten one green sprig and dutifully pronounced it excellent, "now Madame is going to taste Monsieur Paul's special terrine, one that is not even on the summer menu, when a hundred covers are laid here daily and we have a headwaiter and a wine waiter, and cabinet ministers telegraph for tables! Madame will be pleased."

And heedless of my low moans of the walk still before me, of my appreciation and my unhappily human and limited capacity, she cut a thick heady slice from the terrine of meat and stood over me while I ate it, telling me with almost hysterical pleasure of the wild ducks, the spices, the wines that went into it. Even surfeit could not make me deny that it was a rare dish. I ate it all, knowing my luck, and wishing only that I had red wine to drink with it.

I was beginning, though, to feel almost frightened, realizing myself an accidental victim of these stranded gourmets, Monsieur Paul and his hand-maiden. I began to feel that they were using me for a safety valve, much as a thwarted woman relieves herself with tantrums or a fit of weeping. I was serving a purpose, and perhaps a noble one, but I resented it in a way approaching panic.

I protested only to myself when one of Monsieur Paul's special cheeses was cut for me, and ate it doggedly, like a slave. When the girl said that Monsieur Paul himself was preparing a special filter of coffee for me, I smiled servile acceptance; wine and the weight of food and my own character could not force me to argue with maniacs. When, before the coffee came, Monsieur Paul presented me, through his idolater, with the most beautiful apple tart I had ever seen, I allowed it to be cut and served to me. Not a wince or a murmur showed the waitress my distressed fearfulness. With a stuffed care-ful smile on my face, and a clear nightmare in my head of trussed wanderers prepared for his altar by this hermit-priest of gastronomy, I listened to the girl's passionate plea for fresh pastry dough.

"You cannot, you *cannot*, Madame, serve old pastry!" She seemed ready to beat her breast as she leaned across the table. "Look at that delicate crust! You may feel that you have eaten too much." (I nodded idiotic agreement.) "But this pastry is like feathers—it is like snow. It is in fact good for you, a digestive! And why?" She glared sternly at me. "Because Monsieur Paul did not even open the flour bin until he saw you coming! He could not, he *could* not have baked you one of his special apple tarts with old dough!"

She laughed, tossing her head and curling her mouth voluptuously.

IV

Somehow I managed to refuse a second slice, but I trembled under her surmise that I was ready for my special filter.

The wine and the fortitude had fled me, and I drank the hot coffee as a suffering man gulps ether, deeply and gratefully.

I remember, then, chatting with surprising glibness, and sending to Monsieur Paul flowery compliments, all of them sincere and well won, and I remember feeling only amusement when a vast glass of *marc* appeared before me and then gradually disappeared, like the light in the warm room full of water-sounds. I felt surprise to be alive still, and suddenly very grateful to the wild-lipped waitress, as if her presence had sustained me through duress. We discussed food and wine. I wondered bemusedly why I had been frightened.

The *marc* was gone. I went into the crowded bedroom for my jacket. She met me in the darkening hall when I came out, and I paid my bill, a large one. I started to thank her, but she took my hand, drew me into the dining room, and without words poured more spirits into my glass. I drank to Monsieur Paul while she watched me intently, her pale eyes bulging in the dimness and her lips pressed inward as if she too tasted the hot, aged *marc*.

The cat rose from his ferny bed, and walked contemptuously out of the room.

Suddenly the girl began to laugh, in a soft shy breathless way, and came close to me.

"Permit me!" she said, and I thought she was going to kiss me. But instead she pinned a tiny bunch of snowdrops and dark bruised cyclamens against my stiff jacket, very quickly and deftly, and then ran from the room with her head down.

I waited for a minute. No sounds came from anywhere in the old mill, but the endless rushing of the full stream seemed to strengthen, like the timid blare of an orchestra under a falling curtain.

She's a *funny* one, I thought. I touched the cool blossoms on my coat and went out, like a ghost from ruins, across the courtyard toward the dim road to Avallon.

LAWRENCE DURRELL

Something à la Carte?

The tragedy of Mungo Piers-Foley is one (said Antrobus) which should give every Thoughtful Person Pause. It did me. It still does. By the purest inadvertency he found himself cast into the Bottomless Pit. He was a bit absentminded that day. Yet what happened to him could happen to any of us.

Mungo was posted to us from the Blues as Military Attaché, and he was a gallant and carefree young colonel, full of the spice of life. You felt that he had a rich inner nature if only he could be persuaded to open his mouth. He was one of those mournful cylindrical men with hair parted in the middle—men who say little but think a lot. Yet who knows what they think? I don't. But he was an officer and a gentleman of unblemished reputation and a sportsman to boot. Not only to boot, to saddle as well. He had what is known as a splendid seat. He rode to hounds. However pointless the point-to-point, Mungo would be there, clearing hurdle after hurdle on his thoroughbred mule. He played polo without ever once hitting his horse. Myself I don't know much about horses, and what little I know seems to me singularly charmless. The last time I went hacking with Polk-Mowbray I got left in a tree for roughly the same reasons as Absalom. But that is neither here nor there . . .

Mungo had won a huge collection of cups and saucers which he wore on his mantelpiece. He shot. He dynamited fish. An all-round sportsman if ever there was one. We were proud of him in the Mission. All this, of course, only made his tragedy harder cheese than ever. It happened while he was in Paris for a week to help reorganize the NATO cavalry to face the threat of a rocket age. On the morning of his return he lurched into my office looking like a lot of overlooked washing-up. "Antrobus," he said, "hear my story. I am finished, old thing, absolutely finished. I've just put in my resignation and left Polk-Mowbray in tears." He sat down and fumbled for one of my cigars.

"It happened while I was in Paris," he said. "Quite inadvertent, the whole dashed thing. It could have happened to anyone. I popped into the Octagon for a bite. It wasn't until the *addition* came that I realized. Old man, *I had eaten a piece of horse!*"

I sprang up, startled. "You *what?*" I cried incredulously, realizing that I was in the presence of tragedy.

"Horse," he repeated wearily, passing his hand over his forehead. "As I live, Antrobus, a slice carved from a gee-gee. It all seems like a horrible dream. Yet I must say it cut quite sweetly and the sauce was so dashed good that I didn't realize it. It was only when the bill came that the whole of my past life flashed before my eyes. Dear God—a horse! And I a Colonel in the Blues! I was so surprised you could have poured me out with a spoon."

I groaned in sympathy. He gave a harsh cracked laugh and went on. "To think of it, I who have lived for, and practically on, horses. The irony of it all. To find myself sitting there, involuntarily wrapped round a succulent slice of fetlock, feeling the world's biggest bounder. And with a touch of mustard, too." He shuddered at the memory.

"But surely," I said, looking as always for the Silver Lining, "you are hardly to be blamed, Mungo. Surely you could have absorbed just one slice and then Hushed Everything Up? No one could find it in his heart to blame you."

He shook his head sadly. "I thought of that," he said, "but my conscience wouldn't give me any rest, Antrobus. After all, here I am, a founder-member of the Society For The Prevention Of Everything To Nags. Old Boy, I was largely instrumental in getting all those country houses set aside for aged horses, for getting them into the Health Service, for getting them painted by Munnings before they Passed On. Why, we were hoping to get one into Parliament this year . . . How could I strike my colors, go back on my basic principles? I admit I thought of it. After all, I have eaten many strange things in unguarded moments. I once ate some smoked grandmother in the Outer Celebes, but that was to save the regimental goat. And once at Government House in Gibraltar I *think* I ate a portion of infant monkey. But it was never proved. The ADC refused to confess. But all this is a far cry from horses, old chap. A different world. No, I confess that I sobbed aloud as I paid that bill."

For a moment he was silent, and then went on. "After that, Antrobus, there came an endless chain of sleepless nights. I brooded, old man. No peace. At times I thought I might go and throw myself on the mercy of Elizabeth David, confessing everything to her frankly, hiding nothing, asking for absolution. But when I mugged up her books I found no references to anything more questionable than eels or bloater paste—revolting enough, but mundane compared to what I was up against. No, there was no way out. I realized that I should have to Face the Music. So I did. I confess it hurt. I resigned from Whites and Boodles. I had myself crossed off every Stud Book in the Shires. The Athenaeum will see me no more. I even closed my account with the Army, Navy and Air-Force Stores. I transferred my overdraft. I confessed all to the Pytchley and did a public penance at Hurlingham. Then I broke my saddle over my knee . . . and all was over. I am a broken man, Antrobus. I simply came back to collect my gongs and brasses. I only popped in to say good-bye. I somehow felt you would understand."

I was deeply moved. But what could I say to comfort and console poor Mungo? Little enough in all conscience. He still had a fortnight to carry his bat until a replacement arrived and all this time he spent in strict purdah, refusing all invitations. There was only one little incident which, in the light of subsequent events, seems to me significant. It proved how deeply he had been marked by this Major Experience. His inhibitions had begun to slough off. De Mandeville reported that Mungo had been seen in a local hotel dining on *octopus*. I could hardly believe it. *Octopus!* The stuff that comes like ectoplasm! But this was the only straw in the wind. After that, silence closed in. Then Mungo left us and passed out of memory. As the years went by I often thought of him with a twinge of compassion. Doubtless he was in some far-enough-flung colony to dine openly on yams and white mice. I saluted his gallantry in my heart.

But now here is the grisly sequel to my tale. Spalding used to go to Kenya every year to see his family and shoot a bit. One year he went up-country on *safari*. In the heart of the jungle, in a clearing, before a modest hut of wattle, he came upon a dinner-jacketed figure having a preprandial. "Mungo!" he cried. Yes, it was Mungo. He had hidden his shame in that remote corner. They embraced warmly and Spalding was glad to see that his character still had a few fibers intact—for he was correctly dressed for dinner. They sat down on camp-stools and discussed a two-to-one Martini which Mungo mixed with all his old flair. Though he had aged he still looked fairly steady on his pins, and he still made the sort of Martini which fairly whistles through the rigging. Heartening signs, these.

It was only when the brain-fever birds began to call and the little radio in the corner struck eight o'clock that Spalding Suddenly Understood that it wasn't, it couldn't be, the old Mungo . . . For his host said, quite distinctly: "Why not stay and have pot-luck with me tonight? We have elephant for dins." *Elephant!*

Spalding paled—he had been very strictly brought up. Was it possible that Mungo was sitting out here in the wilds gorging himself on elephant? (And if so, how was it done? It must take ages to marinate?) He gulped loudly. "Did I understand you to say elephant, Mungo?" he said.

"Yes," said Mungo, with a kind of loose grin. "You see, old boy, there is no such thing as a *cuisine* in Africa. Once one leaves the Old Country one achieves a kind of Universality, a Oneness with Nature. HERE EVERYTHING IS EDIBLE." He spread his arms to the night, knocking over his glass. "If you don't like elephant," he went on, "I can organize squirrel or chipmunk or boa-constrictor. It's all one. I just send out a little man with a blow-pipe and it's all yours."

Spalding shuddered and muttered a prayer under his breath. "Yes," went on Mungo, "I gave away my Boulestin and both my Elizabeth Davids. They are no use here except for missionaries who have Outworn Concepts. Personally I use Buffon's Natural History to give me ideas for my meals. Why, just to leaf through Section One (Primates) stimulates the appropriate juice, gives one an appetite. I say, you've turned awfully pale. You aren't ill, are you?"

"No, no," said Spalding, "it is simply the kerosene light shining on my rather high and pale forehead."

Mungo settled himself on his camp-stool and said: "Yes, old boy. If once the readers of *The Times* found out just how Edible everything is, it would be all up with the Wine and Food Society." Then in a slow, dreamy voice, full of naked *luxe* and *volupté*, he began to recite softly: 'Leeches *à la rémoulade* . . . Giraffe *Truffée aux Oignons* . . . Boa-Constrictor *Chasseur* . . . *Ragoût de Flamingo* with *Water-Rat Flambé* . . ." He was sunk in a deep trance.

Spalding could bear it no longer. He tip-toed out of the clearing and ran like a madman in the direction of Nairobi . . .

Now I didn't tell you this story (said Antrobus) simply to upset you. No. Moreover, I hope you won't repeat it. I should hate it to get back to the Household Cavalry. It simply illustrates the sort of thing one is up against in the Service. The next Christmas, when my Aunt Hetty asked me to choose two quotations for a sampler she was making me, it was really with Mungo in mind that I made my choice. One text reads: "By their Menus shall ye know them." And the other: "Nothing Exceeds like Excess" . . .

I trust you take my point?

HORTENSE CALISHER

Mrs. Fay Dines on Zebra

Arietta Minot Fay, at thirty-seven, still lived in the house in which she, her father and all their known male forebears but the first had been born, a white, Hudson River–bracketed house, much winged and gabled but with a Revolutionary cottage at its core, set in a tiny village, once only a road, on the west shore of the Hudson River, about twenty-five miles from New York. Arietta's first forebear, Yves Minot, had come to the States in the entourage of Lafayette (some said as a body-servant, although this had never been proved) and had managed to stay near the general's person throughout all the general's campaigns except Valley Forge. In 1779, when the general had gone back briefly to France, Yves had stayed behind, first to marry one of the local Dutch girls (receiving the cottage and a large parcel of land as her dowry) and later to leave her at home while he ventured into battle or other forays, whenever he was so minded. In 1824, when Lafayette returned to America for a final visit, Yves was still there, flourishing in all but sons (because of land inheritance, the Minot line usually ran carefully to one) and had accompanied the general on his famous triumphal tour, again in some capacity typical of the Minots, something unidentifiable, profitable and without a doubt enjoyable.

Arietta, if asked to hazard a guess as to what this might have been, usually replied, with the family talent for presenting itself accurately, that Yves's function probably had something to do with a cap and bells. For, all the Minots took for granted what they had been, were, and hoped to go on being. They were jesters, *fonctionnaires* attending the private person only, quartermasters supplying the ego, minor affections and spirits of those who were rich enough to keep living standards equal to their own *bon viveur* tastes, had the intelligence to relish the thrusts of which they were wisely capable, and above all were important enough to enable the Minots to admire them. This was the Minot vanity and their backbone through the years: that managing always to attach themselves to the most honorable patrons, they had meanwhile restricted their own knavish tricks to the surface diablerie required of their profession—that is, to entertainment only. Beneath the skin they were not knaves, beyond a certain French clarity as to the main chance, which in turn had instructed them that a supernormal honesty, shrewdly displayed, was invaluable to him who lived on perquisites.

For no Minot had ever had a salary, or had gone, as phrase is, "to work." Every male Minot had attended a university as a matter of course, to be refined for his trade, and occasionally to pick up there some symbiotic relationship that had lasted him for life. Arietta's father, of the first generation to have no sons, had done his best by sending her to Vassar, where three members of the Rensselaer (an old dining-club of which he was secretary) had sent their girls that same year—the three men representing respectively money with family, money with politics, and—since the Minots had had to lower their standards along with the rest of the world, though belatedly—money with money. For until her father's time—and he, poor man, was in no way responsible for the monstrous change in the world—all had gone marvelously well with the Minots in both comfort and reputation. And deservedly, for all had worked hard. Although their perquisites had often been extraordinarily vague, ranging from small properties given them to manage and subsequently inherited either in part or in toto, from careers as retainers (they retained so gracefully) or as incumbents of benefices that never had to be explained to them or by them, all the way down to the latter-day vulgarities of stockmarket tips—no Minot had ever boondoggled at the earning of what he received. Until well past the First World War, one could imagine two important men murmuring of a third, as in another context they might mention that his chef was the great-nephew of Brillat-Savarin—"Lucky man, he has a Minot."

Even in the non-Venetian world of post-'29, the world that had begun to be so hard on those useful types for which there never seemed to be any but foreign names: the *cavalière servante*, the *fidus Achates*, the *condottiere*, the . . . Minot—the family had still managed, amiably using its talents where there was still scope for them, but for the first time dangerously using its resources when there was not. Over a hundred years in this country had weakened their French pith, making them less antipathetic than they should have been to eating their capital and selling their land. Marrying by inclination had been an even earlier symptom to appear, but here perhaps they had been lucky, for like so many reared nobly, their inclinations had always been a little bit coarse—and this had kept the line remarkably healthy. This meant that Arietta, when she came on the market, did so from a long line of non-idiots, non-hemophiliacs with a minimum life-expectancy of eighty. It also meant that, with one thing and another, she hadn't much expectancy of anything else except the uses to which she might put her share of Minot temperament—that merriment spiked with truth-telling, suppleness just short of servility, and love of ease combined with a wonderfully circuitous energy for pursuing it. Like so many of her ancestors, Arietta was willing to burn any number of ergs in the process, as long as neither dishonor nor the usual channels of attainment were involved.

On this particular summer Saturday evening at about seven o'clock, Arietta, dressed to go out in her one still respectable cocktail dress, sat in the dimming upstairs parlor of the house that had been hers since the death a year ago, within a few months of each other, of her father and her husband, and gazed out on the river, musing, moodily for her, on the narrow area of play offered that temperament by the modern world. Saturday was shopping day for the week, and this morning, hold back as she might on things like paper napkins—they would use the linen ones—she had not been able to avoid spending eighteen dollars on food. Her nine-year-old son Roger, away for the night at a friend's house, would consume that almost unaided during the school week. One of the sweet-voiced robot-ladies from the telephone company had phoned twice during the past few days, and even the Light & Power, usually so kindly, had begun to press her about last winter's heating bill. This week, to the bewilderment of her friends, she had taken to answering the phone in French, ready to aver that "Madame" was away. There had been no cleaning-woman for a year. Behind her, the rooms, receding wing on wing into the hillside with the depressed elegance of a miniature château, showed, besides the distinguished stainings of a hundred and fifty years, the thin, gradual grime of amateur care. The house, free and clear for a century until the thirties, was hers thanks to her father's single quirk of hereditary thrift, hidden from them until the otherwise worthless will was read— mortgage insurance. It was worth about twenty thousand dollars, possibly a little more to one of that new race of antiquarians who had debouched upon these hills aching to "restore" some old place electrically, and able to—viz. the Lampeys, where she was going that evening. But its sale, if she could bring herself to sell, would be slow. Here she sat in it then, in the richest country in the world. In addition to the house, she had a few marketable "old pieces," small ones to be culled from among the massive bedsteads and armoires, but nothing on which to rear a nine-year-old boy. She was sitting at Great-grandmother Marie-Claire's tambour desk; Roger could eat it in two months. She had the pawn tickets for Marie-Claire's rose-diamonds, and for Marie-Claire's daughter-in-law's epergne. And she had $126.35 in the bank.

And in addition she had, of course, herself. It had been her only dowry, and until some six months ago she had never seriously attempted to draw upon it. "What a pity," her golden-haired Uncle Victor—elder brother of her father and the last successful one of his generation—had remarked of her when she was eight, what a pity that Arietta wasn't male, for she seemed to have all the Minot talents, including a marked facial resemblance to the founder of the line. Victor had died, from an overdose of his patron's pheasant and Lafitte, at the minimal age of eighty, spared from knowing that it was even more of a pity that she wasn't a nineteenth-century male. But here she was, and she was neither. The room where she sat now was the *petit salon* that held the conglomeration of family pictures, and without turning to look at that descending gallery of honorable rogues, she could trace in them not only the decline of the private patron—of which all the world was aware— but of his factotum—small, tragic, subdominant theme that the world had ignored.

Above the mantel was Yves, done on ivory, full-length too, which was unusual for the medium. Legend had it that he had insisted on this because, knee-breeched to the end of his life, he had declared a man to be incomplete without a show of calf; certainly their japing angle went with the face above. It was a triangular face in which all the lines went up, a minstrel face whose nose, long for its tilt, must have moved, as hers did, with speech. The enamelist had even managed to indicate in *couleur-de-rose* those same crab-apple bumps of cheek she had when she smiled. Next to him was the Dutch wife, shown in conventional oval to the waist, of which there was much, a great blonde, serene in all but her stays. Beneath the two, depending on lengths of velvet ribbon in the tree of life, were their heirs direct and collateral, daguerreotype to Brownie, spilling from the mantel to the side walls. As a curious phenomenon, one could see one or the other of the two progenitors always recurring, often with such fidelity that there had long been family slang for the two types—"the beefies" for the Dutch ones, and *"les maigres"* for those *mince* creatures who were true Minots. Although there had been no intermarrying, one type had usually managed to marry the other, and his children tended to be his opposites as well.

105

Yes, it is all very interesting, thought Arietta—we are a fascinating lot, rather like the green and yellow peas in Mendel—and her father had often dined out on that story. In time, if there was time, she might dine out on it too. Meanwhile, brooding on the three pictures between Yves and the wedding portrait of herself and Carolingus Fay, deceased, she traced a history much more in Gibbon's line.

Beneath Yves came his Claude, a "beefy," of whom it might have been said (as Henry Adams had said of himself) that "as far as he had a function in life, it was as a stable-companion to statesmen, whether they liked it or not." In Claude's case they had. Next came Louis, her grandfather, who had switched to railroad barons—a light sprig of a man who had passed on, full in years and benefices, while accompanying home the equally aged body of his baron, on the Union Pacific somewhere between Ogden and Omaha, in a private car. Under him, in the sepia gloss of the eighties, were his sons, beefies again: her father in his teens, in the deerstalker's cap so prophetic of his later years, and Victor, already a man with a beautiful Flemish jowl. Victor had already been with "munitions" at the time. At the minimal age of eighty he had died (her father used to joke) not of pheasant but of pique, because his patron's son, seduced by the increasingly corporate air of Delaware, had entered Victor's exquisitely intangible services on a tax sheet, had actually tried to incorporate *him*. If so, it had still been death in the high style, and of it. But with her father, the long descent, gradual as the grime on her bric-a-brac, was clear. He had still had the hereditary talent, but he had been fifteen years younger than Victor. Patrons herded in groups now instead of carrying on singly, and preferred the distressingly plebeian admiration of the many to the fine, patrician allegiance of the one. And gaiety, the mark of the personal, was suspect in a sociological world. Ergo her father. When a Minot was stripped of his devotion and of the truth-telling that was its honorable underside, when he was reduced to picking up crumbs, of "contact" wherever he could, to making public show of his charms like anyone else, then he did so in the only way he knew. Her father had become a diner-out. It was some consolation that, under many lambent chandeliers and between many long-stemmed rows of pink and tawny glasses, he had dined so well.

She glanced at her wrist, remembered that she no longer had a watch, and looked at the river, estimating the seasonal angle of light on the opposite shore. Still too early to walk the short distance to the Lampeys, who, much as they adored her company, touted it, still preferred their guests to arrive, sharply gala, at eight. And these days Arietta aimed to please, had in fact aimed so steadily these past months and so far from her usual haunts, the shabby Saturday night parties of the real denizens of these hills, that it was no wonder if these were already remarking how unexpected it was of Arietta—slated one would have said for years yet to the memory of Carolingus—to be openly hunting a husband, and in such circles as the Lampeys, too. How surprised they would be if they knew that all she was hunting was a job. A job, to be sure, for a Minot—a sinecure not for sloth, but for the spirit. With, of course, perks enough to feed a healthy nine-year-old boy.

She rose and went to the mantel, staring up at Yves—one *"maigre"* looking at another. She was four velvet ribbons removed from him, and—except for Roger, who would be nothing for years yet—the last hope of his line. If from his vantage point he could have approved the resemblance, would he have expected her, a female, nevertheless to do something in his line? Being female, what she had done was, twelve years ago, to marry Carolingus Fay. After Vassar had come a year in Italy with one of the daughters of her father's three friends; the girl had married there, and Arietta, after attending her in a horsehair hat, had returned home. Next, the second girl, married to an Englishman who farmed in Nigeria, had invited her there. Against her father's wishes—it was not cautious for a woman to become too *déracinée*—she had gone, and in her lightsome way had enjoyed it, but marooned there, she had missed much of the war and most of the eligible men. In any case, esprit, or whatever it was she had, was difficult in a woman if it wasn't so much accompanied by looks as contributed to by them. Returning home, with her laugh-lines baked deeper than they should have been for her age, and with some knowledge of cacao and palm oil added to the magpie lore of her clan, she had vegetated in the Hudson Valley for a few restless months—her father's profession so seldom left him home to be cooked for—and then had gone to Baltimore to visit an old cousin.

And there she had met Carolingus. Eighteen years older than she, he had still seemed a man whom many might be glad to marry—a very fine "beefy" with proconsular manners and profile, and all his curls. Actually he had been a cliché, poor dear Carolingus—old Baltimore French, old poor, old hat—and he had been very glad to marry her. For, by heredity, and unfortunately nothing else, he was a patron—an even sadder case than hers. They had recognized each other, or loved—in time it seemed the same thing—at once. The only way he could afford to retain her was to come live in her house, which he did, to her father's delight—their mutual recognition too was a touching affair. Carolingus had been too shy to dine out (he had only the dispensing talent), and in time, with her and her father's full acquiescence, the house and what it held might have been taken by any casual guest to be his. At eighty her father retired, and the two men could not have been happier, jogging along in a life of aristocratic pattern gone native, shooting over their two acres for rabbit instead of grouse, and serving up the game with an excellent dandelion wine. And in their contentment Arietta had been happy too. It was so difficult for a Minot not to be happy, not to see, in whatever dried facts and kernels of incident the day provided, the possibility of a soufflé. Even when Carolingus had not long survived her father, she could not avoid thinking that he was better so, just as she could not help seeing, as the long, curlicued, taupe coffin went down the front steps, that it looked exactly like the éclairs of which he had always been so fond.

And then of course, it had become her turn—to dine out. She had let no one know her real situation; she would have been plied with all usually offered an untrained widow—"rent your lovely rooms to teachers; become a nursery school aide"—all the genteel solutions that would trap her forever. No, she was still child enough of her race to risk all on its chimera: that somewhere there was a post where one might exercise an airy, impalpable training which could never be put down on any resumé, somewhere even in this taxable world.

So far, her efforts to renew her father's contacts in New York had shown her only how faded they were, and how even those old and well-bred enough to remember the breed she sprang from, its always delicate aims, tended to misinterpret when the diner-out was female, however plain. These last months she had been looking about her in the Valley, among people like the Lampeys, whose kindness had the practicality which went with money still fresh in the till. Tonight, for instance, they were having her in to meet a Miss Bissle from Delaware, who was devoting to a state-wide program of hedge roses and bird sanctuaries her one-twenty-fifth share in a great-grandfather's fortune in explosives, and whose secretary-companion had just died. The Lampeys, drawing Arietta out for Miss Bissle's benefit, would no doubt ask her to repeat the story they particularly loved—about the time a zebra, a real zebra, had appeared in her garden—although she had other anecdotes she herself preferred. A humanist, she liked stories about people, and the zebra one was bad art besides, having no ending really, and an explanation that was sadly mundane. She would much rather tell about Claude and Henry Clay, about one of the Great Compromiser's compromises that had never reached the historians. Or about Louis's patron, a philanthropist who gave in kind only, and who, on being approached at his door by a panhandler who wanted money for a glass eye, was able to invite him into a *cabinet de travail* where he had a box of them. But considering the roses and birds, possibly the zebra was more in line.

Across the river, the last evening light shone on the silver roof of a New

York Central streamliner; she had a few minutes' walk and it was time. Courage, she said to herself, thinking of Roger. You are learning your trade a little late, that is all. You still have $126.35 worth of time. And maybe Miss Bissle would be a jolly hedonist who wanted a "good companion," although this was not often the conclusion one drew from watching people who watched birds. Remember, in any case, that when the artist is good, it is still the patron who is on trial. Reaching up toward Yves, she blew the dust from his frame. Why should our art, she thought, the art of happiness, be such a drug on the market these days? On that note, she tilted her head and went out, swinging the skirt of her dress, luckily so dateless, and tapping sharply, almost as if she scolded it, the tambour desk.

Meanwhile, a few minutes away, the Lampeys and their houseguests, Miss Bissle and her second cousin Robert, were speaking of Arietta. Parker and Helen Lampey, a white-haired couple in their sixties, had started life together at Christian College, Missouri, but long since, owing to Parker's rise to the extreme altitudes of international law, had accustomed themselves to the ponderous social mixture to be found there—Swiss bankers, German industrialists, American judge advocates and solid rich like the Bissles. Thirty years of moving intercontinentally had not made them raffish—so far as was known they had never felt an expatriate tingle. What it had done was to give them the eternally pink-cheeked, good-tempered look of summer people; they had in fact been summer people all over the world. By native standards they should have been suffering from all the ills of cosmopolitan riches and ease; actually money, comfort and change had kept them amiable, enabling them to be as kindly as they looked, though considerably more worldly. Parker held several directorships adjacent to Robert, whose share in the family fortune was much larger than Miss Bissle's, and it was through him they had heard of her needs. And had at once thought of Arietta.

"I made Robert come with me," said Miss Bissle, "because Mary Thrace, the last one, you know—drank." She was a large, gray pachyderm of a woman whose eyes blinked slowly. "And I don't at all. You would think that would make it easier to notice in others, wouldn't you? But it doesn't. So I brought Robert."

"Well, I do," said her cousin, looking at his drink through the lower half of his bifocals. "Steadily. So you did just right."

Parker smiled. He knew Robert, a quiet, abstemious sort, widowed early and childless, devoted to rather *sec* philanthropies since. One of those mild, almost expunged men for whom second or third generation fortune was a conscience, not a release.

"Why do men always make themselves out more colorful than they are?" said Miss Bissle, for whom Robert, past fifty, was still a younger cousin.

Helen Lampey glanced at Miss Bissle's shoes, the flat, self-assured feet of a woman who would never know why. Her cousin looked the way most people who wore glasses like that did—round and tame.

"Is this Mrs. Fay outdoorsy?" said Miss Bissle. "Mary Thrace wasn't."

"I don't know that one thinks of her as 'out' or 'in,'" said Helen slowly. "What would you say, Parker?"

"Delightful either place. In Arietta's company, where you are always seems just where you want to be. The father was just the same."

Helen could see Miss Bissle thinking that this was not the way one got things *done*. "She had a year in Africa," she said hastily. "I should think one would have to be . . . outdoorsy . . . there. And of course she grew up right here in the Hudson Valley—why, they caught a copperhead on their place only last year."

"Still has the old place. Old family hereabouts, the Minots," said Parker, rising to replenish the drinks.

"Minot!" Robert said softly. "Did you say—Minot?"

"Yes, ever know any of them? Understand they were quite a family at one time." Busy with the drinks, he did not note Robert's lack of response, covered in any case by Miss Bissle.

"*Trigonocephalous contortrix,*" she said. "They don't eat birds."

Robert sat back in his chair. Yes, I knew a Minot, he thought. I knew Victor. Probably isn't the same family; chances are it couldn't be. Still, what Lampey had just said about the woman they were expecting—that was just the way Victor had been, turning life rosy and immediate wherever he was, and for adults too, as could be seen in the aureole that went round a room with him—not merely for Robert, the small boy on whom he had occasionally shone his great face, fair, hot and flame-colored as Falstaff's sun. Looking back on Victor now from the modern distance, it seemed to Robert that he must have dreamed him—that day on the Brandywine for instance, 1912 it must have been, when Victor had taken him fishing, the same day he had insisted on letting Robert join the men lunching at Robert's grandfather's table before the stockholders' meeting, and had fed the boy wine. Robert could see him now, jutting like a Rubens from even that portly group, the starched ears of the napkin he had tied around his cravat shining blue in the water-light reflected from walls that were white instead of walnut because of his choice, the napkin flecked, as lunch went on, with sauces Victor had conspired with the cook, the heavy company meanwhile tasting him with the same negligent appreciation they gave the food, as now and then he sent a sally rolling down the table like a prism, or bent over Robert, saying, "A little more claret with the water, Robert? . . . And now, if you please—a little more water with the claret." After lunch, Robert had seen him give his grandfather a sheaf of papers, saying, "Here they are, Bi—Robert and I are going out after turtle." As they left, one of the men said, "Bi—where do you get your cigars?"—it was Victor who had started people calling Robert's grandfather "Bi." "Victor gets them for me in Philadelphia." At the man's murmured envy, his grandfather had taken a careful puff, gently guarding the long, firm ash, and had smiled.

And that afternoon on the dock, sitting over the lines that the caramel-colored Negroes in the shack behind them had lent them, had been a time he had remembered always, like a recurrent dream—a day on which absolutely nothing had happened except sun, water and the lax blush of the wine in his limbs. And Victor—doing nothing all afternoon except what he did everywhere, making one feel that whatever you and he were doing at the moment was "it," that where you were was "here." They had caught, Robert recalled, two turtles; he remembered being warned of their bite, and informed, lovingly, of their soup. "Victor," he had asked suddenly, "what are you in?"—meaning chemicals, cotton, tin, this being the way men in those days, at that table, had spoken of what they did. "Oh I'm not 'in,' " had been the laughing answer. "You might say I'm—*with*." Breathing hard, Victor had been peering in at the hamper that held the turtles. Robert had looked down at him. "So shall I be," he had said. "Oh no you won't. You're already stuck with it, like these chaps. You're already *in*." Victor had risen, puffing. "Best you'll be able to do is to have somebody around like me—way Bi does." Robert had considered. "I'll have you then if I may," he had said.

Victor's face had been in shadow, the sun behind him, but after more than forty years Robert could still sense in him the unnameable quality that had sent him fishing in his cravat. "Mmm. If your father doesn't get to you first," he said. And Robert's father had got to him first, as, in Victor's old age, he had got to Victor. Not a hard man, his father, but a dull one, of the powerful new breed that cherished its dullness for its safety, and meant to impose that, along with the rest of its worldly goods, on its sons. "Like that brew we had at lunch?" Victor had said, as they trotted the hamper along the shore. "And well you might," he said, mentioning a name, a year. "Pity I've only daughters," he sighed. "Women've no palate. Perfume kills it." Above them, atop the green dunes of lawn that swept to the water's edge, a small figure waved at them, his grandfather, guests sped, sauntering the veranda alone. "Will I have one, d'ya think?" asked Robert. "Mmm, can't tell yet." Robert considered. His grandfather, colorless and quiet, seemed to him

111

much like his father, who drank only Saratoga water. "Does Bi?" he said with interest. Victor smiled, waving back. "He's got me," he said.

And Grandfather was like me really, not like Father, Robert thought, returning to the Lampeys', where conversation, as so often happened elsewhere, had rippled on without him. He was a dull man too, as I am, but like me with the different and often painful dimension of not valuing it, of knowing that somewhere, sometimes in the same room, conversation twinkled past him like a prism, a rosier life went by. Grandfather was like me. But Grandfather had Victor.

And looking at the door through which Emily's possibility was to come, telling himself that it was midsummer madness—of Victor's daughters one was dead and the other last heard of years ago in a nursing order in Louisiana—he still told himself that he would not be surprised, not at all, if the woman who came through the door were to be huge and serenely fair, a great Flemish barmaid of a woman, with Victor's florid curls.

When Arietta walked through the door, he was surprised, at the depth of his disappointment. For what he saw was a slight woman, almost tiny, whose hair, sugared now like preserved ginger, might once, at youth's best, have been russet, a small creature whose oddly tweaked face—one of those pulled noses, cheeks that looked as if each held the secret cherry of some joke—was the farthest possible from the classic sun-face he remembered. Even if she were some relation, she was nothing like. There was no point in asking, in opening a private memory to future rakings over whenever he paid a duty call on Emily. For what he was looking at, he reminded himself, all he was looking at was Emily's future companion.

As the evening progressed, he was not so sure. For the Lampeys' protégée remained dumb. From their baffled glances he judged that this was not usual; he himself would have guessed that Mrs. Fay's ordinary manner, if she had any, was more mobile. But for whatever reason, her eyes remained veiled, her hands folded in the lap of her pale, somewhat archaic skirt. A certain stubborn aura spread from her, but nothing else, certainly nothing of the subtle emanation they had been promised, and but rarely a word. Only Emily, impervious to this as she was to so much, noticed nothing, intent on numbering the occasional sips Mrs. Fay took of her wine.

Nor could Arietta have explained. She could have said only that almost at once she had felt Miss Bissle to be a person she could never admire. Or tell the truth to, the truth about Miss Bissle being what it was. Not because Miss Bissle was dull—the best patrons necessarily had almost as much dullness as money—but that she did not suffer from it, whereas the real patrons, all the great ones, had a sweetening tremor of self-doubt at the core. If dullness was what had made them keep Minots, then this human (and useful) sweetening was what had made Minots keep them. But I must, thought Arietta. Roger, she said to herself. $126.35. Nevertheless, when Parker deftly introduced Nigeria, on which he had often heard her entertain, she heard herself furnish him three sentences on the cultivation of the cocoa nib, then fall still. It must be stage fright, her first professional engagement. Her father should have told her that the artist's very piety and scruples were a considerable hindrance when the artist came down to dining out. In desperation she gulped the rest of her wine. Opposite her Miss Bissle blinked slowly at Robert, as if to say "I count on you."

"Arietta!" said Helen Lampey. It was half command, half plea. "Do tell us the story about your zebra."

"Zebra?" said Robert. "Have you hunted them, Mrs. Fay?"

"No." Mrs. Fay addressed her small, clenched hands. "That's equatorial Africa." She heard Helen sigh. "Have you?"

Now, what none of them, what no one knew about Robert Bissle was that once in a while, under certain conditions, he lied. Not on the Exchange of course, or in any real situation. It was his only valve, his sole vice, and it escaped him, with the wistful sound of steam from an air-locked radiator, only when, as tonight, he deemed himself in the safe company of those even duller than he. He leaned back—on these occasions he always did. "Zebras are very beautiful creatures. I never molested them save to procure specimens for the museums, or food for the porters, who liked their rather rank flesh."

Mrs. Fay, for almost the first time, raised her eyes and looked closely at him. "Yes?" she said. Her nose, he observed, moved with speech. "Do go on."

"The hartebeest," he said slowly. "Coke's hartebeest, known locally by the Swahili name of kongoni—were at least as plentiful and almost as tame."

"Why Robert!" said Miss Bissle. "I never knew you were in Africa."

"Oh yes," he said, still looking at his neighbor, in whose odd face—he had not noticed until now—all the lines went up. "One year when your back was turned." He plunged on. "A few months before my arrival, a mixed herd of zebra and hartebeest rushed through the streets of Nairobi, several being killed by the inhabitants, and one of the victims falling just outside the Episcopal church."

"Handy," said Helen Lampey, in spite of having been informed that the Episcopal was Miss Bissle's own. She was watching Arietta and Robert— Arietta *with* Robert, smiling her pawkiest smile at him, and saying, "Yes, yes, do go on."

Robert took off his glasses. No, there was no resemblance, not even if he imagined a napkin tied round her neck, although for a moment there he had almost fancied an echo saying, "and now, a little more claret." He shook his head. The company, whatever it was, was not as safe as he had thought. "Your turn," he said. "Your zebra."

Arietta unfolded her hands. They trembled slightly. Miss Bissle's cousin, and even richer one had heard—and even more. One of the old breed, she was sure of it—and she had almost missed him. "My zebra?" she said. "Mine was—" She had been about to say *real*. But one let people see one knew the truth about them only after one had won them, sometimes long after. And particularly these people. "Mine was—here," she said. "Right here in the Hudson Valley. In our garden."

"So help me it was," said Parker. "I saw it. Go on, Arietta."

So she did. It had been a Saturday morning, she said, and she had been sitting in her bath, when Roger, seven then, had knocked at the door and said there were policemen in the garden and she had called back, "Tell Daddy." Minutes later, Roger had knocked again and said, "Mum, there's a zebra in the garden," and she had replied—"Tell Daddy." "Now," said Arietta, "Roger is not a fey child. I should have known." She knew every periphrasis of this story, every calculated inflection and aside; this was the point where everyone always began to smile expectantly, and pausing, she saw that they had. "I've never been able to afford to disbelieve him since." For then Carolingus had come up the stairs. "He looked," said Mrs. Fay, delaying softly, expertly, "well—like a man who has just seen a zebra in his garden." As, according to him, he had. She went downstairs—and so had he. She made them see the scene just as she had, the two policemen, Mack Sennett characters both of them, yelling "Stand back there!" from a point well behind Carolingus, and there, cornered in a cul-de-sac near the carriage house, flashing and snorting, the zebra, ribanded in the rhododendrons like a beast out of the *douanier* Rousseau.

"The policemen," she said, "had had no breakfast, so there I found myself, carrying a tray with sugar and cream and my best coffee cake— luckily I had baked on Friday—to two policemen and a zebra, in a back yard twenty-five miles from New York." She rose, circled the room, holding the scene with her hands pressed lightly together, and as if absent-mindedly, poured Parker some coffee out of the Lampeys' silver pot. Outside, in the Lampeys' garden, a barn owl hooted—it was the atmosphere, conspiring gently with her as usual. She waited. At this point someone always asked, "But how?"

"But *how?*" said Miss Bissle.

"Ah, now," said Mrs. Fay, "I have to double back. I have to tell you that across from us, in one of those very modern houses with the kitchen set just under the crown of the road, the family gets up very early. They garden, and the mother-in-law is a past president of the Audubon Society of Atlanta, Georgia." Still circling the room, a diseuse gently fabricating her own spotlight, Mrs. Fay rested one hand, a brief wand, on Miss Bissle's shoulder as she passed her. Robert watched, enthralled. There was nothing to it, yet she held them all. They sat like marionettes whom she was awakening slowly to a mild, quizzical sensation like the pleasure-pain in a sleeping foot. "And at about six o'clock that morning, the head of the County Police picked up the phone and heard a cultivated Southern voice say, 'Ah should like to repo't that jus' now, as we wuh setten at breakfas', we saw a zebra payss bah on the Rivuh Road.' " Parker laughed, and Mrs. Fay picked it up, wove him in quickly. "Ah yes," she said, "can't you hear her? And the chief thought to himself that the River Road is rather the bohemian part of his parish, and that Saturday morning comes, well—after Friday night. So he calls our policeman and says, 'George, people down your neck of the woods seeing zebras.' George decides to wait until, well, two or more people see it. Then Joe Zucca, the old caretaker at Fagan's, telephones, babbling that a striped horse is crashing around his conservatory. And the chase is on. And they bring it to bay in our garden."

Parker guffawed. "There are zebras at the bottom of my garden."

Arietta, reaching her own chair, sat down in it. Someone always said that too. She looked round their faces. Yes, she had them, particularly one. Quickly, quickly now, wind it up. And in a long, virtuoso breath, she wound it all up—how the village had filled the yard, a gold mine if she'd just had the lollipop concession, how her smart-aleck neighbor had stopped by the front gate, offering a drive to town, and when she'd said, "Wait a bit, Tom, we've got a zebra in the back yard," had smirked and said, "Yeah, I heard that one at Armando's—and the horse said, 'I've been trying to get it to take its pajamas off all night.' " And how it had been one of the great satisfactions in life to be able to lead him round to the carriage house. And how the cops had finally got hold of the Hudson River Cowboys Association—yes there was one, those kids in white satin chaps and ten-gallon hats who always rode palominos in the Independence Day Parade—and how they'd come, out of costume alas, but with their horse trailer, and how Carolingus and the cops had finally jockeyed the beast in, using a three-man lasso. And how, at the height of it—children screaming, yokels gaping, three heated men hanging on ropes, the whole garden spiraling like a circus suddenly descended from the sky, and in the center of it all, the *louche* and striped, the incredible—how Arietta's eighty-five-year-old Cousin Beck from Port Washington, a once-a-year and always unheralded visitor, had steamed up the driveway in her ancient Lincoln, into the center of it all. "Oh, Cousine Beck," she'd stammered—in French, she never knew why—"you find us a little *en déshabillé*, we have us *un zèbre.*" And how Beck, taking one look, had eased her old limbs out of the car and grunted, "Arietta, you *are* dependable. Just bring me a chair."

Mrs. Fay folded her hands. Now someone would ask the other question. She gave a sigh. Next to her, her neighbor marveled. No, she was nothing like—no aureole. This one whisked herself in and out, like a conjuror's pocket handkerchief. But the effect was the same. Small sensations, usually ignored, made themselves known, piped like a brigade of mice from their holes. There was a confused keenness in the ear . . . nose . . . air? One saw the draperies, peach-fleshed velour, and waited for their smell. The chandelier tinkled, an owl hooted, and a man could hear his own breath. The present, drawn from all its crevices, was here.

"But where did the beast come from?" said Miss Bissle.

Yes, it would be she, thought Arietta. The cousin, his glasses still off, was staring at her with eyes that were bright and vague. "A runaway," she said in a cross voice. It always made her sulky to have to end the fun this way, with no punch line but fact. "There's an animal importer up the mountain; we found out later. He buys them for zoos." She turned pertly to the cousin. "Perhaps it was one of yours."

"I can't think when, Robert," said Miss Bissle. "I've always known exactly where you were."

Robert, before he replaced his glasses, had a vague impression that Mrs. Fay looked guilty, but she spoke so quickly that he must have been wrong.

"Parker," she said, "did you and Helen ever hear about Great-grandfather Claude, and Mr. Henry Clay?"

They hadn't. Nor had they heard about Louis's patron's glass eye. Robert, saved, sank deeper in his chair. He was his father's son after all, trained to fear the sycophant, and he brooded now on whether Mrs. Fay wanted something of him. Look how she had got round the Lampeys. Was she honest? Victor's tonic honesty, he remembered, had spared no one; he never flattered individually but merely opened to dullards the gross, fine flattery of life alone. And what did he, Robert, want of her? If he closed his eyes, prisms of laughter floated past him, flick-flack, down the long cloth of another table; he could feel, there and here, the lax blush of the present in his limbs. He slouched in it, while Arietta told how, when Carolingus spoke for her, her father had said, "You know she has no *dot.*" And how Carolingus, who was slightly deaf, had replied, "I've no dough either." And how in after years, both always amiably purported to be unsure of who had said which.

And then Robert sat up in his chair. For Arietta was telling the story of the "beefies" and *les maigres.*

So that's it, he thought. I knew it, I knew it all the time. And in the recesses of his mind he felt that same rare satisfaction which came to him whenever he was able to add to a small fund he had kept in a downtown savings bank almost since boyhood, money separate from inheritance, made by his own acumen, on his own. I recognized her, he thought, and the feeling grew on him, as it had been growing all evening, that in the right company he was not such a dullard after all. He leaned back now and watched her— quiet now after her sally, unobtrusive whenever she chose. It was not wit she pretended to; her materials were as simple as a child's. What was the quality she shared with Victor, born to it as the Bissles were born to money, that the others here felt too, for there was Lampey, murmuring ingenuously into his brandy-cup "Wonderful stuff this, isn't it?"—quite oblivious of the fact that it was his own—and there even was Emily, her broad feet lifted from the floor? Whatever Mrs. Fay did, its effect was as Victor's had been, to peel some secondary skin from the ordinary, making wherever one was—if one was with her—loom like an object under a magnifying glass—large, majestic and there. She made one live in the now, as, time out of mind it seemed, he had once done for himself. But he did not know how she did it. Or whether she did. Watching her rise from her chair, begin to make her adieu, the thought came to him that he would not mind spending a lifetime finding out.

"Let me go with you," he said, standing up. "Let me drive you home."

But Emily had arisen too. "Mrs. Fay," she said, her blinking fluttered, "have you had any experience with birds?"

Arietta smiled between them. How lucky she had recognized him, the real thing, poor dear, even if his sad little blague—out of *African Game Trails* of course, old Teddy Roosevelt, on half the bookshelves in Nigeria—was not.

"Do," she said to him, "but let's walk." She turned to Miss Bissle, and let the truth escape from her with gusto. After all it was her own. "No, not really. Of course—I've shot them."

On the short way home, the river, lapping blandly, made conversation. Robert spoke once. "I don't really think Emily would have suited you," he said, and Mrs. Fay replied that it was nice of him to put it that way round.

At Arietta's doorway, they paused. But it was imperative that she find out what was on his mind. Or put something there.

117

"I'd ask you in," she said, "but I've nothing but dandelion wine."

"I've never had any," said Robert. "I'd like to try it."

She led him through the hall, past the rack where Carolingus's leather jacket hung, and her father's, and the squirrel-skin weskit they had cured for Roger, then through the softly ruined downstairs rooms, up the stairs and into the little salon. It was an educative tour; it told him a great deal. And this was the family room; he sensed the intimate patchouli that always clung to the center of a house, even before he looked up and saw them all above the mantel, hanging on their velvet tree. While Arietta went for the wine, he moved forward to examine them. What a higgler's collection they were, in their grim descent from ivory to pasteboard to Kodak, yet a firm insouciance went from face to face, as if each knew that its small idiom was an indispensable footnote to history, to the Sargents, Laverys, de Lászlós that people like him had at home. And *there*, in that small brown-tone. Yes, there.

"Take me round the portraits," he said when she returned, and here too, since she also was on the wall, he learned. He saw that Carolingus must have been of an age near his own. "And who are they?" he said. "You missed that one." They were sitting at a small escritoire on which she had placed the wine, and if he stretched a hand he could touch the faded brown-tone.

"That's my father as a boy, and his older brother, Victor."

What an absurd feeling happiness was. That must be its name. To feel as if such a sum, such a round sum had been deposited in that bank that he need never go there again. Not if he stayed here. As, in time, he thought, he could arrange.

Opposite him, Arietta fingered a drawer inside which the name of the desk's first owner was inscribed—Marie-Claire, who had married for inclination but had got the rose-diamonds too. She stole a glance at her vis-à-vis. After all, she had recognized him, and in time, as she did remember, this and inclination could come to be almost the same. It was strange that he was no "beefy," but she had already had one—and no doubt her tribe, along with the rest of the world, must move on. And he was very responsive. In time, she thought, the house would come to seem to him like his own.

"Wonderful stuff," he was saying, holding up to the light one of the old green bottles into which Carolingus and her father had put the wine.

"Is it really?" said Arietta. "I was never any help to them on it."

"What it wants," he said, "is to be decanted, for the sediment. One does it against a candle flame. I was thinking—I might come by tomorrow. And show you."

"Do—for company," said Mrs. Fay. "Actually, one wine seems to me much like any other. I've got no palate for it. Women don't, my father always used to say."

"No, they don't." He was looking at her so deeply that she was startled. "Perfume kills it," he said, and so intensely that, odd averral as it was, it hung over them both like an avowal of love.

Downstairs, she led him out the front door, and watched him to the end of the lane. Roger's spaniel yipped, and over the hill another dog set up an answering cry. In the darkness, as she closed the door, she smiled, one of old Teddy's sentences lumbering through her mind. "The hunter who wanders these lands sees the monstrous river-horse snorting, the snarling leopard and the coiled python, the zebras barking in the moonlight." As she went back up the stairs, she wondered whether she would ever tell him. Some truths, as an honest companion, one spoke in jest; others, as a woman, one kept to oneself. At the moment it didn't matter. Standing in the doorway of the little salon, she stretched her arms. "I've dined out!" she said to the pictures, to herself. "I've dined on zebra, and on hartebeest, and yes, I think, on . . . husband. I've dined well."

Outside the hedge at the end of the lane, Robert watched the door close. He knew just how it would begin tomorrow; he would begin by asking her, as he had never asked anyone, to call him "Bi." There would always be a temptation to say more—who, for instance, would understand about that day on the Brandywine better than she? But he must remember with all she was—she was also a woman. They liked to be chosen for themselves. He must always be as mindful of that as of his incredible luck. And what utter luck it was! He swelled with the urge to tell someone about it. But there were not many in the world today who could appreciate precisely its nature. It was even possible that he himself was the last one extant of all those who once had. Standing in the shadow of the hedge, he whispered it to himself, as once a man had whispered it to his grandfather, over the cigar. "Lucky man," he said to himself, "you have a Minot!"

JAMES VILLAS

I Took Die Kur

It was on a Friday afternoon in the Oak Bar of the Plaza Hotel in New York that I once again realized I was headed for big trouble. Headache, a touch of vertigo, incredible fatigue, listlessness. All the symptoms that would indicate in most people either a severe illness or total nervous collapse I recognized in myself as simply another attack brought on by gastronomic overindulgence and social stress. Most revealing of all was the pain on the right, below the rib cage, a depressingly dull discomfort that betrayed an all too familiar ailment. This time, however, the pain was more than slight, and when I casually slipped my hand underneath my vest to give the liver a little nudge, what I felt could have best been described as a medium-sized truffle.

Utterly demoralized, I was about to order another glass of Champagne (without doubt the best *temporary* remedy for this type of condition) when a Lucullan colleague and hard-core hedonist arrived. He looked worse than I felt, so we ordered two goblets of bubbly.

"Do you realize," he moaned, "the amount of food and wine we consumed last night at The Forum (of the Twelve Caesars)?"

"Don't remind me!" I said. "It was fabulous. But please, let's discuss something else."

"Like what?"

"Like the fastest and easiest way to get me back on my feet, calm my nerves, and soothe a swollen liver, that's what!"

"Well, I can tell you how," my comrade asserted with what I considered a rather dubious tone of authority. "You need to take the cure."

"Cure! What cure?"

"Just the Cure, simple and clear. In Germany, at Baden-Baden. They have this new Anti-Stress program at the legendary Brenner's Park-Hotel. It helps you calm down, lose weight, dry out, stop smoking, and generally restore your physiological and mental balance. It's what the Germans call an *Entschlackungskur*, which means something about cleaning out a stopped-up grease trap."

"Just one minute," I interrupted. "Is all this about doctors and special diets and all that sort of thing? If you think for one minute I'm traveling thousands of miles just to have some German quack throw me in hot mineral waters and tell me to lay off the goodies—well, the idea goes against every one of my principles."

"Listen," he insisted. "Be reasonable. You're tired, overworked, glutted from all the eating and drinking, a victim of big-city and social pressures, and you refuse to change. I think it would be fun to try this type of therapy. After all, it won't last forever, and apparently it can be taken with a bit of style."

Still I hesitated, finding it a little hard to believe that in the short period of a week the most fashionable of Germany's 153 spas could virtually rejuvenate the body and perk up the soul. On the other hand, my friend usually knew about these things, and I figured I really didn't have that much to lose—except about ten pounds of undesirable adipose tissue I'd been richly nourishing over the past couple of years. Besides, if such a mission was planned very carefully—and taken gradually to avoid metabolic shock—it just might turn out to be a marvelous vacation, with or without the added attraction of a possibly successful cure. A few weeks later I was on my way.

Since, of course, Paris happens to be between New York and Baden-Baden, I took advantage of the opportunity, checked into the Ritz, and was shown to my favorite room overlooking the garden. Appointments were impeccable as usual, and on the mantel above the marble fireplace were a large Murano vase holding twenty fresh red tulips, a tiny tin of Russian beluga sunk in ice, a chilled bottle of the hotel's reserve Champagne, and a single greeting card: "Charles C. Ritz." Just as I spooned the first bit of caviar and started to open the bubbly, the phone rang.

"*Mon cher ami*, how was the trip?" began M. Ritz in his inimitable style of alternating French and idiomatic English. "Now what's this I hear about your taking a cure in Germany? *Absurde, mon cher, absurde* that you should let yourself get in that condition. But while you're here there are a few things you must taste, like the new sausage I recently found! And wait till you see how we're preparing our *saumon à la Champagne*. And the new Italian asparagus. Best they've ever sent me. Why not come down now to taste them?"

Knowing that you never argue with the son of César, I consumed a few more delectable grains of beluga, a few more sips of wine, and hastened to the first of many such epicurean tastings, none of which exactly enhanced my already jaded system. When I wasn't sampling or sipping at the Ritz the next few days, I was sampling the *ris de veau* at Aux Lyonnais, the stuffed goose neck at Le Pizou, the *soupe de poissons* at Marius et Janette, and the *soufflé à la liqueur de framboise* at Taillevent.

After four sublime days of gourmandism in Paris, I headed by train to Strasbourg, spending most of the first hour of the trip readjusting the rear belt of my vest. Waiting at the station was the Brenner's Park's Herr Axmacher, the hotel's assistant manager and one of those rare Germans who are visibly undernourished. "And now, off we go to Baden-Baden, where you'll feel like new in just a few days."

"Uh, Herr Axmacher," I stuttered, "apparently someone forgot to tell you, and I know it sounds a little strange, but I'd hoped we could stop on our way for a little lunch at this Alsatian restaurant. Just a small out-of-the-way place I'm sure you'd enjoy."

"But I thought you'd come to take the cure."

"Oh, make no mistake, Herr Axmacher, I have. But it is lunchtime and we're so close to this charming little place."

About forty minutes later our Mercedes pulled up in front of France's most remotely located (and possibly finest) temple of gastronomy. Waiting to greet us inside the spacious, colorful, and rustic dining room was Jean-Pierre Haeberlin, one of the two brothers who own and operate the Auberge de l'Ill. Herr Axmacher appeared a bit stunned, but after a few glasses of chilled Muscat d'Alsace, we got down to serious business, indulging ourselves shamelessly in the ritual of *la haute cuisine*. I had advised Jean-Pierre that as much as possible had to be tasted, especially the specialties of the region. The drama began. Frogs'-leg soup, *brioche de foie gras*, and one giant hot truffle wrapped in foie gras, baked in puff pastry, and served with a Madeira sauce. We were off to a good start and fully ready to sample a salmon soufflé and a bottle of Hügel's vintage Riesling.

Hopes and spirits and appetites remained strong, and although my German host-become-guest still surveyed the scene with a look of incredulity, he managed to help do justice to a truffled guinea hen, as well as a bottle of local pinot noir. After dipping our silver into luscious chocolate profiteroles, we retired to the flower-lined terrace for coffee, flutes of '64 Taittinger Blanc de Blancs, and a few puffs of Montecristos. The "little lunch" had lasted four hours.

An hour later, we had crossed the Rhine and were deep in the majestic Black Forest. By the time we approached the Oos Valley into which Baden-Baden is tucked, I was in a postprandial daze, quite convinced that my liver would explode any moment. Then I caught my first glimpse of noble Baden-Baden. It is a domain of dignity and grace, a refuge from the commonplace, a leafy world of tranquillity. Passing through the small town, I admired all the elegant shops, the old Memorial Church, the dazzling casino designed a century ago by Parisian architects, the sylvan promenades on the banks of the River Oos, the veritable multitude of signs with doctors' names, and the imposing Friedrichsbad and Augustabad, considered by many to be the best-equipped and most-fashionable thermal baths in the world. By the time we pulled up at the hotel, there was no doubt in my mind that Baden-Baden was, indeed, the queen of German spas.

Entering my room at the Brenner's Park was like moving into another age—or, to be more precise, into the setting of a Thomas Mann novel. Fresh flowers and fruit, period furniture, a decades-old crystal chandelier, heavy lush draperies and Persian carpets, a small mahogany boot stand, a tall eight-prong clothes tree—and no detestable television set. It all evoked a spacious comfort and way of life that elsewhere today is hardly more than a dream. By contrast, the gray-marble bathroom was equipped with all modern conveniences: six-foot tub with bath thermometer, magnifying mirror, and, of course, a scale. My private terrace overlooked the quiet forest called the Lichtentaler Allee, and when I stepped out to view the well-dressed curists taking a late-afternoon promenade at the edge of the small river, I understood why so many for so long have chosen this hidden corner of the world to unwind, forget, and reacquire a sense of well-being.

The first night I had a typically restless sleep, only to be awakened early the next morning (and each succeeding morning) by the hotel's seventy-year-old veteran masseur, whose hands have remained supple and strong from kneading the muscles of such ailing guests of the past as Henry Ford, Mary Pickford, Lillian Gish, and Neville Chamberlain.

"*Guten Morgen,*" he greeted me. "Now you will have your first massage, before you get up, before you have breakfast, before you have the chance to start your day with unnecessary worries or concerns. It's all a question of good circulation." And with that dictum Herr Meier thrust open the terrace doors to let in fresh air, then began pushing, pulling, stretching, and pounding every joint, muscle, connecting tissue, and blood vessel in my body.

"Breathe deep," he instructed.

I tried and gasped.

The workout continued a good thirty minutes, after which Herr Meier directed me to get up, go on the terrace for more deep breathing, then drink one of the bottles of mineral water that had been placed next to the bowl of fruit. The taste could best be described as a slick salty water, but it contained *no* salt.

"You must drink our water all during the day," he said sternly. "Everywhere, anywhere. Here in your room, over at the Trinkhalle and Kurhaus, in the bathhouses, anywhere you find it. The water heals, soothes, purges, and stimulates the circulation. The cure is worthless without the water. And you must walk—everywhere, anywhere, *Auf Wiedersehen.*"

Herr Meier left as abruptly as he'd entered, leaving me in what I was sure was a state of total collapse. After, however, a recuperative half hour on the chaise longue, I regained my strength, ordered breakfast, and breathed a little more ozone.

My breakfast came: fresh orange juice made from blood oranges, a split of the house Champagne, fat little German sausages scattered around a mound of scrambled eggs, and a tray of breads and jams. Delightful. Little did I know that this was the last real breakfast I'd see for a week, for within a couple of hours I had received one official *Kurkarte*; one anti-stress booklet entitling me to consultations with a doctor and to social events at the Kurhaus, theater, and casino; one map of the town; and one slip of paper on which was written the name and address of Dr. Werner Hess.

Since I was told I should walk everywhere, I began making my way through the charming streets to keep my first medical appointment, noticing once again on every block the incredible number of druggists, physicians' offices, and young people carrying the same batch of cure material I had. (Everything in Baden-Baden is *Kur* something or something *Kur*.) Arriving at Dr. Hess's office, I informed the doctor of my basic problems, only to be asked in perfect English why I indulged to excess.

"Because I enjoy it," I explained. "And, besides, it's part of my chosen profession to eat and drink."

"So you're not here to learn how to curtail forever your social and gastronomic habits?" he continued.

"Sir, I don't think that would be possible even if I had the volition. I know it sounds bad, but no, that's out of the question. What I'm really looking for is what you call an *Entschlackungskur*, which, if I'm not mistaken, has something to do with what we call a complete overhaul."

Dr. Hess declared me a peculiar case, but after giving me a semicomplete physical (which did, indeed, reveal a swollen liver and eleven pounds of overweight), he sat me down and came forth with a lecture that I both respect and will never forget.

"Listen, young man, I can sympathize fully with your predicament, but your defensive attitude is all wrong. Here no one is going to force you to do anything; we only suggest and hope you'll care enough to force yourself. To respect the type of highly specialized therapy that's been developed here over the past two thousand years, you must first respect your own mind and body. I can, of course, prescribe certain treatments and waters, but unless you acquire the right mental attitude you're simply wasting your time and mine. Less than five percent of all who come here are Americans, and most of them have your same defenses at first. They eye spa therapy with suspicion and contempt, but after they've completed a program and seen what can be accomplished in as little time as a week, most return year after year."

Dr. Hess talked for forty-five minutes, and by the time I left his office I couldn't have been any more dead serious about anything than I was about *Die Kur*. The man was honest and highly intelligent, but, above all, I had the impression that he, unlike most doctors in the United States, cared about something more than how many patients he could shuffle in and out within the period of an hour. I received no boring moral recriminations regarding my smoking, eating, drinking, and lack of exercise. But somehow Dr. Hess convinced me that while I was at Baden-Baden I should change my thinking considerably, go the way of the other curists, curb—but not discontinue!—my natural inclinations, and really make an effort to follow his suggestions.

And for one solid, blessed week that's the way I lived. Each morning there was a massage, followed by a light breakfast on my sunny terrace, deep breathings, and as much water as I could drink—and I did drink gallons of that water! Later I would ascend the grand staircase of the Friedrichsbad and, following the sign language of attendants, find my locker, strip, and join the other ailing and non-ailing curists moving from one balneotherapeutic phase to the next in the Grand Communal Bath. (Germans, young and old alike, take balneotherapy for preventive as well as corrective purposes.)

First I sat in a dry-heat room and gazed up at colorful tiled tableaux of swans and butterflies. After ten minutes I was led to bake in a much hotter room, this one tiled with figures of cattle and fowl resting amiably under palm trees. Curious indeed, but so comforting and civilized. Dripping with perspiration, I was next directed to spend a specified amount of time (huge wall clocks were omnipresent) in three separate bathing pools, the first scalding hot, the second ice cold, the third warm. This was followed by fifteen minutes of lying flat on a marble slab and breathing moist thermal air heated to a demonic temperature by a steaming natural fountain.

So weak I could hardly walk, I was stretched out on a wooden table, lathered with soap made from beef fat, scrubbed from head to toe with a floor brush to remove dead skin cells, and rinsed with bucketfuls of warm water. My body was delightfully numb—or so I thought until an attendant steered me under a frigid shower before draping me in a floor-length towel and leading me to the "rest saloon." There, in a dark, carpeted room with a domelike ceiling, I was shown to a bed and wrapped like a mummy in a sheet and a wool blanket. I slept soundly for an hour, dressed, stopped at one of the cone-shaped thermal fountains for a few glasses of hot mineral water from the Nürtinger Heinrichsquelle spring (good for the liver, bile, stomach, and intestines), and walked back to the hotel without a worry in the world.

Strangely enough, after the first day I scarcely thought about lunch, and, even more strangely, I hadn't the slightest thirst for Champagne or any other alcoholic beverage. If I had hunger pangs, I simply dropped into the Schwarzwald Grill at the hotel for a little fruit or cheese, but in a couple of days I skipped lunch altogether, took excursions through the Black Forest and vineyards, and discussed in detail my thermal treatments with others over glasses of water at the Trinkhalle (a fashionable classic temple where everyone gathers to socialize over water instead of cocktails).

Midafternoons were spent at the Augustabad, an ultramodern bathhouse where it's not uncommon to see two or three chauffeured Rolls-Royces parked in front waiting for curists. There I was packed in mud, given underwater jet massage, bubbled in pine baths, scrubbed with more soap, walked through alternating hot and cold water in troughs with rock beds, and, most remarkable of all, hosed down while I held on to a bar for dear life. It was all fascinating. After these treatments, I was usually so limp I could hardly make it to the water fountains before returning to the hotel for a nap. But what mattered was I felt good, great, fantastic—so much so that I was overly eager to take long late-afternoon walks.

In the evenings, in black tie or a dark suit, I sipped a single highball made with lots of mineral water and learned the cure-saving trick of never studying the hotel's menu. After a light dinner, there was coffee in the lounge and more cure conversation with newly acquired friends from France, Scandinavia, England, and, of course, Switzerland and Germany, but by 10 P.M. we were out for a final walk, breathing deeply on terraces, or making ready for bed. It was all quite that simple, uninvolved, and delightful.

By the end of that almost mythical week, I was rested and "unstressed." My liver was proclaimed normal in size by Dr. Hess, and I'd knocked off exactly nine pounds. Now, I'm still not sure just how, when, or why it all happened. But it did happen. I enjoyed every minute, and I highly recommend the place to those of high moral caliber. For I'm unhappy to report that today I'm the same wreck I was before leaving for Baden-Baden. What brought on the decline? Well, I suppose it all began the moment the Mercedes left that land of the Rhine Maidens, and I was feeling a bit peckish, and there was this little restaurant.

JIM HARRISON

Bird Hunting

Many of our life-giving rituals are deeply private, whether their nature is sexual, religious, or involved in far simpler pleasures. I like, in May—perhaps love is a better word—to stand in a clearing near dark and watch the mating flight of the male woodcock, the sweeping contorted spiral, then the whirl back to earth. Not incidentally, this dance tells you where the birds will be in the fall during hunting season as they mate and breed in the vicinity of their singing grounds. And when migratory groups gather and accumulate they tend to favor these same clearings. The French philosopher Bachelard ascribed a peculiar magic to certain things and locations—attics, haylofts, seashells, a cabin in the dark with a window square of yellow light. Since the age of seven, when I began hunting, I've favored the bottoms of rivers and lakes and forest clearings.

Five months later, in early October, four men stand in such a clearing, perhaps fifteen miles from any human settlement. The October sun is thin and weak at this latitude in Michigan's Upper Peninsula, an area remote and charmless except to a few. The four men are planning the evening's menu and staring at the five bird dogs sprawled in a pool of sunlight. There are two yellow Labrador bitches, one owned by myself and the other by a French count I've been hunting with more than a dozen years. My neighbor, whom I think of as "Dogman," has a German shorthair, an English setter and an English pointer. This lovely pile of animals would make a flawless painting if my bitch Sand, bred from the English Sandringham line, weren't making love to the males with punishing force. It is her way of celebrating the hunt and they cry out as she smothers them. It is hopeless to try to call her off—there is apparently no obedience training when it comes to sheer lust. The fourth hunter among us, an artist from Montana, is especially amused. He is unable to own a bird dog for reasons of temperament.

"Like me, she is a generic love," the artist says. He is the most focused menu planner of the group. During the hunt he stops and stares a lot because he is fat, but also because he is an artist and likes to study the sere umbers, the siennas, the subdued Tuscan riot that is a Michigan October. He suggests for dinner that he quickly do some Hunanese pork backribs for an appetizer, then we can marinate chunks of grouse and sweetbreads in cream and Tabasco in order to stretch the grouse. After we've browned these chunks we'll add a cup of vastly reduced game stock and a cup of the marinade. We would have had more grouse but no one had the energy to brave the densest thickets where they seemed to be that day. Meanwhile the Dogman would grill ten of the plucked woodcock over a wood fire until medium rare, basting them with butter, lemon and pepper. The more elegant *salmis de bécasses* would be made by the Count later when we traveled south to my farmhouse. This evening as a last course the Count would offer two racks of lamb with some garlicky flageolet and a salad to tamp it all down. Three Montrachets and four Châteauneuf du Pape would be the rinse. I can't be disturbing my remaining great wines by travel. They would come later.

A minor regional novelist recently said that *"cuisine minceur is the moral equivalent of the fox-trot."* Perhaps. In any event you simply can't hike through rugged territory for eight hours and be satisfied with three poached mussels and an asparagus mousse. It is another ritual, though never talked about as such, that the food go as well as the hunting, with each occasionally making up deficiencies in the other. When we're on the road together, say on the way to Montana to fish brown trout, the Count will polish off a plate of bad restaurant food, then hiss "filth" for anyone who cares to hear or not. This is also, not incidentally, his response to any political discussion.

The hunt had gone well for a day that had begun too warm for the dogs, but by late morning the wind had swung around to the northwest off Lake Superior. The artist and I formed the "B" team, in that Sand must be kept separate from the others as she tries to hog the good cover. There is something marvelous about a dog with a sure sense of function, and an intelligent, experienced animal recognizes cover. Good cover for grouse and woodcock, though not identical, is a practical matter of finding their main eating areas. In short, they both hang out where they eat: patches of aspen in clearings, edges of the forest with berry-bearing bushes, tag-alder swales along creeks, near pin cherry, chokecherry, thorn apple, beechnut, red and white dog-wood. In other areas abandoned farms are good for reasons of fertility of undergrowth. In my region of the U.P. there are not abandoned farms because farms themselves are scarce—there's one about thirty miles south of here. The main local livelihood is logging, a positive influence on game quantity; as opposed to what most people think, a fully mature forest is relatively sterile in terms of mammalian and game-bird life.

The artist and I are never disturbed over the idea that the others will overshoot us. To be good at bird hunting you need a combination of excellent dog work, an ability to shoot well, and a knowledge of cover. The Dogman's shorthair could find birds in a busy roller rink. I once saw this dog, Cochise by name, crawl beneath a brush pile in search of a wounded grouse, his tail pointing up at the heavens through a mat of cedar brush. I am mindful that the fine novelist, Hemingway, wasted an entire African hunt brooding over the idea that his partner was doing better. Frankly, everyone in his secret heart must know who is the best. I'm not letting Gabriel García Márquez and Saul Bellow ruin my life as a novelist because they're better at it. If the Count and Dogman return garlanded with birds we will rejoice at the table.

We do have one advantage and that rests in the fact that I spend a lot of the summer locating birds, driving hundreds of miles on forest two-tracks. In the past five years I have pretty much covered a strip of land a hundred and fifty miles long by thirty miles wide bordering Lake Superior. Sand is upset that I don't shoot the birds off-season but if she finds a covey of grouse she'll become affectionate back in the car. I fight her off, telling her, "I'm not of your kind, I'm an American Poet."

The artist has new boots and his feet hurt after the first half-hour aspen walk with two flushed birds and no hits. We drive to a tag-alder swale only a mile or so from the village. We are excited enough by this area to stop talking about food and love for a short while. Even the dog is beside herself when we pull to a stop beside the marsh. We each take a side with Sand casting back and forth in the improbably dark tag-alder thicket. Educated luck! Within a half hour a dozen woodcock have burst from cover and we have bagged five. The artist is beside himself and throws himself on the ground laughing and necking with the dog. "Sand, we are American Sportsmen," he yells to the blue sky and a red-tailed hawk a thousand feet above us. On the way back to the car Sand flushes a grouse from a clump of goldenrod. The grouse falls to the artist's long shot. To maintain this state of grace we go to the bar for a few drinks then back to the cabin for lunch and a short midday nap. We envision the

Count and Dogman on a forced march to bag the number of birds we have done effortlessly. We discuss the merits of a pasta dish I had devised in May with a sauce of wild leeks and morels, sweetbreads and cream. I have some dried morels and domestic leeks at the cabin. It will make a serviceable lunch, adding some julienned prosciutto.

In the state of post-nap grogginess our victories seem less specific. We jounce over a dozen miles of logging road to rendezvous with the Count and Dogman at a bend in the river. We are somewhat disappointed to see that they are drinking on the riverbank, and eating a pâté the Count had in his cooler made out of Hungarian grouse and teal he had shot in Montana. They have seven woodcock and two grouse. They are pleasantly surprised at our bag and head off to hunt another hour. When they're gone we finish the pâté and head off lazily down the road with neither of us willing to break brush. We shoot only one of five flushed birds, destroying the morning's invulnerability. Even the dog seems disappointed in us. Hearing distant shooting I climb to a bare hillock and look through my monocular (I'm blind in one eye so in a moment of brilliance gave up binoculars after thirty years). The Dogman and Count approach a swale perhaps a thousand yards distant. My monocular is a small round movie screen focused on the three pointers on tightly honored point. There is a flush and the Count swings left and right and two birds fall. Unlike the artist and I the Count and Dogman take turns. Now I see my own dog, Sand, streaking toward the real action as the Count's retriever fetches the birds. I turn with the monocular and focus on the artist dozing under an oak tree, his left hand brushing acorns from beneath his ample bottom. I am not exactly "one with the earth" but I'm feeling good. Simultaneous visions of a fashion model and a duck I had cooked with marrow and exactly thirty-three cloves of garlic sweep through my mind. It is our first day of hunting together, much like the Glorious Twelfth in England. I can feel my happiness emanating in bands to the hunters in the distance.

Back at the cabin, while the artist is preparing his fiery ribs of the Orient, I inoculate the cracks of the log walls using a large marinade hypodermic and a solution of Tabasco and Canadian whiskey. This drives away bats which have been using the walls as both bedroom and toilet. They fly around drunkenly like poets on grants. I sip this concoction to feel life even more strongly. I am quickly losing the self-absorption that made me all the money in the first place, a self-absorption that paradoxically only regains its value after you lose it for a while. I am wearing a Texas tailored camouflage jump suit with which I sneak up on snowshoe rabbits for illegal summertime French fricassees. I have also seen a curious female coyote five times but never before she has seen me first, wondering perhaps at this burly man creeping through the swamp in clumsy imitation of other beasts.

I turn from my bat chores and look at my friends busy in the kitchen, feeding dogs, dressing after a shower. We in the Midwest have to face up to the idea that no one on America's dream coasts will visit us except for very special occasions. True, we have the Great Lakes but they have the Atlantic and the Pacific. They also have restaurants. Tom McGuane, the novelist, said to me about the Midwest, "Mortimer Snerd must have bred five thousand times a day to build that heartland race." True, but the land as I find it, and daily walk it, is virtually peopleless, with vast undifferentiated swamps, ridges, old circular logging roads; a region of cold fogs, monstrous weather changes, third-growth forests devoid of charm, models, and actresses, or ballerinas, but somehow superbly likable.

After the meal and a goblet of calvados we sit before the fire and watch the Count tease his teeth and upper lip with a thumb, a small piece of blanket on his shoulder. Technically speaking he is *not* "sucking his thumb." He has reminded me that for years I have preferred to watch television through the tiny squares of an afghan thrown over my head. *Pourquoi?* Beats me. The artist becomes morose, commenting that after years of experience in the nearby village he is sure that if he wore a Dolly Parton wig he would be the most attractive woman in town. He has offered local ladies paintings for their favors and the paintings are worth thousands.

"They don't want paintings, they want a husband," says the Dogman. "Besides, you're as ugly as we all are. I drink because I'm ugly. You don't try hard enough. Romania wasn't built in a day."

It is easy to tire of this masculine nonsense, and after a week, when the supply of good wine runs out, we head south to my farm in Leelanau County, a rather spectacular area itself; a hilly landscape of cherry orchards jutting out as a peninsula into Lake Michigan. With a northern front the weather has turned cold and somber which will drive the woodcock south on their migratory route. For years we have found them arriving in our favorite areas between October sixth and tenth.

A Native American myth insists that the Great Spirit made the wood-cock up last out of the leftover parts of other birds. *Philohela minor* is colored in shades of brown, black, and gray which says nothing until you envision the mottled shades of autumn—foliage burned by frost, wet leaves, bare earth. They smell musky and their breasts are plumper than a quail's. The French prefer their flavor over all other game birds, spreading their entrails on large croutons. Jeanne Moreau told me that as a young actress she would save a month to buy a brace of woodcock. The Count doesn't know yet but

I've purchased two cases of Echêzeaux, his favorite. Childish surprises are still the best.

My farmhouse owns the still ample remains of my Warner Bros. Memorial Wine Cellar, though my oldest daughter has hidden a '49 Latour and some '61 Lafites against my excesses. She has made and brought from New York a goose *confit*. My agent has sent a pound of caviar. A bow-hunter friend has sent over a half of venison. I have ordered a quarter of prime veal and a freshly killed local lamb. The Dogman is taking a few days off from grouse and woodcock to get some wild ducks, hopefully teal and mallard. A farmer drops off the dozen barnyard chickens and ducks we called about in August. It's too early to get any fresh truffles from New York but we'll have to make do. We'll poach two local salmon for dinner to lighten up a bit, and I'll make gravlax out of a third. I bought seven pounds of garlic, my favorite number!

And so it goes. We hunt hard during the short Indian summer days and cook hard during the long evenings. I suspect this will strike some as primitive. Years ago we had to hunt much harder and the Count reminds me of how my wife and two daughters would hear the car and run out of the house to see the bag. One day, the best ever, we came home with nine grouse, seven woodcock, and a few rabbits. He says that ten years later whenever he sees a girl wearing braces he thinks of my daughter at thirteen, peering at the game birds with utter delight. Then she would set about plucking enough birds for dinner, and we would hang the others a few days, a desirable practice for flavor.

A week of the local hunting leaves us with a caloric load that we can't quite walk off in our daily hunting. I would like to say that somehow our genes are issuing messages to store up for the coming winter but this is ardent nonsense. In times past certain of the deadly sins achieved a certain spirituality when taken far enough. I resolve to make notes on the spirituality of gluttony but the idea is a bit too remote to attract anything more than thoughts of Rasputin's talents for sex and drink, Nixon's for fibbing, Rabelais's, Toulouse-Lautrec's, and Curnonsky's for food. Before we leave for the austerity of the north we watch the Count working deep into the night. He is assembling a rough pâté in a clear glass tureen made out of gorgeous layers of ground veal flavored with apples and calvados, duck, venison, woodcock and grouse. This little dish is being made as a precaution against our living too simply back in the U.P. That evening the Count had made an enormous *salmis de bécasses*, the most exacting of woodcock dishes, and one would think exhaustion would have driven him to bed, but he lacks our very American cheap resolve to eat nothing to purge too much. During eating, the

French discuss future eating. After the dinner we had decided that Sand should lick the platter, a traditional reward for a dog that has done well in the field. When the platter was put down on the rug with its dark freight of extra sauce she had approached wiggling, her eyes closed in pleasure, and limping with fatigue. After two long, tentative laps the hunger became generalized and she flopped on the platter, rolling in the juices. It was comic and touching. A dog is entitled to a favorite time of year just as we are.

Once I fell down just as a dog came on point in thick cover. I was a little worried as years before I had spent a month in traction from a fall during bird season. Two setters honored the first dog's point, skidding to full attention behind the first dog. It was a rainy day in late season and I watched it all from ground level, having come suddenly to the point where I didn't want to shoot any more birds that year. The grouse wild-flushed off into the mist, free to die during the harsh winter, or live another year.

The season is over and my heart is as full as Neruda's interminable artichoke. Everyone is gone and I draft a novel, further taxing my overused system. I go to a Mexican health farm for two weeks but am terribly embarrassed when I catch a few local workers staring at me at some exercises. Twenty years ago I was a laborer building small buildings as they are now. We were very poor then and a half a venison meant a great deal. I skip the exercises and walk alone every day in the mountains. I hunt rattlesnakes without harming them. After flushing coveys of quail I begin to devise ways of snaring a few to enhance the expensive vegetarian diet at the spa. In New York and Los Angeles, or anywhere in the world, I mostly hunt good restaurants.

My own hunting and fishing are largely misunderstood activities cataloged under the banal notion of "macho," whereas I tend to view them as a continuation of my birthright. The forest, after all, isn't my Louvre. The Louvre is my Louvre. I walk there from my rooms at the Lotti. There are ideas currently afoot about the positive effects of "male bonding," inferring there might be something to such activities as they have had a regular place in the male life since prehistory. There is a studied silliness in responding to old ideas brought up in new dime store frocks by newspaper feature editors. Hemingway went for record kudu and marlin in public, while Faulkner in self-designed obscurity hunted and fished with friends, played polo, chased foxes, sailed, and drank a bit.

Just the other night, in the middle of August while I was writing this, I went calling coyotes with a friend. In the right mood coyotes will respond to our imitation of their call, also to a loon's call which is more difficult to imitate. Despite what taxonomists say, these creatures are related, if only spiritually. To the east the moon was full and enormous at midnight; to the north there was the pale green fluttering sheen of aurora borealis, the northern lights; in the west a large thunderstorm and line squall was forming and bolts of lightning cracked the sky in the forms of undersea coral. We were in a thousand-acre clearing with a thousand huge, gray white pine stumps, cut a century ago. My friend called and the coyotes responded in this mythological landscape with breathless abandon intermingled with the thunder. On the long ride back in the rain one sensed the sky was full of black anti-rainbows. Around a puddle in the trail three woodcock preened and fed. I eased out of the car and stopped quite close to them, their eyes fiery and blinded by the headlights. I spoke to the birds a few minutes, then watched them flush through the glittery beads of rain into the darkness. A wonderful hunt.

ISAAC BASHEVIS SINGER

Short Friday

In the village of Lapschitz lived a tailor named Shmul-Leibele with his wife, Shoshe. Shmul-Leibele was half tailor, half furrier, and a complete pauper. He had never mastered his trade. When filling an order for a jacket or a gaberdine, he inevitably made the garment either too short or too tight. The belt in the back would hang either too high or too low, the lapels never matched, the vent was off center. It was said that he had once sewn a pair of trousers with the fly off to one side. Shmul-Leibele could not count the wealthy citizens among his customers. Common people brought him their shabby garments to have patched and turned, and the peasants gave him their old pelts to reverse. As is usual with bunglers, he was also slow. He would dawdle over a garment for weeks at a time. Yet despite his shortcomings, it must be said that Shmul-Leibele was an honorable man. He used only strong thread and none of his seams ever gave. If one ordered a lining from Shmul-Leibele, even one of common sackcloth or cotton, he bought only the very best material, and thus lost most of his profit. Unlike other tailors who hoarded every last bit of remaining cloth, he returned all scraps to his customers.

Had it not been for his competent wife, Shmul-Leibele would certainly have starved to death. Shoshe helped him in whatever way she could. On Thursdays she hired herself out to wealthy families to knead dough, and on summer days went off to the forest to gather berries and mushrooms, as well as pinecones and twigs for the stove. In winter she plucked down for brides' featherbeds. She was also a better tailor than her husband, and when he began to sigh, or dally and mumble to himself, an indication that he could no longer muddle through, she would take the chalk from his hand and show him how to continue. Shoshe had no children, but it was common knowledge that it wasn't she who was barren, but rather her husband who was sterile, since all of her sisters had borne children, while his only brother was likewise childless. The townswomen repeatedly urged Shoshe to divorce him, but she turned a deaf ear, for the couple loved one another with a great love.

Shmul-Leibele was small and clumsy. His hands and feet were too large for his body, and his forehead bulged on either side as is common in simpletons. His cheeks, red as apples, were bare of whiskers, and but a few hairs sprouted from his chin. He had scarcely any neck at all; his head sat upon his shoulders like a snowman's. When he walked, he scraped his shoes along the ground so that every step could be heard far away. He hummed continuously and there was always an amiable smile on his face. Both winter and summer he wore the same caftan and sheepskin cap with earlaps. Whenever there was any need for a messenger, it was always Shmul-Leibele who was pressed into service, and however far away he was sent, he always went willingly. The wags saddled him with a variety of nicknames and made him the butt of all sorts of pranks, but he never took offense. When others scolded his tormentors, he would merely observe: "What do I care? Let them have their fun. They're only children, after all. . . ."

Sometimes he would present one or another of the mischief makers with a piece of candy or a nut. This he did without any ulterior motive, but simply out of goodheartedness.

Shoshe towered over him by a head. In her younger days she had been considered a beauty, and in the households where she worked as a servant they spoke highly of her honesty and diligence. Many young men had vied for her hand, but she had selected Shmul-Leibele because he was quiet and because he never joined the other town boys who gathered on the Lublin road at noon Saturdays to flirt with the girls. His piety and retiring nature pleased her. Even as a girl Shoshe had taken pleasure in studying the Pentateuch, in nursing the infirm at the almshouse, in listening to the tales of the old women who sat before their houses darning stockings. She would fast on the last day of each month, the Minor Day of Atonement, and often attended the services at the women's synagogue. The other servant girls mocked her and thought her old-fashioned. Immediately following her wedding she shaved her head and fastened a kerchief firmly over her ears, never permitting a stray strand of hair from her matron's wig to show as did some of the other young women. The bath attendant praised her because she never frolicked at the ritual bath, but performed her ablutions according to the laws. She purchased only indisputably kosher meat, though it was a half-cent more per pound, and when she was in doubt about the dietary laws she sought out the rabbi's advice. More than once she had not hesitated to throw out all the food and even to smash the earthen crockery. In short, she was a capable, God-fearing woman, and more than one man envied Shmul-Leibele his jewel of a wife.

Above all of life's blessings the couple revered the Sabbath. Every Friday noon Shmul-Leibele would lay aside his tools and cease all work. He was always among the first at the ritual bath, and he immersed himself in the water four times for the four letters of the Holy Name. He also helped the beadle set the candles in the chandeliers and the candelabra. Shoshe scrimped throughout the week, but on the Sabbath she was lavish. Into the heated oven went cakes, cookies and the Sabbath loaf. In winter, she prepared puddings made of chicken's neck stuffed with dough and rendered fat. In summer she made puddings with rice or noodles, greased with chicken fat and sprinkled with sugar or cinnamon. The main dish consisted of potatoes and buckwheat, or pearl barley with beans, in the midst of which she never failed to set a marrowbone. To insure that the dish would be well cooked, she sealed the oven with loose dough. Shmul-Leibele treasured every mouthful, and at every Sabbath meal he would remark: "Ah, Shoshe love, it's food fit for a king! Nothing less than a taste of Paradise!" to which Shoshe replied, "Eat hearty. May it bring you good health."

Although Shmul-Leibele was a poor scholar, unable to memorize a chapter of the Mishnah, he was well versed in all the laws. He and his wife frequently studied The Good Heart in Yiddish. On half-holidays, holidays and on each free day, he studied the Bible in Yiddish. He never missed a sermon, and though a pauper, he bought from peddlers all sorts of books of moral instructions and religious tales, which he then read together with his wife. He never wearied of reciting sacred phrases. As soon as he arose in the morning he washed his hands and began to mouth the preamble to the prayers. Then he would walk over to the study house and worship as one of the quorum. Every day he recited a few chapters of the Psalms, as well as those prayers which the less serious tended to skip over. From his father he had inherited a thick prayer book with wooden covers, which contained the rites and laws pertaining to each day of the year. Shmul-Leibele and his wife heeded each and every one of these. Often he would observe to his wife: "I shall surely end up in Gehenna, since there'll be no one on earth to say Kaddish over me." "Bite your tongue, Shmul-Leibele," she would counter. "For one, everything is possible under God. Secondly, you'll live until the Messiah comes. Thirdly, it's just possible that I will die before you and you will marry a young woman who'll bear you a dozen children." When Shoshe said this, Shmul-Leibele would shout: "God forbid! You must remain in good health. I'd rather rot in Gehenna!"

Although Shmul-Leibele and Shoshe relished every Sabbath, their greatest satisfaction came from the Sabbaths in wintertime. Since the day before the Sabbath evening was a short one, and since Shoshe was busy until late Thursday at her work, the couple usually stayed up all of Thursday night. Shoshe kneaded dough in the trough, covering it with cloth and a pillow so that it might ferment. She heated the oven with kindling-wood and dry twigs. The shutters in the room were kept closed, the door shut. The bed and bench-bed remained unmade, for at daybreak the couple would take a nap. As long as it was dark Shoshe prepared the Sabbath meal by the light of a candle. She plucked a chicken or a goose (if she had managed to come by one cheaply), soaked it, salted it and scraped the fat from it. She roasted a liver for Shmul-Leibele over the glowing coals and baked a small Sabbath loaf for him. Occasionally she would inscribe her name upon the loaf with letters of dough, and then Shmul-Leibele would tease her: "Shoshe, I am eating you up. Shoshe, I have already swallowed you." Shmul-Leibele loved warmth, and he would climb up on the oven and from there look down as his spouse cooked, baked, washed, rinsed, pounded and carved. The Sabbath loaf would turn out round and brown. Shoshe braided the loaf so swiftly that it seemed to dance before Shmul-Leibele's eyes. She bustled about efficiently with spatulas, pokers, ladles and goosewing dusters, and at times even snatched up a live coal with her bare fingers. The pots perked and bubbled. Occasionally a drop of soup would spill and the hot tin would hiss and squeal. And all the while the cricket continued its chirping. Although Shmul-Leibele had finished his supper by this time, his appetite would be whetted afresh, and Shoshe would throw him a knish, a chicken gizzard, a cookie, a plum from the plum stew or a chunk of the pot-roast. At the same time she would chide him, saying that he was a glutton. When he attempted to defend himself she would cry: "Oh, the sin is upon me, I have allowed you to starve. . . ."

At dawn they would both lie down in utter exhaustion. But because of their efforts Shoshe would not have to run herself ragged the following day, and she could make the benediction over the candles a quarter of an hour before sunset.

The Friday on which this story took place was the shortest Friday of the year. Outside, the snow had been falling all night and had blanketed the house up to the windows and barricaded the door. As usual, the couple had stayed up until morning, then had lain down to sleep. They had arisen later than usual, for they hadn't heard the rooster's crow, and since the windows were covered with snow and frost, the day seemed as dark as night. After whispering, "I thank Thee," Shmul-Leibele went outside with a broom and shovel to clear a path, after which he took a bucket and fetched water from the well. Then, as he had no pressing work, he decided to lay off for the whole day. He went to the study house for the morning prayers, and after breakfast wended his way to the bathhouse. Because of the cold outside, the patrons kept up an eternal plaint: "A bucket! A bucket!" and the bath attendant poured more and more water over the glowing stones so that the steam grew constantly denser. Shmul-Leibele located a scraggly willow-broom, mounted to the highest bench and whipped himself until his skin glowed red. From the bathhouse, he hurried over to the study house where the beadle had already swept and sprinkled the floor with sand. Shmul-Leibele set the candles and helped spread the tablecloths over the tables. Then he went home again and changed into his Sabbath clothes. His boots, resoled but a few days before, no longer let the wet through. Shoshe had done her washing for the week, and had given him a fresh shirt, underdraw-ers, a fringed garment, even a clean pair of stockings. She had already performed the benediction over the candles, and the spirit of the Sabbath emanated from every corner of the room. She was wearing her silk kerchief with the silver spangles, a yellow-and-gray dress, and shoes with gleaming, pointed tips. On her throat hung the chain that Shmul-Leibele's mother, peace be with her, had given her to celebrate the signing of the wedding contract. The marriage band sparkled on her index finger. The candlelight reflected in the window panes, and Shmul-Leibele fancied that there was a duplicate of this room outside and that another Shoshe was out there lighting the Sabbath candles. He yearned to tell his wife how full of grace she was, but there was no time for it, since it is specifically stated in the prayer book that it is fitting and proper to be amongst the first ten worshipers at the synagogue; as it so happened, going off to prayers he was the tenth man to arrive. After the congregation had intoned the Song of Songs, the cantor sang, "Give thanks," and "O come, let us exult." Shmul-Leibele prayed with fervor. The words were sweet upon his tongue, they seemed to fall from his lips with a life of their own, and he felt that they soared to the eastern wall, rose above the embroidered curtain of the Holy Ark, the gilded lions, and the tablets, and floated up to the ceiling with its painting of the twelve constellations. From there, the prayers surely ascended to the Throne of Glory.

The cantor chanted, "Come, my beloved," and Shmul-Leibele trum-peted along in accompaniment. Then came the prayers, and the men recited

"It is our duty to praise . . ." to which Shmul-Leibele added a "Lord of the Universe." Afterwards, he wished everyone a good Sabbath: the rabbi, the ritual slaughterer, the head of the community, the assistant rabbi, everyone present. The *cheder* lads shouted, "Good Sabbath, Shmul-Leibele," while they mocked him with gestures and grimaces, but Shmul-Leibele answered them all with a smile, even occasionally pinched a boy's cheek affectionately. Then he was off for home. The snow was piled high so that one could barely make out the contours of the roofs, as if the entire settlement had been immersed in white. The sky, which had hung low and overcast all day, now grew clear. From among white clouds a full moon peered down, casting a daylike brilliance over the snow. In the west, the edge of a cloud still held the glint of sunset. The stars on this Friday seemed larger and sharper, and through some miracle Lapschitz seemed to have blended with the sky. Shmul-Leibele's hut, which was situated not far from the synagogue, now hung suspended in space, as it is written: "He suspendeth the earth on nothingness." Shmul-Leibele walked slowly since, according to law, one must not hurry when coming from a holy place. Yet he longed to be home. "Who knows?" he thought. "Perhaps Shoshe has become ill? Maybe she's gone to fetch water and, God forbid, has fallen into the well? Heaven save us, what a lot of troubles can befall a man."

On the threshold he stamped his feet to shake off the snow, then opened the door and saw Shoshe. The room made him think of Paradise. The oven had been freshly whitewashed, the candles in the brass candelabras cast a Sabbath glow. The aromas coming from the sealed oven blended with the scents of the Sabbath supper. Shoshe sat on the bench-bed apparently awaiting him, her cheeks shining with the freshness of a young girl's. Shmul-Leibele wished her a happy Sabbath and she in turn wished him a good year. He began to hum, "Peace upon ye minstering angels . . ." and after he had said his farewells to the invisible angels that accompany each Jew leaving the synagogue, he recited: "That worthy woman." How well he understood the meaning of these words, for he had read them often in Yiddish, and each time reflected anew on how aptly they seemed to fit Shoshe.

Shoshe was aware that these holy sentences were being said in her honor, and thought to herself, "Here am I, a simple woman, an orphan, and yet God has chosen to bless me with a devoted husband who praises me in the holy tongue."

Both of them had eaten sparingly during the day so that they would have an appetite for the Sabbath meal. Shmul-Leibele said the benediction over the raisin wine and gave Shoshe the cup so that she might drink. Afterwards, he rinsed his fingers from a tin dipper, then she washed hers, and they both dried their hands with a single towel, each at either end.

Shmul-Leibele lifted the Sabbath loaf and cut it with the bread knife, a slice for himself and one for his wife.

He immediately informed her that the loaf was just right, and she countered: "Go on, you say that every Sabbath."

"But it happens to be the truth," he replied.

Although it was hard to obtain fish during the cold weather, Shoshe had purchased three-fourths of a pound of pike from the fishmonger. She had chopped it with onions, added an egg, salt and pepper and cooked it with carrots and parsley. It took Shmul-Leibele's breath away, and after it he had to drink a tumbler of whiskey. When he began the table chants, Shoshe accompanied him quietly. Then came the chicken soup with noodles and tiny circlets of fat which glowed on the surface like golden ducats. Between the soup and the main course, Shmul-Leibele again sang Sabbath hymns. Since goose was cheap at this time of year, Shoshe gave Shmul-Leibele an extra leg for good measure. After the dessert, Shmul-Leibele washed for the last time and made a benediction. When he came to the words: "Let us not be in need either of the gifts of flesh and blood nor of their loans," he rolled his eyes upward and brandished his fists. He never stopped praying that he be allowed to continue to earn his own livelihood and not, God forbid, become an object of charity.

After grace, he said yet another chapter of the Mishnah, and all sorts of other prayers which were found in his large prayer book. Then he sat down to read the weekly portion of the Pentateuch twice in Hebrew and once in Aramaic. He enunciated every word and took care to make no mistake in the difficult Aramaic paragraphs of the Onkelos. When he reached the last section, he began to yawn and tears gathered in his eyes. Utter exhaustion overcame him. He could barely keep his eyes open and between one passage and the next he dozed off for a second or two. When Shoshe noticed this, she made up the bench-bed for him and prepared her own featherbed with clean sheets. Shmul-Leibele barely managed to say the retiring prayers and began to undress. When he was already lying on his bench-bed he said: "A good Sabbath, my pious wife. I am very tired. . . ." and turning to the wall, he promptly began to snore.

Shoshe sat a while longer gazing at the Sabbath candles which had already begun to smoke and flicker. Before getting into bed, she placed a pitcher of water and a basin at Shmul-Leibele's bedstead so that he would not rise the following morning without water to wash with. Then she, too, lay down and fell asleep.

They had slept an hour or two or possibly three—what does it matter, actually?—when suddenly Shoshe heard Shmul-Leibele's voice. He waked her and whispered her name. She opened one eye and asked, "What is it?"

"Are you clean?" he mumbled.

She thought for a moment and replied, "Yes."

He rose and came to her. Presently he was in bed with her. A desire for her flesh had roused him. His heart pounded rapidly, the blood coursed in his veins. He felt a pressure in his loins. His urge was to mate with her immediately, but he remembered the law which admonished a man not to copulate with a woman until he had first spoken affectionately to her, and he now began to speak of his love for her and how this mating could possibly result in a male child.

"And a girl you wouldn't accept?" Shoshe chided him, and he replied, "Whatever God deigns to bestow would be welcome."

"I fear this privilege isn't mine anymore," she said with a sigh.

"Why not?" he demanded. "Our mother Sarah was far older than you."

"How can one compare oneself to Sarah? Far better you divorce me and marry another."

He interrupted her, stopping her mouth with his hand. "Were I sure that I could sire the twelve tribes of Israel with another, I still would not leave you. I cannot even imagine myself with another woman. You are the jewel of my crown."

"And what if I were to die?" she asked.

"God forbid! I would simply perish from sorrow. They would bury us both on the same day."

"Don't speak blasphemy. May you outlive my bones. You are a man. You would find somebody else. But what would I do without you?"

He wanted to answer her, but she sealed his lips with a kiss. He went to her then. He loved her body. Each time she gave herself to him, the wonder of it astonished him anew. How was it possible, he would think, that he, Shmul-Leibele, should have such a treasure all to himself? He knew the law, one dared not surrender to lust for pleasure. But somewhere in a sacred book he had read that it was permissible to kiss and embrace a wife to whom one had been wed according to the laws of Moses and Israel, and he now caressed her face, her throat and her breasts. She warned him that this was frivolity. He replied, "So I'll lie on the torture rack. The great saints also loved their wives." Nevertheless, he promised himself to attend to ritual bath the following morning, to intone psalms and to pledge a sum to charity. Since she loved him also and enjoyed his caresses, she let him do his will.

After he had satiated his desire, he wanted to return to his own bed, but a heavy sleepiness came over him. He felt a pain in his temples. Shoshe's head ached as well. She suddenly said, "I'm afraid something is burning in the oven. Maybe I should open the flue?"

"Go on, you're imagining it," he replied. "It'll become too cold in here."

And so complete was his weariness that he fell asleep, as did she.

That night Shmul-Leibele suffered an eerie dream. He imagined that he had passed away. The Burial-Society brethren came by, picked him up, lit candles by his head, opened the windows, intoned the prayer to justify God's ordainment. Afterwards, they washed him on the ablution board, carried him on a stretcher to the cemetery. There they buried him as the gravedigger said Kaddish over his body.

"That's odd," he thought, "I hear nothing of Shoshe lamenting or begging forgiveness. Is it possible that she would so quickly grow unfaithful? Or has she, God forbid, been overcome by grief?"

He wanted to call her name, but he was unable to. He tried to tear free of the grave, but his limbs were powerless. All of a sudden he awoke.

"What a horrible nightmare!" he thought. "I hope I come out of it all right."

At that moment Shoshe also awoke. When he related his dream to her, she did not speak for a while. Then she said, "Woe is me. I had the very same dream."

"Really? You too?" asked Shmul-Leibele, now frightened. "This I don't like."

He tried to sit up, but he could not. It was as if he had been shorn of all his strength. He looked towards the window to see if it were day already, but there was no window visible, nor any windowpane. Darkness loomed everywhere. He cocked his ears. Usually he would be able to hear the chirping of a cricket, the scurrying of a mouse, but this time only a dead silence prevailed. He wanted to reach out to Shoshe, but his hand seemed lifeless.

"Shoshe," he said quietly. "I've grown paralyzed."

"Woe is me, so have I," she said. "I cannot move a limb."

They lay there for a long while, silently, feeling their numbness. Then Shoshe spoke: "I fear that we are already in our graves for good."

"I'm afraid you're right," Shmul-Leibele replied in a voice that was not of the living.

"Pity me, when did it happen? How?" Shoshe asked. "After all, we went to sleep hale and hearty."

"We must have been asphyxiated by the fumes from the stove," Shmul-Leibele said.

"But I said I wanted to open the flue."

"Well, it's too late for that now."

"God have mercy upon us, what do we do now? We were still young people. . . ."

"It's no use. Apparently it was fated."

"Why? We arranged a proper Sabbath. I prepared such a tasty meal. An entire chicken neck and tripe."

"We have no further need of food."

Shoshe did not immediately reply. She was trying to sense her own entrails. No, she felt no appetite. Not even for a chicken neck and tripe. She wanted to weep, but she could not.

"Shmul-Leibele, they've buried us already. It's all over."

"Yes, Shoshe, praised be the true Judge! We are in God's hands."

"Will you be able to recite the passage attributed to your name before the Angel Dumah?"

"Yes."

"It's good that we are lying side by side," she muttered.

"Yes, Shoshe," he said, recalling a verse: *Lovely and pleasant in their lives, and in their death they were not divided.*

"And what will become of our hut? You did not even leave a will."

"It will undoubtedly go to your sister."

Shoshe wished to ask something else, but she was ashamed. She was curious about the Sabbath meal. Had it been removed from the oven? Who had eaten it? But she felt that such a query would not be fitting of a corpse. She was no longer Shoshe the dough-kneader, but a pure, shrouded corpse with shards covering her eyes, a cowl over her head and myrtle twigs between her fingers. The Angel Dumah would appear at any moment with his fiery staff, and she would have to be ready to give an account of herself.

Yes, the brief years of turmoil and temptation had come to an end. Shmul-Leibele and Shoshe had reached the true world. Man and wife grew silent. In the stillness they heard the flapping of wings, a quiet singing. An angel of God had come to guide Shmul-Leibele the tailor and his wife, Shoshe, into Paradise.

ISAK DINESEN

✳ *Babette's Feast*

I. *TWO LADIES OF BERLEVAAG*

In Norway there is a fjord—a long narrow arm of the sea between tall mountains—named Berlevaag Fjord. At the foot of the mountains the small town of Berlevaag looks like a child's toy-town of little wooden pieces painted gray, yellow, pink and many other colors.

Sixty-five years ago two elderly ladies lived in one of the yellow houses. Other ladies at that time wore a bustle, and the two sisters might have worn it as gracefully as any of them, for they were tall and willowy. But they had never possessed any article of fashion; they had dressed demurely in gray or black all their lives. They were christened Martine and Philippa, after Martin Luther and his friend Philip Melanchton. Their father had been a Dean and a prophet, the founder of a pious ecclesiastic party or sect, which was known and looked up to in all the country of Norway. Its members renounced the pleasures of this world, for the earth and all that it held to them was but a kind of illusion, and the true reality was the New Jerusalem toward which they were longing. They swore not at all, but their communication was yea yea and nay nay, and they called one another Brother and Sister.

The Dean had married late in life and by now had long been dead. His disciples were becoming fewer in number every year, whiter or balder and harder of hearing; they were even becoming somewhat querulous and quarrelsome, so that sad little schisms would arise in the congregation. But they still gathered together to read and interpret the Word. They had all known the Dean's daughters as little girls; to them they were even now very small sisters, precious for their dear father's sake. In the yellow house they felt that their Master's spirit was with them; here they were at home and at peace.

These two ladies had a French maid-of-all-work, Babette.

It was a strange thing for a couple of Puritan women in a small Norwegian town; it might even seem to call for an explanation. The people of Berlevaag found the explanation in the sisters' piety and kindness of heart. For the old Dean's daughters spent their time and their small income in works of charity; no sorrowful or distressed creature knocked on their door in vain. And Babette had come to that door twelve years ago as a friendless fugitive, almost mad with grief and fear.

But the true reason for Babette's presence in the two sisters' house was to be found further back in time and deeper down in the domain of human hearts.

II. *MARTINE'S LOVER*

As young girls, Martine and Philippa had been extraordinarily pretty, with the almost supernatural fairness of flowering fruit trees or perpetual snow. They were never to be seen at balls or parties, but people turned when they passed in the streets, and the young men of Berlevaag went to church to watch them walk up the aisle. The younger sister also had a lovely voice, which on Sundays filled the church with sweetness. To the Dean's congregation earthly love, and marriage with it, were trivial matters, in themselves nothing but illusions; still it is possible that more than one of the elderly Brothers had been prizing the maidens far above rubies and had suggested as much to their father. But the Dean had declared that to him in his calling his daughters were his right and left hand. Who could want to bereave him of them? And the fair girls had been brought up to an ideal of heavenly love; they were all filled with it and did not let themselves be touched by the flames of this world.

All the same they had upset the peace of heart of two gentlemen from the great world outside Berlevaag.

There was a young officer named Lorens Loewenhielm, who had led a gay life in his garrison town and had run into debt. In the year of 1854, when Martine was eighteen and Philippa seventeen, his angry father sent him on a month's visit to his aunt in her old country house of Fossum near Berlevaag, where he would have time to meditate and to better his ways. One day he rode into town and met Martine in the marketplace. He looked down at the pretty girl, and she looked up at the fine horseman. When she had passed him and disappeared he was not certain whether he was to believe his own eyes.

In the Loewenhielm family there existed a legend to the effect that long ago a gentleman of the name had married a Huldre, a female mountain spirit of Norway, who is so fair that the air round her shines and quivers. Since then, from time to time, members of the family had been second-sighted. Young Lorens till now had not been aware of any particular spiritual gift in his own nature. But at this one moment there rose before his eyes a sudden, mighty vision of a higher and purer life, with no creditors, dunning letters or parental lectures, with no secret, unpleasant pangs of conscience and with a gentle, golden-haired angel to guide and reward him.

Through his pious aunt he got admission to the Dean's house, and saw that Martine was even lovelier without a bonnet. He followed her slim figure with adoring eyes, but he loathed and despised the figure which he himself cut in her nearness. He was amazed and shocked by the fact that he could find nothing at all to say, and no inspiration in the glass of water before him. "Mercy and Truth, dear brethren, have met together," said the Dean. "Righteousness and Bliss have kissed one another." And the young man's thoughts were with the moment when Lorens and Martine should be kissing each other. He repeated his visit time after time, and each time seemed to himself to grow smaller and more insignificant and contemptible.

When in the evening he came back to his aunt's house he kicked his shining riding-boots to the corners of his room; he even laid his head on the table and wept.

On the last day of his stay he made a last attempt to communicate his feelings to Martine. Till now it had been easy for him to tell a pretty girl that he loved her, but the tender words stuck in his throat as he looked into this maiden's face. When he had said good-bye to the party, Martine saw him to the door with a candlestick in her hand. The light shone on her mouth and threw upwards the shadows of her long eyelashes. He was about to leave in dumb despair when on the threshold he suddenly seized her hand and pressed it to his lips.

"I am going away forever!" he cried. "I shall never, never see you again! For I have learned here that Fate is hard, and that in this world there are things which are impossible!"

When he was once more back in his garrison town he thought his adventure over, and found that he did not like to think of it at all. While the other young officers talked of their love affairs, he was silent on his. For seen from the officers' mess, and so to say with its eyes, it was a pitiful business. How had it come to pass that a lieutenant of the hussars had let himself be defeated and frustrated by a set of long-faced sectarians, in the bare-floored rooms of an old Dean's house?

Then he became afraid; panic fell upon him. Was it the family madness which made him still carry with him the dream-like picture of a maiden so fair that she made the air round her shine with purity and holiness? He did not want to be a dreamer; he wanted to be like his brother-officers.

So he pulled himself together, and in the greatest effort of his young life made up his mind to forget what had happened to him in Berlevaag. From now on, he resolved, he would look forward, not back. He would concentrate on his career, and the day was to come when he would cut a brilliant figure in a brilliant world.

His mother was pleased with the result of his visit to Fossum, and in her letters expressed her gratitude to his aunt. She did not know by what queer, winding roads her son had reached his happy moral standpoint.

The ambitious young officer soon caught the attention of his superiors and made unusually quick advancement. He was sent to France and to Russia, and on his return he married a lady-in-waiting to Queen Sophia. In these high circles he moved with grace and ease, pleased with his surroundings and with himself. He even in the course of time benefited from words and turns which had stuck in his mind from the Dean's house, for piety was now in fashion at Court.

In the yellow house of Berlevaag, Philippa sometimes turned the talk to the handsome, silent young man who had so suddenly made his appearance, and so suddenly disappeared again. Her elder sister would then answer her gently, with a still, clear face, and find other things to discuss.

III. PHILIPPA'S LOVER

A year later a more distinguished person even than Lieutenant Loewenhielm came to Berlevaag.

The great singer Achille Papin of Paris had sung for a week at the Royal Opera of Stockholm, and had carried away his audience there as everywhere. One evening a lady of the Court, who had been dreaming of a romance with the artist, had described to him the wild, grandiose scenery of Norway. His own romantic nature was stirred by the narration, and he had laid his way back to France round the Norwegian coast. But he felt small in the sublime surroundings; with nobody to talk to he fell into that melancholy in which he saw himself as an old man, at the end of his career, till on a Sunday, when he could think of nothing else to do, he went to church and heard Philippa sing.

Then in one single moment he knew and understood all. For here were the snowy summits, the wild flowers and the white Nordic nights, translated into his own language of music, and brought him in a young woman's voice. Like Lorens Loewenhielm he had a vision.

"Almighty God," he thought, "Thy power is without end, and Thy mercy reacheth unto the clouds! And here is a prima donna of the opera who will lay Paris at her feet."

Achille Papin at this time was a handsome man of forty, with curly black hair and a red mouth. The idolization of nations had not spoilt him; he was a kind-hearted person and honest toward himself.

He went straight to the yellow house, gave his name—which told the Dean nothing—and explained that he was staying in Berlevaag for his health, and the while would be happy to take on the young lady as a pupil.

He did not mention the Opera of Paris, but described at length how beautifully Miss Philippa would come to sing in church, to the glory of God.

For a moment he forgot himself, for when the Dean asked whether he was a Roman Catholic he answered according to truth, and the old clergyman, who had never seen a live Roman Catholic, grew a little pale. All the same the Dean was pleased to speak French, which reminded him of his young days when he had studied the works of the great French Lutheran writer, Lefèvre d'Etaples. And as nobody could long withstand Achille Papin when he had really set his heart on a matter, in the end the father gave his consent, and remarked to his daughter: "God's paths run across the sea and the snowy mountains, where man's eye sees no track."

So the great French singer and the young Norwegian novice set to work together. Achille's expectation grew into certainty and his certainty into ecstasy. He thought: "I have been wrong in believing that I was growing old. My greatest triumphs are before me! The world will once more believe in miracles when she and I sing together!"

After a while he could not keep his dreams to himself, but told Philippa about them.

She would, he said, rise like a star above any diva of the past or present. The Emperor and Empress, the Princes, great ladies and *bels esprits* of Paris would listen to her, and shed tears. The common people too would worship her, and she would bring consolation and strength to the wronged and oppressed. When she left the Grand Opera upon her master's arm, the crowd would unharness her horses, and themselves draw her to the Café Anglais, where a magnificent supper awaited her.

Philippa did not repeat these prospects to her father or her sister, and this was the first time in her life that she had had a secret from them.

The teacher now gave his pupil the part of Zerlina in Mozart's opera *Don Giovanni* to study. He himself, as often before, sang Don Giovanni's part.

He had never in his life sung as now. In the duet of the second act—which is called the seduction duet—he was swept off his feet by the heavenly music and the heavenly voices. As the last melting note died away he seized Philippa's hands, drew her toward him and kissed her solemnly, as a bridegroom might kiss his bride before the altar. Then he let her go. For the moment was too sublime for any further word or movement; Mozart himself was looking down on the two.

Philippa went home, told her father that she did not want any more singing lessons and asked him to write and tell Monsieur Papin so.

The Dean said: "And God's paths run across the rivers, my child."

When Achille got the Dean's letter he sat immovable for an hour. He thought: "I have been wrong. My day is over. Never again shall I be the divine Papin. And this poor weedy garden of the world has lost its nightingale!"

A little later he thought: "I wonder what is the matter with that hussy? Did I kiss her, by any chance?"

In the end he thought: "I have lost my life for a kiss, and I have no remembrance at all of the kiss! Don Giovanni kissed Zerlina, and Achille Papin pays for it! Such is the fate of the artist!"

In the Dean's house Martine felt that the matter was deeper than it looked, and searched her sister's face. For a moment, slightly trembling, she too imagined that the Roman Catholic gentleman might have tried to kiss Philippa. She did not imagine that her sister might have been surprised and frightened by something in her own nature.

Achille Papin took the first boat from Berlevaag.

Of this visitor from the great world the sisters spoke but little; they lacked the words with which to discuss him.

IV. A LETTER FROM PARIS

Fifteen years later, on a rainy June night of 1871, the bell-rope of the yellow house was pulled violently three times. The mistresses of the house opened the door to a massive, dark, deadly pale woman with a bundle on her arm, who stared at them, took a step forward and fell down on the doorstep in a dead swoon. When the frightened ladies had restored her to life she sat up, gave them one more glance from her sunken eyes and, all the time without a word, fumbled in her wet clothes and brought out a letter which she handed to them.

The letter was addressed to them all right, but it was written in French. The sisters put their heads together and read it. It ran as follows:

Ladies!
Do you remember me? Ah, when I think of you I have the heart filled with wild lilies-of-the-valley! Will the memory of a Frenchman's devotion bend your hearts to save the life of a Frenchwoman?

The bearer of this letter, Madame Babette Hersant, like my beautiful Empress herself, has had to flee from Paris. Civil war has raged in our streets. French hands have shed French blood. The noble Communards, standing up for the Rights of Man, have been crushed and annihilated. Madame Hersant's husband and son, both eminent ladies' hairdressers, have been shot. She herself was arrested as a Pétroleuse—(which word is used here for women who set fire to houses with petroleum)—and has narrowly escaped the blood-stained hands of General Galliffet. She has lost all she possessed and dares not remain in France.

A nephew of hers is cook to the boat *Anna Colbioernsson*, bound for Christiania—(as I believe, the capital of Norway)—and he has obtained shipping opportunity for his aunt. This is now her last sad resort!

Knowing that I was once a visitor to your magnificent country she comes to me, asks me if there be any good people in Norway and begs me, if it be so, to supply her with a letter to them. The two words of 'good people' immediately bring before my eyes your picture, sacred to my heart. I send her to you. How she is to get from Christiania to Berlevaag I know not, having forgotten the map of Norway. But she is a Frenchwoman, and you will find that in her misery she has still got resourcefulness, majesty and true stoicism.

I envy her in her despair: she is to see your faces.

As you receive her mercifully, send a merciful thought back to France.

For fifteen years, Miss Philippa, I have grieved that your

voice should never fill the Grand Opera of Paris. When
tonight I think of you, no doubt surrounded by a gay and
loving family, and of myself: gray, lonely, forgotten by those
who once applauded and adored me, I feel that you may have
chosen the better part in life. What is fame? What is glory?
The grave awaits us all!

And yet, my lost Zerlina, and yet, soprano of the snow!
As I write this I feel that the grave is not the end. In Paradise I
shall hear your voice again. There you will sing, without fears
or scruples, as God meant you to sing. There you will be the
great artist that God meant you to be. Ah! how you will
enchant the angels.

Babette can cook.

Deign to receive, my ladies, the humble homage of the
friend who was once

Achille Papin

At the bottom of the page, as a P.S., were neatly printed the first two
bars of the duet between Don Giovanni and Zerlina, like this:

The two sisters till now had kept only a small servant of fifteen to help
them in the house and they felt that they could not possibly afford to take
on an elderly, experienced housekeeper. But Babette told them that she
would serve Monsieur Papin's good people for nothing, and that she would
take service with nobody else. If they sent her away she must die. Babette
remained in the house of the Dean's daughters for twelve years, until the
time of this tale.

V. STILL LIFE

Babette had arrived haggard and wild-eyed like a hunted animal, but in
her new, friendly surroundings she soon acquired all the appearance of a
respectable and trusted servant. She had appeared to be a beggar; she turned
out to be a conqueror. Her quiet countenance and her steady, deep glance
had magnetic qualities; under her eyes things moved, noiselessly, into their
proper places.

Her mistresses at first had trembled a little, just as the Dean had once done, at the idea of receiving a Papist under their roof. But they did not like to worry a hard-tried fellow-creature with catechization; neither were they quite sure of their French. They silently agreed that the example of a good Lutheran life would be the best means of converting their servant. In this way Babette's presence in the house became, so to say, a moral spur to its inhabitants.

They had distrusted Monsieur Papin's assertion that Babette could cook. In France, they knew, people ate frogs. They showed Babette how to prepare a split cod and an ale-and-bread-soup; during the demonstration the Frenchwoman's face became absolutely expressionless. But within a week Babette cooked a split cod and an ale-and-bread-soup as well as anybody born and bred in Berlevaag.

The idea of French luxury and extravagance next had alarmed and dismayed the Dean's daughters. The first day after Babette had entered their service they took her before them and explained to her that they were poor and that to them luxurious fare was sinful. Their own food must be as plain as possible; it was the soup-pails and baskets for their poor that signified. Babette nodded her head; as a girl, she informed her ladies, she had been cook to an old priest who was a saint. Upon this the sisters resolved to surpass the French priest in asceticism. And they soon found that from the day when Babette took over the housekeeping its cost was miraculously reduced, and the soup-pails and baskets acquired a new, mysterious power to stimulate and strengthen their poor and sick.

The world outside the yellow house also came to acknowledge Babette's excellence. The refugee never learned to speak the language of her new country, but in her broken Norwegian she beat down the prices of Berlevaag's flintiest tradesmen. She was held in awe on the quay and in the marketplace.

The old Brothers and Sisters, who had first looked askance at the foreign woman in their midst, felt a happy change in their little sisters' life, rejoiced at it and benefited by it. They found that troubles and cares had been conjured away from their existence, and that now they had money to give away, time for the confidences and complaints of their old friends and peace for meditating on heavenly matters. In the course of time not a few of the brotherhood included Babette's name in their prayers, and thanked God for the speechless stranger, the dark Martha in the house of their two fair Marys. The stone which the builders had almost refused had become the headstone of the corner.

The ladies of the yellow house were the only ones to know that their cornerstone had a mysterious and alarming feature to it, as if it was somehow related to the Black Stone of Mecca, the Kaaba itself.

Hardly ever did Babette refer to her past life. When in early days the sisters had gently condoled her upon her losses, they had been met with that majesty and stoicism of which Monsieur Papin had written. "What will you ladies?" she had answered, shrugging her shoulders. "It is Fate."

But one day she suddenly informed them that she had for many years held a ticket in a French lottery, and that a faithful friend in Paris was still renewing it for her every year. Some time she might win the *grand prix* of ten thousand francs. At that they felt that their cook's old carpetbag was made from a magic carpet; at a given moment she might mount it and be carried off, back to Paris.

And it happened when Martine or Philippa spoke to Babette that they would get no answer, and would wonder if she had even heard what they said. They would find her in the kitchen, her elbows on the table and her temples on her hands, lost in the study of a heavy black book which they secretly suspected to be a popish prayer-book. Or she would sit immovable on the three-legged kitchen chair, her strong hands in her lap and her dark eyes wide open, as enigmatical and fatal as a Pythia upon her tripod. At such moments they realized that Babette was deep, and that in the soundings of her being there were passions, there were memories and longings of which they knew nothing at all.

A little cold shiver ran through them, and in their hearts they thought: "Perhaps after all she had indeed been a Pétroleuse."

VI. BABETTE'S GOOD LUCK

The fifteenth of December was the Dean's hundredth anniversary.

His daughters had long been looking forward to this day and had wished to celebrate it, as if their dear father were still among his disciples. Therefore it had been to them a sad and incomprehensible thing that in this last year discord and dissension had been raising their heads in his flock. They had endeavored to make peace, but they were aware that they had failed. It was as if the fine and lovable vigor of their father's personality had been evaporating, the way Hoffmann's anodyne will evaporate when left on the shelf in a bottle without a cork. And his departure had left the door ajar to things hitherto unknown to the two sisters, much younger than his spiritual children. From a past half a century back, when the unshepherded sheep had been running astray in the mountains, uninvited dismal guests pressed through the opening on the heels of the worshippers and seemed to darken the little rooms and to let in the cold. The sins of old Brothers and Sisters came, with late piercing repentance like a toothache, and the sins of

155

others against them came back with bitter resentment, like a poisoning of the blood.

There were in the congregation two old women who before their conversion had spread slander upon each other, and thereby to each other ruined a marriage and an inheritance. Today they could not remember happenings of yesterday or a week ago, but they remembered this forty-year-old wrong and kept going through the ancient accounts; they scowled at each other. There was an old Brother who suddenly called to mind how another Brother, forty-five years ago, had cheated him in a deal; he could have wished to dismiss the matter from his mind, but it stuck there like a deep-seated, festering splinter. There was a gray, honest skipper and a furrowed, pious widow, who in their young days, while she was the wife of another man, had been sweethearts. Of late each had begun to grieve, while shifting the burden of guilt from his own shoulders to those of the other and back again, and to worry about the possible terrible consequences, through all eternity, to himself, brought upon him by one who had pretended to hold him dear. They grew pale at the meetings in the yellow house and avoided each other's eyes.

As the birthday drew nearer, Martine and Philippa felt the responsibility growing heavier. Would their ever-faithful father look down to his daughters and call them by name as unjust stewards? Between them they talked matters over and repeated their father's saying: that God's paths were running even across the salt sea, and the snow-clad mountains, where man's eye sees no track.

One day of this summer the post brought a letter from France to Madame Babette Hersant. This in itself was a surprising thing, for during these twelve years Babette had received no letter. What, her mistresses wondered, could it contain? They took it into the kitchen to watch her open and read it. Babette opened it, read it, lifted her eyes from it to her ladies' faces and told them that her number in the French lottery had come out. She had won ten thousand francs.

The news made such an impression on the two sisters that for a full minute they could not speak a word. They themselves were used to receiving their modest pension in small instalmènts; it was difficult to them even to imagine the sum of ten thousand francs in a pile. Then they pressed Babette's hand, their own hands trembling a little. They had never before pressed the hand of a person who the moment before had come into possession of ten thousand francs.

After a while they realized that the happenings concerned themselves as well as Babette. The country of France, they felt, was slowly rising before their servant's horizon, and correspondingly their own existence was sinking beneath their feet. The ten thousand francs which made her rich—how poor did they not make the house she had served! One by one old forgotten cares and worries began to peep out at them from the four corners of the kitchen. The congratulations died on their lips, and the two pious women were ashamed of their own silence.

During the following days they announced the news to their friends with joyous faces, but it did them good to see these friends' faces grow sad as they listened to them. Nobody, it was felt in the Brotherhood, could really blame Babette: birds will return to their nests and human beings to the country of their birth. But did that good and faithful servant realize that in going away from Berlevaag she would be leaving many old and poor people in distress? Their little sisters would have no more time for the sick and sorrowful. Indeed, indeed, lotteries were ungodly affairs.

In due time the money arrived through offices in Christiania and Berlevaag. The two ladies helped Babette to count it, and gave her a box to keep it in. They handled, and became familiar with, the ominous bits of paper.

They dared not question Babette upon the date of her departure. Dared they hope that she would remain with them over the fifteenth of December?

The mistresses had never been quite certain how much of their private conversation the cook followed or understood. So they were surprised when on a September evening Babette came into the drawing room, more humble or subdued than they had ever seen her, to ask a favor. She begged them, she said, to let her cook a celebration dinner on the Dean's birthday.

The ladies had not intended to have any dinner at all. A very plain supper with a cup of coffee was the most sumptuous meal to which they had ever asked any guest to sit down. But Babette's dark eyes were as eager and pleading as a dog's; they agreed to let her have her way. At this the cook's face lighted up.

But she had more to say. She wanted, she said, to cook a French dinner, a real French dinner, for this one time. Martine and Philippa looked at each other. They did not like the idea; they felt that they did not know what it might imply. But the very strangeness of the request disarmed them. They had no arguments wherewith to meet the proposition of cooking a real French dinner.

Babette drew a long sigh of happiness, but still she did not move. She had one more prayer to make. She begged that her mistresses would allow her to pay for the French dinner with her own money.

"No, Babette!" the ladies exclaimed. How could she imagine such a thing? Did she believe that they would allow her to spend her precious money on food and drink—or on them? No, Babette, indeed.

Babette took a step forward. There was something formidable in the move, like a wave rising. Had she stepped forth like this, in 1871, to plant a red flag on a barricade? She spoke, in her queer Norwegian, with classical French eloquence. Her voice was like a song.

Ladies! Had she ever, during twelve years, asked you a favor? No! And why not? Ladies, you who say your prayers every day, can you imagine what it means to a human heart to have no prayer to make? What would Babette have had to pray for? Nothing! Tonight she had a prayer to make, from the bottom of her heart. Do you not then feel tonight, my ladies, that it becomes you to grant it her, with such joy as that with which the good God has granted you your own?

The ladies for a while said nothing. Babette was right; it was her first request these twelve years; very likely it would be her last. They thought the matter over. After all, they told themselves, their cook was now better off than they, and a dinner could make no difference to a person who owned ten thousand francs.

Their consent in the end completely changed Babette. They saw that as a young woman she had been beautiful. And they wondered whether in this hour they themselves had not, for the very first time, become to her the "good people" of Achille Papin's letter.

VII. *THE TURTLE*

In November Babette went for a journey.

She had preparations to make, she told her mistresses, and would need a leave of a week or ten days. Her nephew, who had once got her to Christiania, was still sailing to that town; she must see him and talk things over with him. Babette was a bad sailor; she had spoken of her one sea-voyage, from France to Norway, as of the most horrible experience of her life. Now she was strangely collected; the ladies felt that her heart was already in France.

After ten days she came back to Berlevaag.

Had she got things arranged as she wished? the ladies asked. Yes, she answered, she had seen her nephew and given him a list of the goods which he was to bring her from France. To Martine and Philippa this was a dark saying, but they did not care to talk of her departure, so they asked her no more questions.

Babette was somewhat nervous during the next weeks. But one December day she triumphantly announced to her mistresses that the goods had come to Christiania, had been transshipped there, and on this very day had arrived at Berlevaag. She had, she added, engaged an old man with a wheel-barrow to have them conveyed from the harbor to the house.

But what goods, Babette? the ladies asked. Why, Mesdames, Babette replied, the ingredients for the birthday dinner. Praise be to God, they had all arrived in good condition from Paris.

By this time Babette, like the bottled demon of the fairy tale, had swelled and grown to such dimensions that her mistresses felt small before her. They now saw the French dinner coming upon them, a thing of incalculable nature and range. But they had never in their life broken a promise; they gave themselves into their cook's hands.

All the same when Martine saw a barrow load of bottles wheeled into the kitchen, she stood still. She touched the bottles and lifted up one. "What is there in this bottle, Babette?" she asked in a low voice. "Not wine?" "Wine, Madame!" Babette answered. "No, Madame. It is a Clos Vougeot 1846!" After a moment she added: "From Philippe, in Rue Montorgueil!" Martine had never suspected that wines could have names to them, and was put to silence.

Late in the evening she opened the door to a ring, and was once more faced with the wheelbarrow, this time with a red-haired sailor-boy behind it, as if the old man had by this time been worn out. The youth grinned at her as he lifted a big, undefinable object from the barrow. In the light of the lamp it looked like some greenish-black stone, but when set down on the kitchen floor it suddenly shot out a snake-like head and moved it slightly from side to side. Martine had seen pictures of tortoises, and had even as a child owned a pet tortoise, but this thing was monstrous in size and terrible to behold. She backed out of the kitchen without a word.

She dared not tell her sister what she had seen. She passed an almost sleepless night; she thought of her father and felt that on his very birthday she and her sister were lending his house to a witches' sabbath. When at last she fell asleep she had a terrible dream, in which she saw Babette poisoning the old Brothers and Sisters, Philippa and herself.

Early in the morning she got up, put on her gray cloak and went out in the dark street. She walked from house to house, opened her heart to her Brothers and Sisters, and confessed her guilt. She and Philippa, she said, had meant no harm; they had granted their servant a prayer and had not foreseen what might come of it. Now she could not tell what, on her father's birthday, her guests would be given to eat or drink. She did not actually mention the turtle, but it was present in her face and voice.

The old people, as has already been told, had all known Martine and Philippa as little girls; they had seen them cry bitterly over a broken doll.

Martine's tears brought tears into their own eyes. They gathered in the afternoon and talked the problem over.

Before they again parted they promised one another that for their little sisters' sake they would, on the great day, be silent upon all matters of food and drink. Nothing that might be set before them, be it even frogs or snails, should wring a word from their lips.

"Even so," said a white-bearded Brother, "the tongue is a little member and boasteth great things. The tongue can no man tame; it is an unruly evil, full of deadly poison. On the day of our master we will cleanse our tongues of all taste and purify them of all delight or disgust of the senses, keeping and preserving them for the higher things of praise and thanksgiving."

So few things ever happened in the quiet existence of the Berlevaag brotherhood that they were at this moment deeply moved and elevated. They shook hands on their vow, and it was to them as if they were doing so before the face of their Master.

VIII. *THE HYMN*

On Sunday morning it began to snow. The white flakes fell fast and thick; the small windowpanes of the yellow house became pasted with snow.

Early in the day a groom from Fossum brought the two sisters a note. Old Mrs. Loewenhielm still resided in her country house. She was now ninety years old and stone-deaf, and she had lost all sense of smell or taste. But she had been one of the Dean's first supporters, and neither her infirmity nor the sledge journey would keep her from doing honor to his memory. Now, she wrote, her nephew, General Lorens Loewenhielm, had unexpectedly come on a visit; he had spoken with deep veneration of the Dean, and she begged permission to bring him with her. It would do him good, for the dear boy seemed to be in somewhat low spirits.

Martine and Philippa at this remembered the young officer and his visits; it relieved their present anxiety to talk of old happy days. They wrote back that General Loewenhielm would be welcome. They also called in Babette to inform her that they would now be twelve for dinner; they added that their latest guest had lived in Paris for several years. Babette seemed pleased with the news, and assured them that there would be food enough.

The hostesses made their little preparations in the sitting room. They dared not set foot in the kitchen, for Babette had mysteriously nosed out a cook's mate from a ship in the harbor—the same boy, Martine realized, who had brought in the turtle—to assist her in the kitchen and to wait at table, and now the dark woman and the red-haired boy, like some witch with her familiar spirit, had taken possession of these regions. The ladies could not tell what fires had been burning or what cauldrons bubbling there from before daybreak.

Table linen and plate had been magically mangled and polished, glasses and decanters brought, Babette only knew from where. The Dean's house did not possess twelve dining-room chairs, the long horsehair-covered sofa had been moved from the parlor to the dining room, and the parlor, ever sparsely furnished, now looked strangely bare and big without it.

Martine and Philippa did their best to embellish the domain left to them. Whatever troubles might be in wait for their guests, in any case they should not be cold; all day the sisters fed the towering old stove with birch-knots. They hung a garland of juniper round their father's portrait on the wall, and placed candlesticks on their mother's small working table beneath it; they burned juniper-twigs to make the room smell nice. The while they wondered if in this weather the sledge from Fossum would get through. In the end they put on their old black best frocks and their confirmation gold crosses. They sat down, folded their hands in their laps and committed themselves unto God.

The old Brothers and Sisters arrived in small groups and entered the room slowly and solemnly.

This low room with its bare floor and scanty furniture was dear to the Dean's disciples. Outside its windows lay the great world. Seen from in here the great world in its winter-whiteness was ever prettily bordered in pink, blue and red by the row of hyacinths on the window-sills. And in summer, when the windows were open, the great world had a softly moving frame of white muslin curtains to it.

Tonight the guests were met on the doorstep with warmth and sweet smell, and they were looking into the face of their beloved Master, wreathed with evergreen. Their hearts like their numb fingers thawed.

One very old Brother, after a few moments' silence, in his trembling voice struck up one of the Master's own hymns:

> *"Jerusalem, my happy home*
> *name ever dear to me . . ."*

One by one the other voices fell in, thin quivering women's voices, ancient seafaring Brothers' deep growls, and above them all Philippa's clear soprano, a little worn with age but still angelic. Unwittingly the choir had seized one another's hands. They sang the hymn to the end, but could not bear to cease and joined in another:

> *"Take not thought for food or raiment*
> *careful one, so anxiously . . ."*

The mistresses of the house somewhat reassured by it, the words of the third verse:

> *"Wouldst thou give a stone, a reptile*
> *to thy pleading child for food? . . ."*

went straight to Martine's heart and inspired her with hope.

In the middle of this hymn sledge bells were heard outside; the guests from Fossum had arrived.

Martine and Philippa went to receive them and saw them into the parlor. Mrs. Loewenhielm with age had become quite small, her face colorless like parchment, and very still. By her side General Loewenhielm, tall, broad and ruddy, in his bright uniform, his breast covered with decorations, strutted and shone like an ornamental bird, a golden pheasant or a peacock, in this sedate party of black crows and jackdaws.

IX. GENERAL LOEWENHIELM

General Loewenhielm had been driving from Fossum to Berlevaag in a strange mood. He had not visited this part of the country for thirty years. He had come now to get a rest from his busy life at Court, and he had found no rest. The old house of Fossum was peaceful enough and seemed somehow pathetically small after the Tuileries and the Winter Palace. But it held one disquieting figure: young Lieutenant Loewenhielm walked in its rooms.

General Loewenhielm saw the handsome, slim figure pass close by him. And as he passed, the boy gave the elder man a short glance and a smile, the haughty, arrogant smile which youth gives to age. The General might have smiled back, kindly and a little sadly, as age smiles at youth, if it had not been that he was really in no mood to smile; he was, as his aunt had written, in low spirits.

General Loewenhielm had obtained everything that he had striven for in life and was admired and envied by everyone. Only he himself knew of a queer fact, which jarred with his prosperous existence: that he was not perfectly happy. Something was wrong somewhere, and he carefully felt his mental self all over, as one feels a finger over to determine the place of a deep-seated, invisible thorn.

He was in high favor with royalty, he had done well in his calling, he had friends everywhere. The thorn sat in none of these places.

His wife was a brilliant woman and still good-looking. Perhaps she neglected her own house a little for her visits and parties; she changed her servants every three months and the General's meals at home were served unpunctually. The General, who valued good food highly in life, here felt a slight bitterness against the lady, and secretly blamed her for the indigestion from which he sometimes suffered. Still the thorn was not here either.

Nay, but an absurd thing had lately been happening to General Loewenhielm: he would find himself worrying about his immortal soul. Did he have any reason for doing so? He was a moral person, loyal to his king, his wife and his friends, an example to everybody. But there were moments when it seemed to him that the world was not a moral, but a mystic, concern. He looked into the mirror, examined the row of decorations on his breast and sighed to himself: "Vanity, vanity, all is vanity!"

The strange meeting at Fossum had compelled him to make out the balance-sheet of his life.

Young Lorens Loewenhielm had attracted dreams and fancies as a flower attracts bees and butterflies. He had fought to free himself of them; he had fled and they had followed. He had been scared of the Huldre of the family legend and had declined her invitation to come into the mountain; he had firmly refused the gift of second sight.

The elderly Lorens Loewenhielm found himself wishing that one little dream would come his way, and a gray moth of dusk look him up before nightfall. He found himself longing for the faculty of second sight, as a blind man will long for the normal faculty of vision.

Can the sum of a row of victories in many years and in many countries be a defeat? General Loewenhielm had fulfilled Lieutenant Loewenhielm's wishes and had more than satisfied his ambitions. It might be held that he had gained the whole world. And it had come to this, that the stately, worldly-wise older man now turned toward the naïve young figure to ask him, gravely, even bitterly, in what he had profited? Somewhere something had been lost.

When Mrs. Loewenhielm had told her nephew of the Dean's anniversary and he had made up his mind to go with her to Berlevaag, his decision had not been an ordinary acceptance of a dinner invitation.

He would, he resolved, tonight make up his account with young Lorens Loewenhielm, who had felt himself to be a shy and sorry figure in the house of the Dean, and who in the end had shaken its dust off his riding boots. He would let the youth prove to him, once and for all, that thirty-one years ago he had made the right choice. The low rooms, the haddock and the glass of water on the table before him should all be called in to bear evidence that in their milieu the existence of Lorens Loewenhielm would very soon have become sheer misery.

He let his mind stray far away. In Paris he had once won a *concours hippique* and had been feted by high French cavalry officers, princes and dukes among them. A dinner had been given in his honor at the finest restaurant of the city. Opposite him at table was a noble lady, a famous beauty whom he had long been courting. In the midst of dinner she had lifted her dark velvet eyes above the rim of her champagne glass and without words had promised to make him happy. In the sledge he now all of a sudden remembered that he had then, for a second, seen Martine's face before him and had rejected it. For a while he listened to the tinkling of the sledge bells, then he smiled a little as he reflected how he would tonight come to dominate the conversation round that same table by which young Lorens Loewenhielm had sat mute.

Large snowflakes fell densely; behind the sledge the tracks were wiped out quickly. General Loewenhielm sat immovable by the side of his aunt, his chin sunk in the high fur collar of his coat.

X. BABETTE'S DINNER

As Babette's red-haired familiar opened the door to the dining room, and the guests slowly crossed the threshold, they let go one another's hands and became silent. But the silence was sweet, for in spirit they still held hands and were still singing.

Babette had set a row of candles down the middle of the table; the small flames shone on the black coats and frocks and on the one scarlet uniform, and were reflected in clear, moist eyes.

General Loewenhielm saw Martine's face in the candlelight as he had seen it when the two parted, thirty years ago. What traces would thirty years of Berlevaag life have left on it? The golden hair was now streaked with silver; the flower-like face had slowly been turned into alabaster. But how serene was the forehead, how quietly trustful the eyes, how pure and sweet the mouth, as if no hasty word had ever passed its lips.

When all were seated, the eldest member of the congregation said grace in the Dean's own words:

> *"May my food my body maintain,*
> *may my body my soul sustain,*

*may my soul in deed and word
give thanks for all things to the Lord."*

At the word of "food" the guests, with their old heads bent over their folded hands, remembered how they had vowed not to utter a word about the subject, and in their hearts they reinforced the vow: they would not even give it a thought! They were sitting down to a meal, well, so had people done at the wedding of Cana. And grace has chosen to manifest itself there, in the very wine, as fully as anywhere.

Babette's boy filled a small glass before each of the party. They lifted it to their lips gravely, in confirmation of their resolution.

General Loewenhielm, somewhat suspicious of his wine, took a sip of it, startled, raised the glass first to his nose and then to his eyes, and sat it down bewildered. "This is very strange!" he thought. "Amontillado! And the finest Amontillado that I have ever tasted." After a moment, in order to test his senses, he took a small spoonful of his soup, took a second spoonful and laid down his spoon. "This is exceedingly strange!" he said to himself. "For surely I am eating turtle-soup—and what turtle-soup!" He was seized by a queer kind of panic and emptied his glass.

Usually in Berlevaag people did not speak much while they were eating. But somehow this evening tongues had been loosened. An old Brother told the story of his first meeting with the Dean. Another went through that sermon which sixty years ago had brought about his conversion. An aged woman, the one to whom Martine had first confided her distress, reminded her friends how in all afflictions any Brother or Sister was ready to share the burden of any other.

General Loewenhielm, who was to dominate the conversation of the dinner table, related how the Dean's collection of sermons was a favorite book of the Queen's. But as a new dish was served he was silenced. "Incredible!" he told himself. "It is Blinis Demidoff!" He looked round at his fellow-diners. They were all quietly eating their Blinis Demidoff, without any sign of either surprise or approval, as if they had been doing so every day for thirty years.

A Sister on the other side of the table opened on the subject of strange happenings which had taken place while the Dean was still amongst his children, and which one might venture to call miracles. Did they remember, she asked, the time when he had promised a Christmas sermon in the village the other side of the fjord? For a fortnight the weather had been so bad that no skipper or fisherman would risk the crossing. The villagers were giving up hope, but the Dean told them that if no boat would take him, he would come to them walking upon the waves. And behold! Three days before Christmas the storm stopped, hard frost set in, and the fjord froze from shore to shore—and this was a thing which had not happened within the memory of man!

The boy once more filled the glasses. This time the Brothers and Sisters knew that what they were given to drink was not wine, for it sparkled. It must be some kind of lemonade. The lemonade agreed with their exalted state of mind and seemed to lift them off the ground, into a higher and purer sphere.

General Loewenhielm again set down his glass, turned to his neighbor on the right and said to him: "But surely this is a Veuve Cliquot 1860?" His neighbor looked at him kindly, smiled at him and made a remark about the weather.

Babette's boy had his instructions; he filled the glasses of the Brotherhood only once, but he refilled the General's glass as soon as it was emptied. The General emptied it quickly time after time. For how is a man of sense to behave when he cannot trust his senses? It is better to be drunk than mad.

Most often the people in Berlevaag during the course of a good meal would come to feel a little heavy. Tonight it was not so. The *convives* grew lighter in weight and lighter of heart the more they ate and drank. They no longer needed to remind themselves of their vow. It was, they realized, when man has not only altogether forgotten but has firmly renounced all ideas of food and drink that he eats and drinks in the right spirit.

General Loewenhielm stopped eating and sat immovable. Once more he was carried back to that dinner in Paris of which he had thought in the sledge. An incredibly recherché and palatable dish had been served there; he had asked its name from his fellow diner, Colonel Galliffet, and the Colonel had smilingly told him that it was named "Cailles en Sarcophage." He had further told him that the dish had been invented by the chef of the very café in which they were dining, a person known all over Paris as the greatest culinary genius of the age, and—most surprisingly—a woman! "And indeed," said Colonel Galliffet, "this woman is now turning a dinner at the Café Anglais into a kind of love affair—into a love affair of the noble and romantic category in which one no longer distinguishes between bodily and spiritual appetite or satiety! I have, before now, fought a duel for the sake of a fair lady. For no woman in all Paris, my young friend, would I more willingly shed my blood!" General Loewenhielm turned to his neighbor on the left and said to him: "But this is Cailles en Sarcophage!" The neighbor, who had been listening to the description of a miracle, looked at him absent-mindedly, then nodded his head and answered: "Yes, Yes, certainly. What else would it be?"

From the Master's miracles the talk round the table had turned to the smaller miracles of kindliness and helpfulness daily performed by his daughters. The old Brother who had first struck up the hymn quoted the Dean's saying: "The only things which we may take with us from our life on earth are those which we have given away!" The guests smiled—what nabobs would not the poor, simple maidens become in the next world!

General Loewenhielm no longer wondered at anything. When a few minutes later he saw grapes, peaches and fresh figs before him, he laughed to his neighbor across the table and remarked: "Beautiful grapes!" His neighbor replied: " 'And they came onto the brook of Eshcol, and cut down a branch with one cluster of grapes. And they bare it two upon a staff.' "

Then the General felt that the time had come to make a speech. He rose and stood up very straight.

Nobody else at the dinner table had stood up to speak. The old people lifted their eyes to the face above them in high, happy expectation. They were used to seeing sailors and vagabonds dead drunk with the crass gin of the country, but they did not recognize in a warrior and courtier the intoxication brought about by the noblest wine of the world.

XI. GENERAL LOEWENHIELM'S SPEECH

"Mercy and truth, my friends, have met together," said the General. "Righteousness and bliss shall kiss one another."

He spoke in a clear voice which had been trained in drill grounds and had echoed sweetly in royal halls, and yet he was speaking in a manner so new to himself and so strangely moving that after his first sentence he had to make a pause. For he was in the habit of forming his speeches with care, conscious of his purpose, but here, in the midst of the Dean's simple congregation, it was as if the whole figure of General Loewenhielm, his breast covered with decorations, were but a mouthpiece for a message which meant to be brought forth.

"Man, my friends," said General Loewenhielm, "is frail and foolish. We have all of us been told that grace is to be found in the universe. But in our human foolishness and short-sightedness we imagine divine grace to be finite. For this reason we tremble . . ." Never till now had the General stated that he trembled; he was genuinely surprised and even shocked at hearing his own voice proclaim the fact. "We tremble before making our choice in life, and after having made it again tremble in fear of having chosen wrong. But the moment comes when our eyes are opened, and we see and realize that grace is infinite. Grace, my friends, demands nothing from us but that we shall await it with confidence and acknowledge it in gratitude. Grace, brothers, makes no conditions and singles out none of us in particular; grace takes us all to its bosom and proclaims general amnesty. See! that which we have chosen is given us, and that which we have refused is, also and at the same time, granted us. Ay, that which we have rejected is poured upon us abundantly. For mercy and truth have met together, and righteousness and bliss have kissed one another!"

The Brothers and Sisters had not altogether understood the General's speech, but his collected and inspired face and the sound of well-known and cherished words had seized and moved all hearts. In this way, after thirty-one years, General Loewenhielm succeeded in dominating the conversation at the Dean's dinner table.

Of what happened later in the evening nothing definite can here be stated. None of the guests later on had any clear remembrance of it. They only knew that the rooms had been filled with a heavenly light, as if a number of small halos had blended into one glorious radiance. Taciturn old people received the gift of tongues; ears that for years had been almost deaf were opened to it. Time itself had merged into eternity. Long after midnight the windows of the house shone like gold, and golden song flowed out into the winter air.

The two old women who had once slandered each other now in their hearts went back a long way, past the evil period in which they had been stuck, to those days of their early girlhood when together they had been preparing for confirmation and hand in hand had filled the roads round Berlevaag with singing. A Brother in the congregation gave another a knock in the ribs, like a rough caress between boys, and cried out: "You cheated me on that timber, you old scoundrel!" The Brother thus addressed almost collapsed in a heavenly burst of laughter, but tears ran from his eyes. "Yes, I did so, beloved Brother," he answered. "I did so." Skipper Halvorsen and Madam Oppegaarden suddenly found themselves close together in a corner and gave one another that long, long kiss, for which the secret uncertain love affair of their youth had never left them time.

The old Dean's flock were humble people. When later in life they thought of this evening it never occurred to any of them that they might have been exalted by their own merit. They realized that the infinite grace of which General Loewenhielm had spoken had been allotted to them, and they did not even wonder at the fact, for it had been but the fulfillment of an ever-present hope. The vain illusions of this earth had dissolved before their eyes like smoke, and they had seen the universe as it really is. They had been given one hour of the millennium.

Old Mrs. Loewenhielm was the first to leave. Her nephew accompanied her, and their hostesses lighted them out. While Philippa was helping the old lady into her many wraps, the General seized Martine's hand and held it for a long time without a word. At last he said:

"I have been with you every day of my life. You know, do you not, that it has been so?"

"Yes," said Martine, "I know that it has been so."

"And," he continued, "I shall be with you every day that is left to me. Every evening I shall sit down, if not in the flesh, which means nothing, in spirit, which is all, to dine with you, just like tonight. For tonight I have learned, dear sister, that in this world anything is possible."

"Yes, it is so, dear brother," said Martine. "In this world anything is possible."

Upon this they parted.

When at last the company broke up it had ceased to snow. The town and the mountains lay in white, unearthly splendor and the sky was bright with thousands of stars. In the street the snow was lying so deep that it had become difficult to walk. The guests from the yellow house wavered on their feet, staggered, sat down abruptly or fell forward on their knees and hands and were covered with snow, as if they had indeed had their sins washed white as wool, and in this regained innocent attire were gamboling like little lambs. It was, to each of them, blissful to have become as a small child; it was also a blessed joke to watch old Brothers and Sisters, who had been taking themselves so seriously, in this kind of celestial second childhood. They stumbled and got up, walked on or stood still, bodily as well as spiritually hand in hand, at moments performing the great chain of a beatified *lanciers*.

"Bless you, bless you, bless you," like an echo of the harmony of the spheres rang on all sides.

Martine and Philippa stood for a long time on the stone steps outside the house. They did not feel the cold. "The stars have come nearer," said Philippa.

"They will come every night," said Martine quietly. "Quite possibly it will never snow again."

In this, however, she was mistaken. An hour later it again began to snow, and such a heavy snowfall had never been known in Berlevaag. The next morning people could hardly push open their doors against the tall snowdrifts. The windows of the houses were so thickly covered with snow, it was told for years afterwards, that many good citizens of the town did not realize that daybreak had come, but slept on till late in the afternoon.

XII. *THE GREAT ARTIST*

When Martine and Philippa locked the door they remembered Babette. A little wave of tenderness and pity swept through them: Babette alone had had no share in the bliss of the evening.

So they went out into the kitchen, and Martine said to Babette: "It was quite a nice dinner, Babette."

Their hearts suddenly filled with gratitude. They realized that none of their guests had said a single word about the food. Indeed, try as they might, they could not themselves remember any of the dishes which had been served. Martine bethought herself of the turtle. It had not appeared at all, and now seemed very vague and far away; it was quite possible that it had been nothing but a nightmare.

Babette sat on the chopping block, surrounded by more black and greasy pots and pans than her mistresses had ever seen in their life. She was as white and as deadly exhausted as on the night when she first appeared and had fainted on their doorstep.

After a long time she looked straight at them and said: "I was once cook at the Café Anglais."

Martine said again: "They all thought that it was a nice dinner." And when Babette did not answer a word she added: "We will all remember this evening when you have gone back to Paris, Babette."

Babette said: "I am not going back to Paris."

"You are not going back to Paris?" Martine exclaimed.

"No," said Babette. "What will I do in Paris? They have all gone. I have lost them all, Mesdames."

The sisters' thoughts went to Monsieur Hersant and his son, and they said: "Oh, my poor Babette."

"Yes, they have all gone," said Babette. "The Duke of Morny, the Duke of Decazes, Prince Narishkine, General Galliffet, Aurélian Scholl, Paul Daru, the Princesse Pauline! All!"

The strange names and titles of people lost to Babette faintly confused the two ladies, but there was such an infinite perspective of tragedy in her announcement that in their responsive state of mind they felt her losses as their own, and their eyes filled with tears.

At the end of another long silence Babette suddenly smiled slightly at them and said: "And how would I go back to Paris, Mesdames? I have no money."

"No money?" the sisters cried as with one mouth.

"No," said Babette.

"But the ten thousand francs?" the sisters asked in a horrified gasp.

"The ten thousand francs have been spent, Mesdames," said Babette. The sisters sat down. For a full minute they could not speak.

"But ten thousand francs?" Martine slowly whispered.

"What will you, Mesdames," said Babette with great dignity. "A dinner for twelve at the Café Anglais would cost ten thousand francs."

The ladies still did not find a word to say. The piece of news was incomprehensible to them, but then many things tonight in one way or another had been beyond comprehension.

Martine remembered a tale told by a friend of her father's who had been a missionary in Africa. He had saved the life of an old chief's favorite wife, and to show his gratitude the chief had treated him to a rich meal. Only long afterwards the missionary learned from his own black servant that what he had partaken of was a small fat grandchild of the chief's, cooked in honor of the great Christian medicine man. She shuddered.

But Philippa's heart was melting in her bosom. It seemed that an unforgettable evening was to be finished off with an unforgettable proof of human loyalty and self-sacrifice.

"Dear Babette," she said softly, "you ought not to have given away all you had for our sake."

Babette gave her mistress a deep glance, a strange glance. Was there not pity, even scorn, at the bottom of it?

"For your sake?" she replied. "No. For my own."

She rose from the chopping block and stood up before the two sisters.

"I am a great artist!" she said.

She waited a moment and then repeated: "I am a great artist, Mesdames."

Again for a long time there was deep silence in the kitchen.

Then Martine said: "So you will be poor now all your life, Babette?"

"Poor?" said Babette. She smiled as if to herself. "No, I shall never be poor. I told you that I am a great artist. A great artist, Mesdames, is never poor. We have something, Mesdames, of which other people know nothing."

While the elder sister found nothing more to say, in Philippa's heart deep, forgotten chords vibrated. For she had heard, before now, long ago, of the Café Anglais. She had heard, before now, long ago, the names on Babette's tragic list. She rose and took a step toward her servant.

"But all those people whom you have mentioned," she said, "those princes and great people of Paris whom you named, Babette? You yourself fought against them. You were a Communard! The General you named had your husband and son shot! How can you grieve over them?"

Babette's dark eyes met Philippa's.

"Yes," she said, "I was a Communard. Thanks be to God, I was a Communard! And those people whom I named, Mesdames, were evil and cruel. They let the people of Paris starve; they oppressed and wronged the poor. Thanks be to God, I stood upon a barricade; I loaded the gun for my menfolk! But all the same, Mesdames, I shall not go back to Paris, now that those people of whom I have spoken are no longer there."

She stood immovable, lost in thought.

"You see, Mesdames," she said, at last, "those people belonged to me, they were mine. They had been brought up and trained, with greater expense than you, my little ladies, could ever imagine or believe, to understand what a great artist I am. I could make them happy. When I did my very best I could make them perfectly happy."

She paused for a moment.

"It was like that with Monsieur Papin too," she said.

"With Monsieur Papin?" Philippa asked.

"Yes, with your Monsieur Papin, my poor lady," said Babette. "He told me so himself: 'It is terrible and unbearable to an artist,' he said, 'to be encouraged to do, to be applauded for doing, his second best.' He said: 'Through all the world there goes one long cry from the heart of the artist: Give me leave to do my utmost!' "

Philippa went up to Babette and put her arms round her. She felt the cook's body like a marble monument against her own, but she herself shook and trembled from head to foot.

For a while she could not speak. Then she whispered:

"Yet this is not the end! I feel, Babette, that this is not the end. In Paradise you will be the great artist that God meant you to be! Ah!" she added, the tears streaming down her cheeks. "Ah, how you will enchant the angels!"

TOBIAS WOLFF

Smorgasbord

"A prep school in March is like a ship in the Doldrums." Our history master said this, as if to himself, while we were waiting for the bell to ring after class. He stood by the window and tapped the glass with his ring in a dreamy, abstracted way meant to make us think he'd forgotten we were there. We were supposed to get the impression that when we weren't around he turned into someone interesting, someone witty and profound, who uttered impromptu bons mots and had a poetic vision of life.

The bell rang.

I went to lunch. The dining hall was almost empty, because it was a free weekend and most of the boys in school had gone to New York, or home, or to their friends' homes, as soon as their last class let out. About the only ones left were foreigners and scholarship students like me and a few other untouchables of various stripes. The school had laid on a nice lunch for us, cheese soufflé, but the portions were small and I went back to my room still hungry. I was always hungry.

Snow and rain fell past my window. The snow on the quad looked grimy; it had melted above the underground heating pipes, exposing long brown lines of mud.

I couldn't get to work. On the next floor down someone kept playing "Mack the Knife." That one song incessantly repeating itself made the dorm seem not just empty but abandoned, as if those who had left were never coming back. I cleaned my room. I tried to read. I looked out the window.

173

I sat down at my desk and studied the new picture my girlfriend had sent me, unable to imagine her from it; I had to close my eyes to do that, and then I could see her, see her solemn eyes and the heavy white breasts she would gravely let me hold sometimes, but not kiss . . . not yet, anyway. But I had a promise. That summer, as soon as I got home, we were going to become lovers. "Become lovers." That was how she'd said it, very deliberately, listening to the words as she spoke them. All year I had repeated them to myself to take the edge off my loneliness and the fits of lust that made me want to scream and drive my fists through walls. We were going to become lovers that summer, and we were going to be lovers all through college, true to each other even if we ended up thousands of miles apart again, and after college we were going to marry and join the Peace Corps and then do something together that would help people. This was our plan. Back in September, the night before I left for school, we wrote it all down along with a lot of other specifics concerning our future: number of children (6), their names, the kinds of dogs we would own, a sketch of our perfect house. We sealed the paper in a bottle and buried it in her back yard. On our Golden Anniversary we were going to dig it up again and show it to our children and grandchildren to prove that dreams can come true.

I was writing her a letter when Crosley came to my room. Crosley was a science whiz. He won the science prize every year and spent his summers working as an intern in different laboratories. He was also a fanatical weight lifter. His arms were so knotty that he had to hold them out from his sides as he walked, as if he were carrying buckets. Even his features seemed muscular. His face was red. Crosley lived down the hall by himself in one of the only singles in the school. He was said to be a thief; that supposedly was the reason he'd ended up without a roommate. I didn't know if it was true, and I tried to avoid forming an opinion on the matter, but whenever we passed each other I felt embarrassed and dropped my eyes.

Crosley leaned in the door and asked me how things were.

I said okay.

He stepped inside and looked around the room, tilting his head to read my roommate's pennants and the titles of our books. I was uneasy. I said, "So what can I do for you?" not meaning to sound as cold as I did but not exactly regretting it either.

He caught my tone and smiled. It was the kind of smile you put on when you pass a group of people you suspect are talking about you. It was his usual expression.

He said, "You know Garcia, right?"

"Garcia? Sure. I think so."

"You know him," Crosley said. "He runs around with Hidalgo and those guys. He's the tall one."

"Sure," I said. "I know who Garcia is."

"Well, his stepmother is in New York for a fashion show or something, and she's going to drive up and take him out to dinner tonight. She told him to bring along some friends. You want to come?"

"What about Hidalgo and the rest of them?"

"They're at some kind of polo deal in Maryland. Buying horses, or ponies."

The notion of someone my age buying ponies to play a game with was so unexpected that I couldn't quite take it in. "Jesus," I said.

Crosley said, "How about it? You want to come?"

I'd never even spoken to Garcia. He was the nephew of a famous dictator, and all his friends were nephews and cousins of other dictators. They lived as they pleased here. Most of them kept cars a few blocks from the campus, though that was completely against the rules, and I'd heard that some of them kept women as well. They were cocky and prankish and charming. They moved everywhere in a body with sunglasses pushed up on their heads and jackets slung over their shoulders, twittering all at once like birds, *chinga* this and *chinga* that. The headmaster was completely buffaloed. After Christmas vacation a bunch of them came down with gonorrhea, and all he did was call them in and advise them that they should not be in too great a hurry to lose their innocence. It became a school joke. All you had to do was say the word *innocence* and everyone would crack up.

"I don't know," I said.

"Come on," Crosley said.

"But I don't even know the guy."

"So what? I don't either."

"Then why did he ask you?"

"I was sitting next to him at lunch."

"Terrific," I said. "That explains you. What about me? How come he asked me?"

"He didn't. He told me to bring someone else."

"What, just anybody? Just whoever happened to present himself to your attention?"

Crosley shrugged.

I laughed. Crosley gave me a look to make sure I wasn't laughing at him, then he laughed too. "Sounds great," I said. "Sounds like a recipe for a really memorable evening."

"You got something better to do?" Crosley asked.

"No," I said.

The limousine picked us up under the awning of the headmaster's house. The driver, an old man, got out slowly and then slowly adjusted his cap before opening the door for us. Garcia slid in beside the woman in back. Crosley and I sat across from them on seats that pulled down. I caught her scent immediately. For some years afterwards I bought perfume for women, and I was never able to find that one.

Garcia erupted into Spanish as soon as the driver closed the door behind me. He sounded angry, spitting words at the woman and gesticulating violently. She rocked back a little, then let loose a burst of her own. I stared openly at her. Her skin was very white. She wore a black cape over a black dress cut just low enough to show her pale throat, and the bones at the base of her throat. Her mouth was red. There was a spot of rouge high on each cheek, not rubbed in to look like real color but left there carelessly, or carefully, to make you think again how white her skin was. Her teeth were small and sharp-looking, and she bared them in concert with certain gestures and inflections. As she talked her little pointed tongue flicked in and out.

She wasn't a lot older than we were. Twenty-five at the most. Maybe younger.

She said something definitive and cut her hand through the air. Garcia began to answer her but she said "No!" and chopped the air again. Then she turned and smiled at Crosley and me. It was a completely false smile. She said, "Where would you fellows like to eat?" Her voice sounded lower in English, even a little harsh, though the harshness could have come from her accent. She called us *fallows*.

"Anywhere is fine with me," I said.

"Anywhere," she repeated. She narrowed her big black eyes and pushed her lips together. I could see that my answer disappointed her. She looked at Crosley.

"There's supposed to be a good French restaurant in Newbury," Crosley said. "Also an Italian place. It depends on what you want."

"No," she said. "It depends on what you want. I am not so hungry."

If Garcia had a preference, he kept it to himself. He sulked in the corner, his round shoulders slumped and his hands between his knees. He seemed to be trying to make a point of some kind.

"There's also a smorgasbord," Crosley said. "If you like smorgasbords."

"Smorgasbord," she said. She repeated the word to Garcia. He frowned, then answered her in a sullen monotone.

I couldn't believe Crosley had suggested the smorgasbord. It was an egregiously uncouth suggestion. The smorgasbord was where the local fatties went to binge. Football coaches brought whole teams there to bulk up. The food was good enough, and God knows there was plenty of it, all you could eat, actually, but the atmosphere was brutally matter-of-fact. The food was good, though. Big platters of shrimp on crushed ice. Barons of beef. Smoked turkey. No end of food, really.

She was smiling. Obviously the concept was new to her. "You—do you like smorgasbords?" she asked Crosley.

"Yes," he said.

"And you?" she said to me.

I nodded. Then, not to seem wishy-washy, I said, "You bet."

"Smorgasbord," she said. She laughed and clapped her hands. "Smorgasbord!"

Crosley gave directions to the driver, and we drove slowly away from the school. She said something to Garcia. He nodded at each of us in turn and gave our names, then looked away again, out the window, where the snowy fields were turning dark. His face was long, his eyes sorrowful as a hound's. He had barely talked to us while we were waiting for the limousine. I didn't know why he was mad at his stepmother, or why he wouldn't talk to us, or why he'd even asked us along, but by now I didn't really care.

She studied us and repeated our names skeptically. "No," she said. She pointed at Crosley and said, "El Blanco." She pointed at me and said, "El Negro." Then she pointed at herself and said, "I am Linda."

"Leen-da," Crosley said. He really overdid it, but she showed her sharp little teeth and said, *"Exactamente."*

Then she settled back against the seat and pulled her cape close around her shoulders. It soon fell open again. She was restless. She sat forward and leaned back, crossed and recrossed her legs, swung her feet impatiently. She had on black high heels fastened by a thin strap; I could see almost her entire foot. I heard the silky rub of her stockings against each other, and breathed in a fresh breath of her perfume every time she moved. That perfume had a certain effect on me. It didn't reach me as just a smell, it was personal, it seemed to issue from her very privacy. It made the hair bristle on my arms. It entered my veins like fine tingling wires, widening my eyes, tightening my spine, sending faint chills across my shoulders and the backs of my knees. Every time she moved I felt a little tug and followed her motion with some slight motion of my own.

When we arrived at the smorgasbord—Swenson's, I believe it was, or maybe Hansen's, some such honest Swede of a name—Garcia refused to get out of the limousine. Linda tried to persuade him, but he shrank back into his corner and would not answer or even look at her. She threw up her hands. "Ah!" she said, and turned away. Crosley and I followed her across the parking lot toward the big red barn. Her dress rustled as she walked. Her heels clicked on the cement.

You could say one thing for the smorgasbord; it wasn't pretentious. It was in a real barn, not some quaint fantasy of a barn with butter-churn lamps and little brass ornaments nailed to the walls on strips of leather. At one end of the barn was the kitchen. The rest of it had been left open and filled with picnic tables. Blazing light bulbs hung from the rafters. In the middle of the barn stood what my English master would have called "the groaning board"—a great table heaped with food, every kind of food you could think of, and more. I had been there several times and it always gave me a small, pleasant shock to see how much food there was.

Girls wearing dirndls hustled around the barn, cleaning up messes, changing tablecloths, bringing fresh platters of food from the kitchen.

We stood blinking in the sudden light. Linda paid up, then we followed one of the waitresses across the floor. Linda walked slowly, gazing around like a tourist. Several men looked up from their food as she passed. I was right behind her, and I looked forbiddingly back at them so they would think she was my wife.

We were lucky; we got a table to ourselves. On crowded nights they usually doubled you up with another party, and that could be an unromantic experience. Linda shrugged off her cape and waved us toward the food. "Go on," she said. She sat down and opened her purse. When I looked back she was lighting a cigarette.

"You're pretty quiet tonight," Crosley said as we filled our plates. "You pissed off about something?"

I shook my head. "Maybe I'm just quiet, Crosley, you know?"

He speared a slice of meat and said, "When she called you El Negro, that didn't mean she thought you were a Negro. She just said that because your hair is dark. Mine is light, that's how come she called me El Blanco."

"I know that, Crosley. Jesus. You think I couldn't figure that out? Give me some credit, okay?" Then, as we moved around the table, I said, "You speak Spanish?"

"*Un poco.* Actually more like *un poquito.*"

"What's Garcia mad about?"

"Money. Something about money."

"Like what?"

He shook his head. "That's all I could get. But it's definitely about money."

I'd meant to start off slow but by the time I reached the end of the table my plate was full. Salad, ham, jumbo shrimp, barbecued beef, Eggs Benny. Crosley's was full too. We walked back toward Linda, who was leaning forward on her elbows and looking around the barn. She took a long drag off her cigarette, lifted her chin, and blew a stream of smoke up toward the rafters. I sat down across from her. "Scoot down," Crosley said, and settled in beside me.

She watched us eat for a while.

"So," she said, "El Blanco. Are you from New York?"

Crosley looked up in surprise. "No, ma'am," he said. "I'm from Virginia."

Linda stabbed out her cigarette. She had long fingernails painted the same deep red as the lipstick smears on her cigarette butt. She said, "I just came from New York and I can tell you that is one crazy place. Just incredible. Listen to this. I am in a taxicab, you know, and we are stopping in this traffic jam for a long time and there is a taxicab next to us with this fellow in it who stares at me. Like this, you know." She made her eyes go round. "Of course I ignore him. So guess what? My door opens and he gets into my cab. 'Excuse me,' he says, 'I want to marry you.' 'That's nice,' I say. 'Ask my husband.' 'I don't care about your husband,' he says. 'Your husband is history. So is my wife.' Of course I had to laugh. 'Okay,' he says. 'You think that's funny? How about this.' Then he says—" Linda looked sharply at each of us. She sniffed and made a face. "He says things you would never believe. Never. He wants to do this and he wants to do that. Well, I act like I am about to scream. I open my mouth like this. 'Hey,' he says, 'Okay, okay. Relax.' Then he gets out and goes back to his taxicab. We are still sitting there for a long time again, and you know what he is doing? He is reading the newspaper. With his hat on. Go ahead, eat," she said to us, and nodded toward the food.

A tall blonde girl was carving fresh slices of roast beef onto a platter. She smiled at us. She was hale and bosomy—I could see the laces on her bodice straining. Her cheeks glowed. Her bare arms and shoulders were ruddy with exertion. Crosley raised his eyebrows at me. I raised mine back but my heart wasn't in it. She was a Viking dream, pure gemütlichkeit, but I was drunk on Garcia's stepmother and in that condition you don't want a glass of milk, you want more of what's making you stumble and fall.

Crosley and I filled our plates again and headed back.

"I'm always hungry," he said.

"I know what you mean," I told him.

Linda smoked another cigarette while we ate. She watched the other tables as if she were at a movie. I tried to eat with a little finesse and so did Crosley, dabbing his lips with a napkin between every bulging mouthful, but some of the people around us had completely slipped their moorings. They ducked their heads low to receive their food, and while they chewed it up they looked around suspiciously and kept their forearms close to their plates. A big family to our left was the worst. There was something competitive and desperate about them; they seemed to be eating their way toward a condition where they would never have to eat again. You would have thought that they were refugees from a great hunger, that outside these walls the land was afflicted with drought and barrenness. I felt a kind of desperation myself; I felt as if I were growing emptier with every bite I took.

There was a din in the air, a steady roar like that of a waterfall.

Linda looked around her with a pleased expression. She bore no likeness to anyone here, but she seemed completely at home. She sent us back for another plate, then dessert and coffee, and while we were finishing up she asked El Blanco if he had a girlfriend.

"No, ma'am," Crosley said. "We broke up," he added, and his red face turned purple. It was clear that he was lying.

"You. How about you?"

I nodded.

"Ha!" she said. "El Negro is the one! So. What's her name?"

"Jane."

"Jaaane," Linda drawled. "Okay, let's hear about Jaaane."

"Jane," I said again.

Linda smiled.

I told her everything. I told her how my girlfriend and I had met and what she looked like and what our plans were—everything. I told her more than everything, because I gave certain coy but definite suggestions about the extremes to which our passion had already driven us. I meant to impress her with my potency, to enflame her, to wipe that smile off her face, but the more I told her the more wolfishly she smiled and the more her eyes laughed at me.

Laughing eyes—now there's a cliché my English master would have eaten me alive for. "How exactly did these eyes laugh?" he would have asked, looking up from my paper while my classmates snorted around me. "Did they titter, or did they merely chortle? Did they give a great guffaw? Did they, perhaps, *scream* with laughter?"

I am here to tell you that eyes can scream with laughter. Linda's did. As I played big hombre for her I could see exactly how complete my failure was, I could hear her saying *Okay, El Negro, go on, talk about your little gorlfren, how pretty she is and so on, but we know what you want, don't we?—you want to*

*suck on my tongue and slobber on my titties and lick my belly and bury your face
in me. That's what you want.*

Crosley interrupted me. "Ma'am . . ." he said, and nodded toward the
door. Garcia was leaning there with his arms crossed and an expression of
fury on his face. When she looked at him he turned and walked out the door.

Her eyes went flat. She sat there for a moment. She began to take a
cigarette from her case, then put it back and stood up. "Let's go," she said.

Garcia was waiting in the car, rigid and silent. He said nothing on the
drive back. Linda swung her foot and stared out the window at the passing
houses and bright, moonlit fields. Just before we reached the school Garcia
leaned forward and began speaking to her in a low voice. She listened
impassively and did not answer. He was still talking when the limousine
stopped in front of the headmaster's house. The driver opened the door.
Garcia fixed his eyes on her. Still impassive, she took her pocketbook out of
her purse. She opened it and looked inside. She meditated over the contents,
then withdrew a bill and offered it to Garcia. It was a one hundred dollar bill.
"Boolshit!" he said, and sat back angrily. With no change of expression she
turned and held the bill out to me. I didn't know what else to do but take
it. She got another one from her pocketbook and presented it to Crosley,
who hesitated even less than I did. Then she gave us the same false smile she
had greeted us with, and said, "Good night, it was a pleasure to meet you.
Good night, good night," she said to Garcia.

The three of us got out of the limousine. I went a few steps and then
slowed down, and began to look back.

"Keep walking!" Crosley hissed.

Garcia let off a string of words as the driver closed the door. I faced
around again and walked with Crosley across the quad. As we approached
our dorm he quickened his pace. "I don't believe it," he whispered. "A
hundred bucks." When we were inside the door he stopped and shouted, "A
hundred bucks! A hundred fucking dollars!"

"Pipe down," someone called.

"All right, all right. Fuck you!" he added.

We went up the stairs to our floor, laughing and banging into each
other. "Do you fucking believe it?" he said.

I shook my head. We were standing outside my door.

"No, really now, listen." He put his hands on my shoulders and looked
into my eyes. He said, "Do you fucking *believe* it?"

I told him I didn't.

"Well neither do I. I don't fucking believe it."

There didn't seem to be much to say after that. I would have invited

Crosley in, but to tell the truth I still thought of him as a thief. We laughed a few more times and said good-night.

My room was cold. I took the bill out of my pocket and looked at it. It was new and stiff, the kind of bill you associate with kidnappings. The picture of Franklin was surprisingly lifelike. I looked at it for a while. A hundred dollars was a lot of money then. I had never had a hundred dollars before, not in one chunk like this. To be on the safe side I taped it to a page in *Profiles in Courage*—page 100, so I wouldn't forget where it was.

I had trouble getting to sleep. The food I had eaten sat like a stone in me, and I was miserable about the things I had said. I understood that I had been a liar and a fool. I kept shifting under the covers, then I sat up and turned on my reading lamp. I picked up the new picture my girlfriend had sent me, and closed my eyes, and when I had some peace of mind I renewed my promises to her.

We broke up a month after I got home. Her parents were away one night, and we seized the opportunity to make love in their canopied bed. This was the fifth time that we had made love. She got up immediately afterwards and started putting her clothes on. When I asked her what the problem was she wouldn't answer me. I thought, Oh Christ, what now? "Come on," I said. "What's the problem?"

She was tying her shoes. She looked up and said, "You don't love me."

It surprised me to hear this, not because she said it but because it was true. Before this moment I hadn't known it was true, but it was—I didn't love her.

For a long time afterwards I told myself that I had never really loved her, but this was a lie.

We're supposed to smile at the passions of the young, and at what we recall of our own passions, as if they were no more than a series of sweet frauds we had fooled ourselves with and then wised up to. Not only the passion of boys and girls for each other but the others, too—passion for justice, for doing right, for turning the world around—all these come in their time under our wintry smiles. But there was nothing foolish about what we felt. Nothing merely young. I just wasn't up to it. I let the light go out.

Sometime later I heard a soft knock at my door. I was still wide awake. "Yeah," I said.

Crosley stepped inside. He was wearing a blue dressing gown of some silky material that shimmered in the dim light of the hallway. He said, "Have you got any Tums or anything?"

"No. I wish I did."

"You too, huh?" He closed the door and sat on my roommate's bunk. "Do you feel as bad as I do?"

"How bad do you feel?"

"Like I'm dying. I think there was something wrong with the shrimp."

"Come on, Crosley. You ate everything but the barn."

"So did you."

"That's right. That's why I'm not complaining."

He moaned and rocked back and forth on the bed. I could hear real pain in his voice. I sat up. "Crosley, are you okay?"

"I guess," he said.

"You want me to call the nurse?"

"God," he said. "No. That's all right." He kept rocking. Then, in a carefully offhand way, he said, "Look, is it okay if I just stay here for a while?"

I almost said no, then I caught myself. "Sure," I told him. "Make yourself at home."

He must have heard my hesitation. "Forget it," he said bitterly. "Sorry I asked." But he made no move to go.

I felt confused, tender toward Crosley because he was in pain, repelled because of what I had heard about him. But maybe what I had heard about him wasn't true. I wanted to be fair, so I said, "Hey Crosley, do you mind if I ask you a question?"

"That depends."

I sat up. Crosley was watching me. In the moonlight his dressing gown was iridescent as oil. He had his arms crossed over his stomach. "Is it true that you got caught stealing?"

"You fucker," he said. He looked down at the floor.

I waited.

He said, "You want to hear about it, just ask someone. Everybody knows all about it, right?"

"I don't."

"That's right, you don't." He raised his head. "You don't know shit about it and neither does anyone else." He tried to smile. His teeth appeared almost luminous in the cold silver light. "The really hilarious part is, I didn't actually get caught stealing it, I got caught putting it back. Not to make excuses. I stole the fucker, all right."

"Stole what?"

"The coat," he said. "Robinson's overcoat. Don't tell me you didn't know that."

I shook my head.

"Then you must have been living in a cave or something. You know Robinson, right? Robinson was my roommate. He had this camel's hair overcoat, this really just beautiful overcoat. I kind of got obsessed with it.

183

I thought about it all the time. Whenever he went somewhere without it I would put it on and stand in front of the mirror. Then one day I just took the fucker. I stuck it in my locker over at the gym. Robinson was really upset. He'd go to his closet ten, twenty times a day, like he thought the coat had just gone for a walk or something. So anyway, I brought it back. He came into the room while I was hanging it up." Crosley bent forward suddenly, then leaned back.

"You're lucky they didn't kick you out."

"I wish they had," he said. "The dean wanted to play Jesus. He got all choked up over the fact that I had brought it back." Crosley rubbed his arms. "Man, did I want that coat. It was ridiculous how much I wanted that coat. You know?" He looked right at me. "Do you know what I'm talking about?"

I nodded.

"Really?"

"Yes."

"Good." Crosley lay back against the pillow, then lifted his feet onto the bed. "Say," he said, "I think I figured out how come Garcia invited me."

"Yeah? How come?"

"He was mad at his stepmother, right? He wanted to punish her."

"So?"

"So I'm the punishment. He probably heard I was the biggest asshole in the school, and figured whoever came with me would have to be an asshole too. That's my theory, anyway."

I started laughing. It hurt my stomach but I couldn't stop. Crosley said, "Come on, man, don't make me laugh," then he started laughing and moaning at the same time.

We lay without talking for a time. Crosley said, "El Negro."

"Yeah."

"What are you going to do with your C-note?"

"I don't know. What are you going to do?"

"Buy a woman."

"Buy a woman?"

"I haven't gotten laid in a really long time. In fact," he said, "I've never gotten laid."

"Me either."

I thought about his words. *Buy a woman.* He could actually do it. I could do it myself. I didn't have to wait, I didn't have to burn like this for month after month until Jane decided she was ready to give me relief. Three months was a long time to wait. It was an unreasonable time to wait for anything if you had no good reason to wait, if you could just buy what you needed. And to think that you could buy this—buy a mouth for your mouth, and arms and legs to wrap you tight. I had never considered this before. I thought of the money in my book. I could almost feel it there. Pure possibility.

Jane would never know. It wouldn't hurt her at all, and in a certain way it might help, because it was going to be very awkward at first if neither of us had any experience. As a man, I should know what I was doing. It would be a lot better that way.

I told Crosley that I liked his idea. "The time has come to lose our innocence," I said.

"*Exactamente*," he said.

And so we sat up and took counsel, leaning toward each other from the beds, holding our swollen bellies, whispering back and forth about how this thing might be done, and where, and when.

ELIZABETH BOWEN

Lunch

"After all," said Marcia, "there are egoists and egoists. You are one sort of egoist, I am the other."

A ladybird had dropped on to her plate from a cluster of leaves above, and she invited it on to her finger and transferred it very carefully to the rail of the verandah.

"Differentiate," said the stranger, watching the progress of the ladybird.

They were lunching on the verandah, and the midday sun fell through a screen of leaves in quivering splashes on to the tablecloth, the elusive pattern of Marcia's dress, the crude enameled brilliance of the salad in a willow-pattern bowl, the dinted plate and cutlery slanting together at angles of confusion. The water was spring water, so cold that a mist had formed on the sides of their tumblers and of the red glass water-jug. They considered helpings of cold lamb, and their heads and faces were in shadow.

Through the open window the interior of the coffee-room was murky and repellent; with its drab, disheveled tables, and chairs so huddled *tête-à-tête* that they travestied intimacy. It was full of the musty reek of cruets and the wraiths of long-digested meals, and of a brooding reproach for their desertion whenever they turned their heads towards it. A mournful waitress, too, reproached them, flicking desultorily about among the crumbs.

From under the verandah the hotel garden slanted steeply down to the road; the burning dustiness beneath them was visible in glimpses between the branches of the lime trees. Cyclists flashed past, and an occasional motor whirled up clouds of dust to settle in the patient limes. Behind their screen of leaves they two sat sheltered and conversant, looking out to where, beyond the village, the country fell away into the hot blue distances of June, and cooled by a faint wind that crept towards them through a rustle and glitter of leaves from hay-fields and the heavy shade of elders.

The jewels flashed in Marcia's rings as she laid down knife and fork, and, drumming with her fingers on the table, proceeded to expatiate on egoists.

"Don't think I'm going to be clever," she implored him, "and talk like a woman in a Meredith book. Well, quite baldly to begin with, one acknowledges that one puts oneself first, doesn't one? There may be other people, but it's ourselves that matter."

He had relaxed his face to a calm attentiveness, and, leaning limply back in his chair, looked at her with tired, kindly eyes, like the eyes of a monkey, between wrinkled lids.

"Granted, if you wish it for the sake of argument. But—"

"But you are protesting inwardly that the other people matter more? They do matter enormously. But the more they matter to you, still the more you're mattering to yourself; it merely raises your standard of values. Have you any children?"

"Six," said the tired man.

"I have three," said Marcia. "And a husband. Quite enough, but I am very fond of them all. That is why I am always so glad to get away from them."

He was cutting his lamb with quiet slashing strokes of his knife, and eating quickly and abstractedly, like a man whose habits of life have made food less an indulgence than a necessity. She believed that she was interesting him.

"My idea in life, my particular form of egoism, is a determination not to be swamped. I resent most fearfully, not the claims my family make on me, but the claims I make on my family. Theirs are a tribute to my indispensability, mine, a proof of my dependence. Therefore I am a perfectly charming woman, but quite extraordinarily selfish. That is how all my friends describe me. I admire their candor, but I never congratulate them on their perspicacity. My egoism is nothing if not blatant and unblushing.

"Now you go on!" she said encouragingly, helping herself to salad. "Tell me about your selfishness, then I'll define how it's different from mine."

He did not appear inspired.

"Yours is a much better kind," she supplemented. "Finer. You have given up everything but the thing that won't be given up. In fact, there's nothing wrong in your sort of egoism. It's only your self-consciousness that brings it to life at all. In the middle of your abject and terrible unselfishness you feel a tiny strain of resistance, and it worries you so much that it has rubbed you sore. It's mere morbidity on your part, that's what I condemn about it. Turn your family out into the street and carouse for a fortnight and you'll be a better man at the end of it. Mine is healthy animal spirits, mine is sheer exuberance; yours is a badgered, hectic, unavowed resistance to the people you love best in the world because, unknowingly, you still love yourself better."

"You wouldn't know the meaning of healthy animal spirits with six children on my income. I suppose what you are trying to say about me, is . . . the turning of the worm?"

"No," said Marcia, "not exactly turning. I wonder if I am making a fool of myself? I don't believe you are an egoist at all. My ideas are beginning to desert me; I am really incapable of a sustained monologue on any subject under the sun. You see, generally I talk in circles; I mean, I say something cryptic, that sounds clever and stimulates the activities of other people's minds, and when the conversation has reached a climax of brilliancy I knock down my hammer, like an auctioneer, on somebody else's epigram, cap it with another, and smile round at them all with calm assurance and finality. By that time everybody is in a sort of glow, each believing that he or she has laid the largest and finest of the conversational eggs.

"Goodness, you've finished! Would you just call through the window and ask that woman if there's anything else to eat? She's been taking such an interest in our conversation and our profiles. Say strawberries if possible, because otherwise I have a premonition it will be blancmange."

The stranger put his head and shoulders through the window. Marcia studied his narrow back in the shabby tweed jacket, his thinning hair and the frayed edges of his collar. One hand gripped the back of his chair; she thought, "How terrible to see a man who isn't sunburned." She listened to his muffled conversation with the waitress, and pushed her plate away, deploring the oiliness of the salad.

With flushed face he reappeared, and two plump arms came through the window after him, removed their plates, and clattered on to the table a big bowl of strawberries and a small greyish blancmange in a thick glass dish.

"I wonder if I'm tiring you," said Marcia remorsefully. "I know you came out here to be quiet, and I've done nothing but sharpen my theories on you ever since we made common cause against the coffee-room—it *was* worth while, too, wasn't it? Never mind, I'll let you go directly after lunch, and you shall find the tranquility you came to look for underneath a lime tree loud with bees. (I never take the slightest interest in Nature, but I always remember the touch about the bees. I came across it in a book.) I see a book in your pocket. If I wasn't here you'd be reading with it propped up against the water-jug, blissfully dipping your strawberries into the salt and wondering why they tasted so funny. But do let's eat them in our fingers, anyway. I never eat them with a spoon unless there's cream . . . My husband says he finds me too exhilarating for a prolonged *tête-à-tête*."

He smiled at her with embarrassment, then leaned his elbow on the warm rail of the verandah and looked down on to the road.

"It's so hot," he said with sudden petulance, "so beastly *hot*. I didn't realize how hot it was going to be or I wouldn't have bicycled out."

"It's not very hot here, is it? Those leaves—"

"No, but I was thinking about the hotness everywhere else. This makes it worse."

"Fancy *bicycling*. Do let me give you some blancmange; I think it is an heirloom. Did you come far?"

"From Lewisham." He added, "I work in a publisher's office."

"A publisher—how interesting! I wonder if you could do anything to help a boy I know; such a charming boy! He has written a book, but—"

He flushed. "I am not a—an influential member of the firm."

"Oh, then, p'raps you couldn't. Tell me, why did you come here today? I mean why *here* specially?"

"Oh, for no reason. Just at random. Why did you?"

"To meet somebody who hasn't turned up. He was going to have brought a lunch-basket and we were to have picnicked down by the river. Oh, nobody I shouldn't meet. You haven't blundered into an elopement. I've got no brain for intrigue. After lunch we were going to have sketched— at least, he would have sketched and I should have talked. He's by way of teaching me. We were to have met at twelve, but I suppose he's forgotten or is doing something else. Probably he wired, but it hadn't come before I started."

"Do you paint?"

"I've got a paint-box." She indicated a diminutive Windsor and Newton and a large water-color block lying at her feet.

"I'm sorry," he said diffidently. "I'm afraid this must be something of a disappointment."

"Not a bit." She clasped her hands on the table, leaning forward. "I've really loved our lunch-party. You *listened*. I've met very few people who could really listen."

"I've met very few people who were worth listening to."

She raised her brows. Her shabby man was growing gallant.

"I am certain," she smiled, "that with your delicate perceptions of the romantic you would rather we remained incognito. Names and addresses are—"

"Banality."

The leaves rustled and her muslins fluttered in a breath of warm wind. In silence they turned their faces out towards the distance.

"I love views," she said, "when there isn't anything to understand in them. There are no subtleties of emotion about June. She's so gloriously elemental. Not a month for self-justification, simply for self-abandonment."

He turned towards her quickly, his whole face flushed and lighted up for speech.

With a grind and screech of brakes a big car drew up under the lime trees.

Marcia leaned over the verandah rail.

"*John,*" she cried. "Oh, John!"

She reached out for her parasol and dived to gather up her sketching things.

"How late you are," she called again, "how *late* you are! Did you have a puncture, or what were you doing?"

She pushed back her chair with a grating sound along the tiled floor of the verandah, and stood looking down bright-eyed at his weary, passive, disillusioned face.

"I was right," she said, "there are two sorts of egoists, and I am both."

ROBIN HEMLEY

All You Can Eat

Sarah, Jamie, and I are at this pancake social given by a local church. Not that we're churchgoers, it's just that we like pancakes. We never use syrup though, only butter. Bad for our teeth, you know. I remember when sweet meant good and wholesome, but now you can't trust anything that doesn't say "sugarless" or "all-natural' on the bottle.

I didn't want to come here in the first place. In fact when Sarah suggested it, I blew up. My weekends are the only times I have to relax, and crowds of churchgoers aggravate me. I work hard at the office all week. I'm up for promotion. Our marriage is going to hell. Our son loves his toys more than us. And what does Sarah want to do? She wants to go to a pancake social just because Aunt Jemima is supposed to attend. The Real Aunt Jemima.

So what? I say. There's no such thing as the Real Aunt Jemima anyway. There's probably a whole horde of these Aunt Jemimas traveling around the country, appearing at pancake socials. But my arguments have no effect on Sarah. We never want to do the same things. My idea of an enjoyable Sunday is staying home and reading the newspaper, watching "Meet the Press" and then "60 Minutes" later on. I'm the type of guy who can't go a day without knowing what's going on in the world. If you wanted, you could quiz me and I'd know everything. Yesterday there was an earthquake in Peru, and it killed three hundred people.

Sarah, on the other hand, couldn't care less about news. All she's interested in is fixing up our house and taking Jamie to places like this. Last week it was the circus. The week before that she took the kid to one of those tacky little sidewalk sales called Art Daze. When we're alone together, we have nothing to say. I want to talk about Iran, and all she can think about is wood paneling in the den.

The meal is one of those all-you-can-eat deals. I've only had about four pancakes and I'm ready to go home, but I can't even suggest it because Aunt Jemima hasn't shown yet. All I can do is stare across the table at this fat man who's too busy pigging out to notice me. He's got his head bent so low to the table that his tie is soaking up the syrup on his plate. That's gluttony for you. As far as I'm concerned, gluttony is the worst sin by a long shot. And he's not the only one pigging out here. It seems like my family is the only one that knows how to eat decently.

The fat man sees me staring and lifts the corner of his mouth in a half smile. "You don't like pancakes?" he says, and adds, "This here's sure a bargain."

I don't have time to answer because the minister gets up on stage and announces that Aunt Jemima is here.

Out she comes, fat and dressed just like you see her on the syrup bottles: red polka-dotted kerchief, frowsy old dress, and a pair of tits that belong in a 4-H fair. The kids don't know who the hell she is, so they keep eating their pancakes like nothing's happening while the old woman thanks everyone, especially the children, God's children, and tells us all how much she loves us.

Sarah leans over to my side and whispers, "I didn't realize she'd be such a racial stereotype."

"What do you expect of someone named Aunt Jemima?" I say.

The minister sits down at the piano, and Aunt Jemima turns around to tell him something, I suppose what key she's in. At that moment, all the parents grab the bottles of syrup on the table and show the kids just who Aunt Jemima is. When she turns around again, they go wild, now that they've seen her face on a mass-produced product. My Jamie starts to clap and yell along with all the others. Over the general roar in the church basement you hear a few parents telling their kids to eat their pancakes before they get cold.

"Before I start my song," says Aunt Jemima in a deep melodious voice, "I want to say a few words to y'all. Now I travel around the country singing to good folk like y'all, but I don't only sing, I have a message to bring. When you see me on a bottle of syrup, what do you really see? You don't just see old Aunt Jemima. You see all the things in life that's sweet and good, all them simple things in life, like maple syrup."

"Simple things in life," I tell Sarah. "Who's she fooling?"

"Relax, Jack," says Sarah. "If you'd stop acting like a skeptic for a minute, you might enjoy yourself. Just remember your blood pressure, okay?"

"I remember," I say. "I don't need you to remind me. But if I have a heart attack and drop dead, I want you to move my body. I don't want to be found dead among a bunch of churchgoers. Next she's going to start talking about family values."

But she doesn't. She goes right into her song, "He's Got the Whole World in His Hands." She's got a deep gospel voice and sways to the music while the minister accompanies her on that old piano with half the keys chipped away. While she sings, she makes motions with her hands. When she gets to the word *world*, she makes a circle. When she says *hands*, she cups her own together and looks piously up at the ceiling. After two verses, she stops and says, "Now I want all you children, God's children, to sing along with me and do all the things I do with my hands. Now when I say children, I don't just mean the young ones," and she gives us her famous syrupy smile. Everyone laughs, even me. I don't know, maybe there's not all that much difference between me and these churchgoers, and anyway, what's the use of arguing with such a sweet old woman? So I grab Sarah's hand, even though we just had an argument before breakfast, and she smiles at me like people do only in movies or rest homes, sort of vacant.

Sarah and I have had a lot of arguments recently. She's always reading these dumb women's magazines and trying out the things that they tell her to do. "101 Ways to Fix Chicken Pot Pie for the Man You Love," and stuff like that. Poor Sarah. She's been trying for the last fifteen years to make me happy, but the more she tries, the more bored I get with her. There are some people who aren't meant to be happy, and I'm one of them. I don't like happy people. Sarah is completely the opposite. Her favorite word is *tickle*. She likes to go to movies that tickle her, and if she ever reads a newspaper, it's only to scan the columnists who tickle her.

A couple of weekends ago, Sarah spent hours shellacking the covers of women's magazines onto the walls of our bathroom. Of course when I saw what she was doing, I was furious. "Sarah," I said. "This is the tackiest thing I've ever seen. I mean, you might as well turn the whole house into a 7-Eleven."

"I just thought it would brighten up the place," she said. "Don't you think it looks cheery?"

"It looks cheery as hell," I said. "I don't need cheeriness when I'm on the john."

Sarah sat down on the edge of the tub. Then she grabbed a pile of magazine covers, threw them over the drain, and turned on the water full blast. A model's face was on top, and the face just bounced up and down under the water pressure like it was doing some kind of strange facial swimming stroke.

For the first time in a while, I was scared for Sarah. I had an aunt who killed herself with sleeping pills, and this seemed to be just the kind of thing someone would do before they offed themselves. So I gave in. I let her shellac the bathroom so that now it looks like a newsstand. Then I took her out to dinner, and I didn't even mention the fact that the Soviet Union had rejected our latest arms proposal, though it was on my mind.

Now Sarah's acting like we've never argued in our lives. She's just giving me that silly smile of hers.

"I'm glad we came," I say to make her happy. "Pass the syrup."

"But you don't like syrup."

"That's true," I say. "I don't know what's come over me. It just looks so sweet, so wholesome."

"Daddy, can I have some syrup?" says Jamie.

"No. You remember your last checkup, don't you?"

"Oh, let him have some," says Sarah. "A little couldn't hurt," and she smiles at me. But she doesn't need to smile. Her hair smiles for her, flipping up on either side of her face, a phony style that went out fifteen years ago.

"Well, it *does* look good," I say. I pour some onto my pancakes and take a bite.

Yum.

Aunt Jemima's well into her song again, and everyone is singing along, following her motions with their hands. When she gets to the part about the "itty bitty baby in His hands," they all rock their arms back and forth. Some of the younger children don't know how to rock a baby and look more like they're sawing some object in half.

Babies. Sarah's wanted to have another child for a while, but I don't. She's so old-fashioned about that sort of thing. If I tried to tell her about exponential population growth and about starvation, she wouldn't understand me at all. She'd probably just smile and say, "But we're not some starving tribe in Africa, honey. We can afford another child." I've known Sarah long enough to know this is exactly what she'd say.

But it's all right. This anger towards Sarah will pass. Right now, I feel happy and know that the whole audience is thinking the same thought: everything is fine. We're all safe together in the hands of this fat old woman. She looks like she could shelter us from anything.

The shy-looking minister at the piano feels it too. He's pounding his fingers up and down on the keyboard, his skinny churchgoing rump half off the bench just like Jerry Lee Lewis. And the whole plaster ceiling is shaking, bits of it raining down on us like God's white teeth. Then the song ends, and everyone is tired and sweating. My brain is sweating from all this thinking. Maybe I should stop thinking and relax, like Sarah says.

I smell my armpits. That roll-on antiperspirant I use really *does* last a long time. As the commercial says, men sweat more than women, but you couldn't tell it by old Aunt Jemima. She's got two wide circles around her armpits, and she says, "It's a mite hot in here."

Everyone agrees. All this combined body heat makes the place hotter than an oven. I look over at Jamie. In between songs, he's wolfing down pancakes like he's never tasted food before. And the syrup. His pancakes are swimming in it. Empty bottles line our long table like dominoes, and our waiter is working his butt off bringing stacks of steaming hot pancakes and bottles of maple syrup to everyone. I've never seen Jamie eat like this. Sarah and I have to feed him protein pills just to keep him from going anemic on us.

And that fat man. He's sure getting his money's worth. I've never seen anyone put away this much food.

I don't know what it is with him and me. We've been having this silent fight ever since we sat down, with him just smiling that weird half smile at me. I don't know why I feel so hostile toward this particular fat man. Maybe it's really guilt. Maybe I'm hostile because I have a lot of fat inside *me*, not the kind you can weigh. I'm really a skinny guy. Invisible fat.

"I sure wish Jamie would eat like this all the time," I tell Sarah.

"Me too," she says. "Maybe we should feed him pancakes morning, noon, and night." She sends me another vacant smile that doesn't mean anything. It's just polite. I look around the room and half the people in here have that same polite smile on their faces.

Anyway, what's she saying? Morning, noon, and night. I don't know about that.

I pour milk into my coffee with a moo-cow creamer, which is sort of disgusting if you think about it. I mean, the people who invented these things must have known that it looks like the cow is puking into your coffee.

I take a few bites of my pancakes, swishing them around in the syrup with my fork. Yum, yum. They're such simple things really, brown on the outside, fluffy white inside. But they're so good. I never realized before that covering them with syrup makes all the difference in the world.

Aunt Jemima is singing another song now, called "Pancake Lady."

None of us know the words, so we just let her sing while we laugh along in between bites.

> *Pancake Lady makes pancakes for me*
> *Pancake Lady makes pancakes for free*
> *Eat 'em up, eat 'em up, one, two, three*
> *Pancake Lady's got a hold on me*

Suddenly Jamie gags and yells with his mouth full, "Look, there's a fly in my pancake. Yuck, there's a fly in my pancake."

Sure enough, Jamie's fork has uncovered a little fly, snugly wedged in a piece of white fluff, its itty feet and its bitty head sticking out.

"Jamie," says Sarah. "Don't make such a fuss over a little fly. You're going to spoil everyone's breakfast."

"Your mother's right," I say. "Have some more syrup and eat your pancakes."

"But I'm not hungry anymore. It's gross. A gross, dead fly in my pancake."

As soon as Jamie says gross, the fat man looks over at him with a pained expression. I put my arm around Jamie's shoulder and hug him to me so that his mouth is squeezed into my armpit. I smile at the fat man and whisper to Jamie, "You're embarrassing me, you little twit. Finish your pancakes or you won't eat for a month."

Jamie's mouth is so firmly planted in my armpit he can barely move his lips. "Daddy, you're hurting me," says a voice like the dummy of an amateur ventriloquist.

The fat man leans across the table and pokes his fork at my son. "Nice little boy you got there," he says. And then he does something disgusting. He sticks out his fat cow tongue, covered with big chunks of chewed-up pancakes. If he wasn't an adult, I'd think he had shown me his slimy food on purpose.

"Oh yes," I say, a little flabbergasted. "He is kind of nice. Jamie, thank the nice fat man."

Oh shit, I didn't mean to say that. I look at the fat man, but he's just smiling at me, taking big bites from his stack of pancakes.

"Daddy," says Jamie, his voice like the sound of a TV in another room. "Please let me go. I'll eat anything."

I free Jamie and tell him, "Now be a good boy and eat your pancakes and syrup."

Jamie looks all right, just a little red in the face. He picks up his fork, pours syrup on his pancakes, and then makes a big ceremony of cutting away the piece with the fly. He slides it with his fork to the side of his plate.

"His mother spoils him," I tell the fat man, and Sarah gives me a "wait until we get home" look.

I glance at Sarah and wonder why she still wears her hair in that phony flip that went out of style fifteen years ago. I just wish we had something like syrup to pour on our marriage.

Yesterday we were talking for the millionth time about having a kid, and I said, "Look, I bet you don't even know who the prime minister of Japan is."

"Maybe I don't," she said. "But that's because I don't bury myself in things that don't matter."

"The world doesn't matter?" I said.

When Sarah argues, she gets irrational. All she did to answer me was to recite this kids' rhyme, "Here's the church, here's the steeple. Open the doors and see all the people." She also made the corresponding motions with her hands, first interlocking her fists, then pointing her index fingers into a spire, and then opening up her hands and wiggling her fingers at me. After that she stuck out her tongue and locked herself in the bathroom. A woman like that certainly can't handle another child. Still, there was something sort of endearing about her at that moment.

Aunt Jemima finishes the song and we all clap for her. I wonder where she's been for the last fifteen years. Things sure do seem a lot simpler when she's around.

I look over at the fat man for a second. This time he looks me directly in the eye, and with a wink, opens his mouth as wide as it will go, showing me a mouthful of stuff that looks like foam rubber.

"Listen, mattress-face," I say. "I've had just about enough of you," and I get ready to send him a punch, though I'm sure he's got enough flesh in that shock-absorbing face to suck up half my arm. I'm halfway off the bench and across the table when Aunt Jemima starts into her next song, "Camptown Races." As soon as I hear that soothing voice, I just can't get up enough energy to be angry anymore. I float back nice and easy to my bench, like a paper cut-out doll.

I lean over to Sarah and whisper, "Speaking of racial stereotypes, what do you think of this one?"

"It's lovely," she says, smiling at me and blinking like she's in some 1960's beach party movie.

Aunt Jemima tells everyone to sing with her, and so we sing.

The kids love this song. Most of them don't know the words, but they sing along anyway. They especially love the line, Doo dah, doo dah, and won't sing anything but these words. The song soon turns into a shouting match among the children, most of them substituting Doo dah, and then Doo doo, for all the words in between. I sort of resent this alteration of the original, but no one else seems to mind. Aunt Jemima looks like she's having a blast, dancing around the stage like a voodoo queen, her enormous hands waving in front of her.

The fat man is yelling Doo doo in my face.

Plaster chips fall from the ceiling as the song ends, and with hardly a break, Aunt Jemima leads us in "The Hokey Pokey." The minister's hands flop up and down on the keyboard like a marionette's. Everyone rises from the benches and crowds in between the tables to do the Hokey Pokey dance. There's not enough room for a circle, so we make two lines facing each other. Like two Zulu armies dancing before a battle, we shake our feet, then our hands, and then we turn ourselves around.

Aunt Jemima's voice rises above us, singing, "That's what it's all about."

I am suddenly disturbed by the fact that I am shaking my hands and feet at the command of an old woman. If someone from the office were to come in now I would certainly be passed over for promotion. They'd make life unbearable. "Glad you're working for us," they'd say. "We need a man around the firm who knows his Hokey Pokey."

But I can't stop doing the dance. This is ten times better than watching "Meet the Press." It's hard to worry about work, divorce, or even the world when you're doing the Hokey Pokey.

When the song finally ends, everyone in the church basement groans. We want more, but Aunt Jemima says she's tired. In fact she looks completely drained. Her kerchief has fallen off, and she doesn't even have enough strength to pick it up. But we want an encore. The crowd's past control, with everyone shouting and hooting for more.

"I'm about ready for some more pancakes and syrup," I tell Sarah over the noise.

"Daddy?" says Jamie. "I'm tired. Can we go home?"

"We'll go home when I say so," I tell him. "We can't leave in the middle of Miss Jemima's last song. She'd be offended."

"You're good people," Aunt Jemima tells us. "Real fine people. Now before I sing my last song, I want to ask you, what's the best food in the whole wide world?"

"Pancakes!" we yell.

"And what tastes better on pancakes than anything else?"

"Syrup!"

Why, there's nothing we wouldn't eat for this fine woman.

With tears in her eyes, she leads us once again in "He's Got the Whole World in His Hands." We're still standing from the Hokey Pokey, and so we sway along.

When she says world, we all make a globe. When she says hands, we cup our hands like we're holding robins' eggs.

Then she sings, "He's got you and me brother in His hands," and clutches her chest. We all clutch our chests. She collapses on the floor, and everyone except for the minister at the piano collapses with her.

Lying on the floor like that, we sing until all the verses are done.

After the song ends, the basement is quiet except for our breathing. Slowly, we rise to our feet, all except Aunt Jemima, who remains on the floor, her arms folded on her chest, her eyes closed. She's quite a gal, joking around like that.

The minister gets up from his piano bench, steps over Aunt Jemima, and yells, "Three cheers for Aunt Jemima."

We all cheer, but she's so modest, she doesn't even respond. She just stays on the floor, that syrupy smile fixed on the ceiling.

I sit down with the rest of the crowd.

Then the waiters spring out of the kitchen, carrying trays of steaming hot pancakes and new bottles of syrup, and we begin to eat again. I have a voracious appetite. So does Jamie. He's shoveling pancakes into his mouth. The piece with the fly is gone. He must have eaten it. In fact, everyone is eating with so much gusto that no one has time to talk. All you can hear is the *squish squish* of people chewing pancakes, like the sound of an army walking in wet shoes.

People are smiling and laughing. I smile at Sarah. That hair style of hers is the most attractive thing in the world right now, except of course, for pancakes with lots of syrup.

I lean her way and say, "I've been thinking, Sarah. I've changed my mind. Let's have a baby."

"Let's have lots and lots of babies," she says.

"Gobs and gobs of babies."

"Daddy?" says Jamie with a cute expression of concern on his face. "If you have lots and lots of babies, will you still love me?"

"Why certainly, young man. That's what it's all about."

"Ooh Daddy," he says. "I love you as much as pancakes."

"With lots of syrup," I reply. "That reminds me. I could use some more."

I ask the nice man across the table to pass the syrup, and he kindly obliges. Then I see that a couple of paramedics have come to take Aunt Jemima away. No one else seems to notice. Maybe I'll find out what happened to her on the news, but then again, maybe I won't. I'm sure she'll be all right. I don't know, it's just a feeling I have, that all of us are safe together.

WILLIAM HAMILTON

Madame Vache

In my memory's permanent collection, I can find her face. On it was an expression of wide, apprehensive astonishment unless she was, as she usually was, eating. Eating, she was comfortable, calm, and relaxed. Her long eyelashes fluttered shut and half shut as her attention was collected by her taste buds. Away from the meal she was, with good reason, lost. Tension, confusion, suspicion, and wonder were all Madame found when she looked up from eating.

Madame Vache was the only cow at Ethelwild, my family's place in the Napa Valley. She was a Hereford cow. Since they aren't milk cows, Herefords are not as heavily uddered as the dairy breeds, so Madame Vache wasn't even obviously a cow. Being the only cow, and not particularly cowlike, must have had an effect on Madame's personality.

She didn't belong to us. She was kept on our land—like some other items too big for him to retain on his own premises—by a man who did carpentry for my family. She was an only cow, uncowlike and on loan.

Our place has not been altered by agriculture. It's much as it must have been when the Wappo Indians were landlord. When I think of a cow grazing, I think of a flat green field under a flat blue sky, all of it flat as a flag, including the profiled cow in the middle. But Madame had to climb among mossy rocks and weave through trees to graze, like the deer around her. We had about a dozen head of horses on the same land, but, they being horses and Madame being a cow, the commonality of their domestication wasn't, apparently, enough of a bond for Madame to travel with them through the woods.

Did I ever see Madame look enviously through the separation of brush and trees between her and that little community of horses, grazing and napping together, kicking and nudging each other, moving off in their inevitably sociable herd? Maybe I only imagine I did, or maybe I project how I would have felt being the only one of something watching others who had others.

Despite our citified presumption that what goes on in nature is strictly natural, it often isn't. Nature can be as artificially social as any other hostess. How do we know that the desperate scurry of insects that starts when you pick up a rock isn't from shame and embarrassment? They're naked, they can't find their bathrobes, and you've just walked in on them. This was exactly the sort of mortification that became apparent whenever I came upon Madame Vache in the hills. If she was lying down, dozing behind a bush when I found her, she would leap to her feet, as embarrassed as a night watchman discovered asleep on the job by the boss.

Her intense and baleful stare would, after a moment, swing left and right as she looked to see how the other cows were handling my intrusion. But of course there were no other cows, and Madame's stare would return to me and fill up with the shame of being reminded of her irremediable and endless difference from all the rest of the world she knew.

She was not only the only cow, and not cowlike and on loan; she was, furthermore, a virgin. She had arrived at Ethelwild a heifer and grown into a cow with no more reference and connection to her species than she had to her surroundings.

Because of these circumstances Madame Vache was, like a hero of Albert Camus or the voice of Søren Kierkegaard's philosophy, an existentialist. Existentialism added poignancy to the expression on her face, as it had to the jacket photographs of Camus I remembered from college. Her singularity, her otherness, and the heroism of resolve-despite-futility blazed in her eyes whenever she wasn't eating or sleeping.

Our carpenter decided to slaughter his cow. This kind of event disturbs people who might like to believe the parcels of meat in a supermarket could be reassembled into cows and freed to graze on flat fields forever, but, being country bred, I had no right to such sentiment. Madame was his cow.

Released from her earthly solitude, Madame was transmogrified by a butcher into all the familiar cuts composing the red garden of a modern market's meat display. The carpenter gave us several packages of Madame Vache. Soon she was served for dinner.

I, who had for years loved her and pondered over her, looked at her steak as if I would find a familiar lineament or even a knowing wink, but I found none. How did my old friend taste? That is the most fascinating part of her story.

Madame Vache was the best piece of beef I ever tasted. Because she browsed like the deer over a completely wild, unplanted range, she was a profoundly different flavor from any beef I knew. She was so fit from her hiker's life that her meat was not marbleized with fat. The meat was tender and clear, and it made me fancy I was tasting some of the long meal in our hills that had been the most enjoyable part of her life.

I was proud of her for tasting so good. I like to think if things had been the other way around, Madame would have enjoyed me as much as I enjoyed her.

VIRGINIA WOOLF

To the Lighthouse

Now all the candles were lit, and the faces on both sides of the table were brought nearer by the candle light, and composed, as they had not been in the twilight, into a party round a table, for the night was now shut off by panes of glass, which, far from giving any accurate view of the outside world, rippled it so strangely that here, inside the room, seemed to be order and dry land; there, outside, a reflection in which things wavered and vanished, waterily.

Some change at once went through them all, as if this had really happened, and they were all conscious of making a party together in a hollow, on an island; had their common cause against that fluidity out there. Mrs. Ramsay, who had been uneasy, waiting for Paul and Minta to come in, and unable, she felt, to settle to things, now felt her uneasiness changed to expectation. For now they must come, and Lily Briscoe, trying to analyze the cause of the sudden exhilaration, compared it with that moment on the tennis lawn, when solidity suddenly vanished, and such vast spaces lay between them; and now the same effect was got by the many candles in the sparely furnished room, and the uncurtained windows, and the bright mask-like look of faces seen by candlelight. Some weight was taken off them; anything might happen, she felt. They must come now, Mrs. Ramsay thought, looking at the door, and at that instant, Minta Doyle, Paul Rayley, and a maid carrying a great dish in her hands came in together. They were awfully late; they were horribly late, Minta said, as they found their way to different ends of the table.

"I lost my brooch—my grandmother's brooch," said Minta with a sound of lamentation in her voice, and a suffusion in her large brown eyes, looking down, looking up, as she sat by Mr. Ramsay, which roused his chivalry so that he bantered her.

How could she be such a goose, he asked, as to scramble about the rocks in jewels?

She was by way of being terrified of him—he was so fearfully clever, and the first night when she had sat by him, and he talked about George Eliot, she had been really frightened, for she had left the third volume of *Middlemarch* in the train and she never knew what happened in the end; but afterwards she got on perfectly, and made herself out even more ignorant than she was, because he liked telling her she was a fool. And so tonight, directly he laughed at her, she was not frightened. Besides, she knew, directly she came into the room, that the miracle had happened; she wore her golden haze. Sometimes she had it; sometimes not. She never knew why it came or why it went, or if she had it until she came into the room and then she knew instantly by the way some man looked at her. Yes, tonight she had it, tremendously; she knew that by the way Mr. Ramsay told her not to be a fool. She sat beside him, smiling.

It must have happened then, thought Mrs. Ramsay; they are engaged. And for a moment she felt what she had never expected to feel again— jealousy. For he, her husband, felt it too—Minta's glow; he liked these girls, these golden-reddish girls, with something flying, something a little wild and harum-scarum about them, who didn't "scrape their hair off," weren't, as he said about poor Lily Briscoe, "skimpy." There was some quality which she herself had not, some luster, some richness, which attracted him, amused him, led him to make favorites of girls like Minta. They might cut his hair for him, plait him watch-chains, or interrupt him at his work, hailing him (she heard them), "Come along, Mr. Ramsay; it's our turn to beat them now," and out he came to play tennis.

But indeed she was not jealous, only, now and then, when she made herself look in her glass a little resentful that she had grown old, perhaps, by her own fault. (The bill for the greenhouse and all the rest of it.) She was grateful to them for laughing at him. ("How many pipes have you smoked today, Mr. Ramsay?" and so on), till he seemed a young man; a man very attractive to women, not burdened, not weighed down with the greatness of his labors and the sorrows of the world and his fame or his failure, but again as she had first known him, gaunt but gallant; helping her out of a boat, she remembered; with delightful ways, like that (she looked at him, and he looked astonishingly young, teasing Minta). For herself—"Put it down there," she said, helping the Swiss girl to place gently before her the huge brown pot in which was the Bœuf en Daube—for her own part she liked her boobies. Paul must sit by her. She had kept a place for him. Really, she sometimes thought she liked the boobies best. They did not bother one with their dissertations. How much they missed, after all, these very clever men! How dried up they did become, to be sure. There was something, she thought as he sat down, very charming about Paul. His manners were delightful to her, and his sharp cut nose and his bright blue eyes. He was so considerate. Would he tell her—now that they were all talking again—what had happened?

"We went back to look for Minta's brooch," he said, sitting down by her. "We"—that was enough. She knew from the effort, the rise in his voice to surmount a difficult word that it was the first time he had said "we." "We" did this, "we" did that. They'll say that all their lives, she thought, and an exquisite scent of olives and oil and juice rose from the great brown dish as Marthe, with a little flourish, took the cover off. The cook had spent three days over that dish. And she must take great care, Mrs. Ramsay thought, diving into the soft mass, to choose a specially tender piece for William Bankes. And she peered into the dish, with its shiny walls and its confusion of savory brown and yellow meats, and its bay leaves and its wine, and thought: This will celebrate the occasion—a curious sense rising in her, at once freakish and tender, of celebrating a festival, as if two emotions were called up in her, one profound—for what could be more serious than the love of man for woman, what more commanding, more impressive, bearing in its bosom the seeds of death; at the same time these lovers, these people entering into illusion glittering eyed, must be danced round with mockery, decorated with garlands.

"It is a triumph," said Mr. Bankes, laying his knife down for a moment. He had eaten attentively. It was rich; it was tender. It was perfectly cooked. How did she manage these things in the depths of the country? he asked her. She was a wonderful woman. All his love, all his reverence had returned; and she knew it.

"It is a French recipe of my grandmother's," said Mrs. Ramsay, speaking with a ring of great pleasure in her voice. Of course it was French. What passes for cookery in England is an abomination (they agreed). It is putting cabbages in water. It is roasting meat till it is like leather. It is cutting off the delicious skins of vegetables. "In which," said Mr. Bankes, "all the virtue of the vegetable is contained." And the waste, said Mrs. Ramsay. A whole French family could live on what an English cook throws away. Spurred on by her sense that William's affection had come back to her, and that everything was all right again, and that her suspense was over, and that now she was free both to triumph and to mock, she laughed, she gesticulated, till Lily thought, How childlike, how absurd she was, sitting up there with all her beauty opened again in her, talking about the skins of vegetables. There was something frightening about her. She was irresistible.

KENNETH GRAHAME

Mr. Badger

They waited patiently for what seemed a very long time, stamping in the snow to keep their feet warm. At last they heard the sound of slow shuffling footsteps approaching the door from the inside. It seemed, as the Mole remarked to the Rat, like some one walking in carpet slippers that were too large for him and down-at-heel; which was intelligent of Mole, because that was exactly what it was.

There was the noise of a bolt shot back, and the door opened a few inches, enough to show a long snout and a pair of sleepy blinking eyes.

"Now, the *very* next time this happens," said a gruff and suspicious voice, "I shall be exceedingly angry. Who is it *this* time, disturbing people on such a night? Speak up!"

"O, Badger," cried the Rat, "let us in, please. It's me, Rat, and my friend Mole, and we've lost our way in the snow."

"What, Ratty, my dear little man!" exclaimed the Badger, in quite a different voice. "Come along in, both of you, at once. Why, you must be perished. Well I never! Lost in the snow! And in the Wild Wood, too, and at this time of night. But come in with you."

The two animals tumbled over each other in their eagerness to get inside, and heard the door shut behind them with great joy and relief.

The Badger, who wore a long dressing-gown, and whose slippers were indeed very down-at-heel, carried a flat candlestick in his paw and had probably been on his way to bed when their summons sounded. He looked kindly down on them and patted both their heads. "This is not the sort of night for small animals to be out," he said paternally. "I'm afraid you've been up to some of your pranks again, Ratty. But come along; come into the kitchen. There's a first-rate fire there, and supper and everything."

He shuffled on in front of them, carrying the light, and they followed him, nudging each other in an anticipating sort of way, down a long, gloomy, and, to tell the truth, decidedly shabby passage, into a sort of a central hall, out of which they could dimly see other long tunnel-like passages branching, passages mysterious and without apparent end. But there were doors in the hall as well—stout oaken comfortable-looking doors. One of these the Badger flung open, and at once they found themselves in all the glow and warmth of a large fire-lit kitchen.

The floor was well-worn red brick, and on the wide hearth burned a fire of logs, between two attractive chimney-corners tucked away in the wall, well out of any suspicion of draught. A couple of high-backed settles, facing each other on either side of the fire, gave further sitting accommodation for the sociably disposed. In the middle of the room stood a long table of plain boards placed on trestles, with benches down each side. At one end of it, where an armchair stood pushed back, were spread the remains of the Badger's plain but ample supper. Rows of spotless plates winked from the shelves of the dresser at the far end of the room, and from the rafters overhead hung hams, bundles of dried herbs, nets of onions, and baskets of eggs. It seemed a place where heroes could fitly feast after victory, where weary harvesters could line up in scores along the table and keep their Harvest Home with mirth and song, or where two or three friends of simple tastes could sit about as they pleased and eat and smoke and talk in comfort and contentment. The ruddy brick floor smiled up at the smoky ceiling; the oaken settles, shiny with long wear, exchanged cheerful glances with each other; plates on the dresser grinned at pots on the shelf, and the merry firelight flickered and played over everything without distinction.

The kindly Badger thrust them down on a settle to toast themselves at the fire, and bade them remove their wet coats and boots. Then he fetched them dressing-gowns and slippers, and himself bathed the Mole's shin with warm water and mended the cut with sticking-plaster till the whole thing was just as good as new, if not better. In the embracing light and warmth, warm and dry at last, with weary legs propped up in front of them, and a suggestive clink of plates being arranged on the table behind, it seemed to the storm-driven animals, now in safe anchorage, that the cold and trackless Wild Wood just left outside was miles and miles away, and all that they had suffered in it a half-forgotten dream.

When at last they were thoroughly toasted, the Badger summoned them to the table, where he had been busy laying a repast. They had felt pretty hungry before, but when they actually saw at last the supper that was spread for them, really it seemed only a question of what they should attack first where all was so attractive, and whether the other things would obligingly wait for them till they had time to give them attention. Conversation was impossible for a long time; and when it was slowly resumed, it was that regrettable sort of conversation that results from talking with your mouth full. The Badger did not mind that sort of thing at all, nor did he take any notice of elbows on the table, or everybody speaking at once. As he did not go into Society himself, he had got an idea that these things belonged to the things that didn't really matter. (We know of course that he was wrong, and took too narrow a view; because they do matter very much, though it would take too long to explain why.) He sat in his armchair at the head of the table, and nodded gravely at intervals as the animals told their story; and he did not seem surprised or shocked at anything, and he never said, "I told you so," or, "Just what I always said," or remarked that they ought to have done so-and-so, or ought not to have done something else. The Mole began to feel very friendly towards him.

When supper was really finished at last, and each animal felt that his skin was now as tight as was decently safe, and that by this time he didn't care a hang for anybody or anything, they gathered round the glowing embers of the great wood fire, and thought how jolly it was to be sitting up *so* late, and *so* independent, and *so* full.

"Well, it's time we were all in bed," said the Badger, getting up and fetching flat candlesticks. "Come along, you two, and I'll show you your quarters. And take your time tomorrow morning—breakfast at any hour you please!"

He conducted the two animals to a long room that seemed half bedchamber and half loft. The Badger's winter stores, which indeed were visible everywhere, took up half the room—piles of apples, turnips, and potatoes, baskets full of nuts, and jars of honey; but the two little white beds on the remainder of the floor looked soft and inviting, and the linen on them, though coarse, was clean and smelled beautifully of lavender; and the Mole and the Water Rat, shaking off their garments in some thirty seconds, tumbled in between the sheets in great joy and contentment.

In accordance with the kindly Badger's injunctions, the two tired animals came down to breakfast very late next morning, and found a bright fire burning in the kitchen, and two young hedgehogs sitting on a bench at the table, eating oatmeal porridge out of wooden bowls. The hedgehogs dropped their spoons, rose to their feet, and ducked their heads respectfully as the two entered.

"There, sit down, sit down," said the Rat pleasantly, "and go on with your porridge. Where have you youngsters come from? Lost your way in the snow, I suppose?"

"Yes, please sir," said the elder of the two hedgehogs respectfully. "Me and little Billy here, we was trying to find our way to school—mother *would* have us go, was the weather ever so—and of course we lost ourselves, sir, and Billy he got frightened and took and cried, being young and faint-hearted. And at last we happened up against Mr. Badger's back door, and made so bold as to knock, sir, for Mr. Badger he's a kind-hearted gentleman, as every one knows—"

"I understand," said the Rat, cutting himself some rashers from a side of bacon, while the Mole dropped some eggs into a saucepan. "And what's the weather like outside? You needn't 'sir' me quite so much," he added.

"O, terrible bad, sir, terrible deep the snow is," said the hedgehog. "No getting out for the likes of you gentlemen today."

"Where's Mr. Badger?" inquired the Mole, as he warmed the coffee pot before the fire.

"The master's gone into his study, sir," replied the hedgehog, "and he said as how he was going to be particular busy this morning, and on no account was he to be disturbed."

This explanation, of course, was thoroughly understood by every one present. The fact is, as already set forth, when you live a life of intense activity for six months in the year, and of comparative or actual somnolence for the other six, during the latter period you cannot be continually pleading sleepiness when there are people about or things to be done. The excuse gets monotonous. The animals well knew that Badger, having eaten a hearty breakfast, had retired to his study and settled himself in an armchair with his legs up on another and a red cotton handkerchief over his face, and was being "busy" in the usual way at this time of the year.

The front doorbell clanged loudly, and the Rat, who was very greasy with buttered toast, sent Billy, the smaller hedgehog, to see who it might be. There was a sound of much stamping in the hall, and presently Billy returned in front of the Otter, who threw himself on the Rat with an embrace and a shout of affectionate greeting.

"Get off!" spluttered the Rat, with his mouth full.

"Thought I should find you here all right," said the Otter cheerfully. "They were all in a great state of alarm along River Bank when I arrived this morning. Rat never been home all night—nor Mole either—something dreadful must have happened, they said; and the snow had covered up all your tracks, of course. But I knew that when people were in any fix they mostly went to Badger, or else Badger got to know of it somehow, so I came straight off here, through the Wild Wood and the snow! My! it was fine, coming through the snow as the red sun was rising and showing against the black treetrunks! As you went along in the stillness, every now and then masses of snow slid off the branches suddenly with a flop! making you jump and run for cover. Snow-castles and snow-caverns had sprung up out of nowhere in the night—and snow bridges, terraces, ramparts—I could have stayed and played with them for hours. Here and there great branches had been torn away by the sheer weight of the snow, and robins perched and hopped on them in their perky conceited way, just as if they had done it themselves. A ragged string of wild geese passed overhead, high on the grey sky, and a few rooks whirled over the trees, inspected, and flapped off homewards with a disgusted expression; but I met no sensible being to ask the news of. About halfway across I came on a rabbit sitting on a stump, cleaning his silly face with his paws. He was a pretty scared animal when I crept up behind him and placed a heavy forepaw on his shoulder. I had to cuff his head once or twice to get any sense out of it at all. At last I managed to extract from him that Mole had been seen in the Wild Wood last night by one of them. It was the talk of the burrows, he said, how Mole, Mr. Rat's particular friend, was in a bad fix; how he had lost his way, and 'They' were up and out hunting, and were chivvying him round and round. 'Then why didn't any of you *do* something?' I asked. 'You mayn't be blessed with brains, but there are hundreds and hundreds of you, big stout fellows, as fat as butter, and your burrows running in all directions, and you could have taken him in and made him safe and comfortable, or tried to, at all events.' 'What, *us*?' he merely said: '*do* something? us rabbits?' So I cuffed him again and left him. There was nothing else to be done. At any rate, I had learned something; and if I had had the luck to meet any of 'Them' I'd have learned something more—or *they* would."

"Weren't you at all—er—nervous?" asked the Mole, some of yesterday's terror coming back to him at the mention of the Wild Wood.

"Nervous?" The Otter showed a gleaming set of strong white teeth as he laughed. "I'd give 'em nerves if any of them tried anything on with me. Here, Mole, fry me some slices of ham, like the good little chap you are. I'm frightfully hungry, and I've got any amount to say to Ratty here. Haven't seen him for an age."

So the good-natured Mole, having cut some slices of ham, set the hedgehogs to fry it, and returned to his own breakfast, while the Otter and the Rat, their heads together, eagerly talked river-shop, which is long shop and talk that is endless, running on like the babbling river itself.

A plate of fried ham had just been cleared and sent back for more, when the Badger entered, yawning and rubbing his eyes, and greeted them all in his quiet, simple way, with kind inquiries for every one. "It must be getting on for luncheon time," he remarked to the Otter. "Better stop and have it with us. You must be hungry, this cold morning."

"Rather!" replied the Otter, winking at the Mole. "The sight of these greedy young hedgehogs stuffing themselves with fried ham makes me feel positively famished."

The hedgehogs, who were just beginning to feel hungry again after their porridge, and after working so hard at their frying, looked timidly up at Mr. Badger, but were too shy to say anything.

"Here, you two youngsters be off home to your mother," said the Badger kindly. "I'll send some one with you to show you the way. You won't want any dinner today, I'll be bound."

He gave them sixpence apiece and a pat on the head, and they went off with much respectful swinging of caps and touching of forelocks.

THOMAS PYNCHON

Banana Breakfasts

An Excerpt from *Gravity's Rainbow*

His name is Capt. Geoffrey ("Pirate") Prentice. He is wrapped in a thick blanket, a tartan of orange, rust, and scarlet. His skull feels made of metal.

Just above him, twelve feet overhead, Teddy Bloat is about to fall out of the minstrels' gallery, having chosen to collapse just at the spot where somebody in a grandiose fit, weeks before, had kicked out two of the ebony balusters. Now, in his stupor, Bloat has been inching through the opening, head, arms, and torso, until all that's keeping him up there is an empty champagne split in his hip pocket, that's got hooked somehow—

By now Pirate has managed to sit up on his narrow bachelor bed, and blink about. How awful. How bloody awful . . . above him, he hears cloth rip. The Special Operations Executive has trained him to fast responses. He leaps off of the cot and kicks it rolling on its casters in Bloat's direction. Bloat, plummeting, hits square amidships with a great strum of bedsprings. One of the legs collapses. "Good morning," notes Pirate. Bloat smiles briefly and goes back to sleep, snuggling well into Pirate's blanket.

Bloat is one of the co-tenants of the place, a maisonette erected last century, not far from the Chelsea Embankment, by Corydon Throsp, an acquaintance of the Rossettis' who wore hair smocks and liked to cultivate pharmaceutical plants up on the roof (a tradition young Osbie Feel has lately revived), a few of them hardy enough to survive fogs and frosts, but most returning, as fragments of peculiar alkaloids, to rooftop earth, along with manure from a trio of prize Wessex Saddleback sows quartered there by

Throsp's successor, and dead leaves off many decorative trees transplanted to the roof by later tenants, and the odd unstomachable meal thrown or vomited there by this or that sensitive epicurean—all got scumbled together, eventually, by the knives of the seasons, to an impasto, feet thick, of unbelievable black topsoil in which anything could grow, not the least being bananas. Pirate, driven to despair by the wartime banana shortage, decided to build a glass hothouse on the roof, and persuade a friend who flew the Rio–to–Ascension–to–Fort-Lamy run to pinch him a sapling banana tree or two, in exchange for a German camera, should Pirate happen across one on his next mission by parachute.

Pirate has become famous for his Banana Breakfasts. Messmates throng here from all over England, even some who are allergic or outright hostile to bananas, just to watch—for the politics of bacteria, the soil's stringing of rings and chains in nets only God can tell the meshes of, have seen the fruit thrive often to lengths of a foot and a half, yes amazing but true.

Pirate in the lavatory stands pissing, without a thought in his head. Then he threads himself into a wool robe he wears inside out so as to keep his cigarette pocket hidden, not that this works too well, and circling the warm bodies of friends makes his way to French windows, slides outside into the cold, groans as it hits the fillings in his teeth, climbs a spiral ladder ringing to the roof garden and stands for a bit, watching the river. The sun is still below the horizon. The day feels like rain, but for now the air is uncommonly clear. The great power station, and the gasworks beyond, stand precisely: crystals grown in morning's beaker, stacks, vents, towers, plumbing, gnarled emissions of steam and smoke. . . .

"Hhahh," Pirate in a voiceless roar watching his breath slip away over the parapets, "hhaahhh!" Rooftops dance in the morning. His giant bananas cluster, radiant yellow, humid green. His companions below dream drooling of a Banana Breakfast. This well-scrubbed day ought to be no worse than any—

Will it? Far to the east, down in the pink sky, something has just sparked, very brightly. A new star, nothing less noticeable. He leans on the parapet to watch. The brilliant point has already become a short vertical white line. It must be somewhere out over the North Sea . . . at least that far . . . icefields below and a cold smear of sun. . . .

What is it? Nothing like this ever happens. But Pirate knows it, after all. He has seen it in a film, just in the last fortnight . . . it's a vapor trail. Already a finger's width higher now. But not from an airplane. Airplanes are not launched vertically. This is the new, and still Most Secret, German rocket bomb.

"Incoming mail." Did he whisper that, or only think it? He tightens the ragged belt of his robe. Well, the range of these things is supposed to be over 200 miles. You can't see a vapor trail 200 miles, now, can you.

Oh. Oh, yes: around the curve of the Earth, farther east, the sun over there, just risen over in Holland, is striking the rocket's exhaust, drops and crystals, making them blaze clear across the sea. . . .

The white line, abruptly, has stopped its climb. That would be fuel cutoff, end of burning, what's their word . . . Brennschluss. We don't have one. Or else it's classified. The bottom of the line, the original star, has already begun to vanish in red daybreak. But the rocket will be here before Pirate sees the sun rise.

The trail, smudged, slightly torn in two or three directions, hangs in the sky. Already the rocket, gone pure ballistic, has risen higher. But invisible now.

Oughtn't he to be doing something . . . get on to the operations room at Stanmore, they must have it on the Channel radars—no: no time, really. Less than five minutes Hague to here (the time it takes to walk down to the teashop on the corner . . . for light from the sun to reach the planet of love . . . no time at all). Run out in the street? Warn the others?

Pick bananas. He trudges through black compost in to the hothouse. He feels he's about to shit. The missile, sixty miles high, must be coming up on the peak of its trajectory by now . . . beginning its fall . . . *now.* . . .

Trusswork is pierced by daylight, milky panes beam beneficently down. How could there be a winter—even this one—gray enough to age this iron that can sing in the wind, or cloud these windows that open into another season, however falsely preserved?

Pirate looks at his watch. Nothing registers. The pores of his face are prickling. Emptying his mind—a Commando trick—he steps into the wet heat of his bananery, sets about picking the ripest and the best, holding up the skirt of his robe to drop them in. Allowing himself to count only bananas, moving barelegged among the pendulous bunches, among these yellow chandeliers, this tropical twilight. . . .

Out into the winter again. The contrail is gone entirely from the sky. Pirate's sweat lies on his skin almost as cold as ice.

He takes some time lighting a cigarette. He won't hear the thing come in. It travels faster than the speed of sound. The first news you get of it is the blast. Then, if you're still around, you hear the sound of it coming in.

What if it should hit *exactly*—ahh, no—for a split second you'd have to feel the very point, with the terrible mass above, strike the top of the skull. . . .

Pirate hunches his shoulders, bearing his bananas down the corkscrew ladder.

Across a blue tile patio, in through a door to the kitchen. Routine: plug in American blending machine won from Yank last summer, some poker game, table stakes, B.O.Q. somewhere in the north, never remember now. . . . Chop several bananas into pieces. Make coffee in urn. Get can of milk from cooler. Puree 'nanas in milk. Lovely. *I would coat all the booze-corroded stomachs of England.* . . . Bit of marge, still smells all right, melt in skillet. Peel more bananas, slice lengthwise. Marge sizzling, in go long slices. Light oven *whoomp* blow us all up someday oh, ha, ha, yes. Peeled whole bananas to go on broiler grill soon as it heats. Find marshmallows. . . .

In staggers Teddy Bloat with Pirate's blanket over his head, slips on a banana peel and falls on his ass. "Kill myself," he mumbles.

"The Germans will do it for you. Guess what I saw from the roof."

"That V-2 on the way?"

"A4, yes."

"I watched it out the window. About ten minutes ago. Looked queer, didn't it. Haven't heard a thing since, have you. It must have fallen short. Out to sea or something."

"Ten minutes?" Trying to read the time on his watch.

"At least." Bloat is sitting on the floor, working the banana peel into a pajama lapel for a boutonniere.

Pirate goes to the phone and rings up Stanmore after all. Has to go through the usual long, long routine, but knows he's already stopped believing in the rocket he saw. God has plucked it for him, out of its airless sky, like a steel banana. "Prentice here, did you have anything like a pip from Holland a moment ago. Aha. Aha. yes, we *saw* it." This could ruin a man's taste for sunrises. He rings off. "They lost it over the coast. They're calling it premature Brennschluss."

"Cheer up," Teddy crawling back toward the busted cot. "There'll be more."

Good old Bloat, always the positive word. Pirate for a few seconds there, waiting to talk to Stanmore, was thinking, Danger's over, Banana Breakfast is saved. But it's only a reprieve. Isn't it. There will indeed be others, each just as likely to land on top of him. No one either side of the front knows exactly how many more. Will we have to stop watching the sky?

Osbie Feel stands in the minstrels' gallery, holding one of the biggest of Pirate's bananas so that it protrudes out the fly of his striped pajama

217

bottoms—stroking with his other hand the great jaundiced curve in triplets against 4/4 toward the ceiling, he acknowledges dawn with the following:

> Time to gather your arse up off the floor,
>> (have a bana-na)
> Brush your teeth and go toddling off to war.
> Wave your hand to sleepy land,
> Kiss those dreams away,
> Tell Miss Grable you're not able,
> Not till V-E Day, oh,
> Ev'rything'll be grand in Civvie Street
>> (have a bana-na)
> Bubbly wine and girls wiv lips so sweet—
> But there's still the German or two to fight,
> So show us a smile that's shiny bright,
> And then, as we may have suggested once before—
> Gather yer blooming arse up off the floor!

There's a second verse, but before he can get quite into it, prancing Osbie is leaped upon and thoroughly pummeled, in part with his own stout banana, by Bartley Gobbitch, DeCoverley Pox, and Maurice ("Saxophone") Reed, among others. In the kitchen, black-market marshmallows slide languid into syrup atop Pirate's double boiler, and soon begin thickly to bubble. Coffee brews. On a wooden pub sign daringly taken, one daylight raid, by a drunken Bartley Gobbitch, across which still survives in intaglio the legend SNIPE AND SHAFT, Teddy Bloat is mincing bananas with a great isosceles knife, from beneath whose nervous blade Pirate with one hand shovels the blonde mash into waffle batter resilient with fresh hens' eggs, for which Osbie Feel has exchanged an equal number of golf balls, these being even rarer this winter than real eggs, other hand blending the fruit in, not overvigorously, with a wire whisk, whilst surly Osbie himself, sucking frequently at a half-pint milk bottle filled with Vat 69 and water, tends to the bananas in the skillet and broiler. Near the exit to the blue patio, DeCoverley Pox and Joaquin Stick stand by a concrete scale model of the Jungfrau, which some enthusiast back during the twenties spent a painstaking year modeling and casting before finding out it was too large to get out of any door, socking the slopes of the famous mountain with red rubber hot-water bags full of ice cubes, the idea being to pulverize the ice for Pirate's banana frappés. With their nights' growths of beard, matted hair, bloodshot eyes, miasmata of foul breath, DeCoverley and Joaquin are wasted gods urging on a tardy glacier.

Elsewhere in the maisonette, other drinking companions disentangle from blankets (one spilling wind from his, dreaming of a parachute), piss into bathroom sinks, look at themselves with dismay in concave shaving mirrors, slap water with no clear plan in mind onto heads of thinning hair, struggle into Sam Brownes, dub shoes against rain later in the day with hand muscles already weary of it, sing snatches of popular songs whose tunes they don't always know, lie, believing themselves warmed, in what patches of the new sunlight come between the mullions, begin tentatively to talk shop as a way of easing into whatever it is they'll have to be doing in less than an hour, lather necks and faces, yawn, pick their noses, search cabinets or bookcases for the hair of the dog that not without provocation and much prior conditioning bit them last night.

Now there grows among all the rooms, replacing the night's old smoke, alcohol and sweat, the fragile, musaceous odor of Breakfast: flowery, permeating, surprising, more than the color of winter sunlight, taking over not so much through any brute pungency or volume as by the high intricacy to the weaving of its molecules, sharing the conjuror's secret by which—though it is not often Death is told so clearly to fuck off—the living genetic chains prove even labyrinthine enough to preserve some human face down ten or twenty generations . . . so the same assertion-through-structure allows this war morning's banana fragrance to meander, repossess, prevail. Is there any reason not to open every window, and let the kind scent blanket all Chelsea? As a spell, against falling objects. . . .

With a clattering of chairs, upended shell cases, benches, and ottomans, Pirate's mob gather at the shores of the great refectory table, a southern island well across a tropic or two from chill Corydon Throsp's mediaeval fantasies, crowded now over the swirling dark grain of its walnut uplands with banana omelets, banana sandwiches, banana casseroles, mashed bananas molded in the shape of a British lion rampant, blended with eggs into batter for French toast, squeezed out a pastry nozzle across the quivering creamy reaches of a banana blancmange to spell out the words C'est magnifique, mais ce n'est pas la guerre (attributed to a French observer during the Charge of the Light Brigade) which Pirate has appropriated as his motto . . . tall cruets of pale banana syrup to pour oozing over banana waffles, a giant glazed crock where diced bananas have been fermenting since the summer with wild honey and muscat raisins, up out of which, this winter morning, one now dips foam mugsfull of banana mead . . . banana croissants and banana kreplach, and banana oatmeal and banana jam and banana bread, and bananas flamed in ancient brandy Pirate brought back last year from a cellar in the Pyrenees also containing a clandestine radio transmitter . . .

219

The phone call, when it comes, rips easily across the room, the hangovers, the grabassing, the clatter of dishes, the shoptalk, the bitter chuckles, like a rude metal double-fart, and Pirate knows it's got to be for him. Bloat, who's nearest, takes it, forkful of *bananes glacées* poised fashionably in the air. Pirate takes up a last dipper of mead, feels it go valving down his throat as if it's time, time in its summer tranquility, he swallows.

"Your employer."

"It's not fair," Pirate moans, "I haven't even done me morning push-ups yet."

The voice, which he's heard only once before—last year at a briefing, hands and face blackened, anonymous among a dozen other listeners—tells Pirate now there's a message addressed to him, waiting at Greenwich.

"It came over in a rather delightful way," the voice high-pitched and sullen, "none of *my* friends are that clever. All *my* mail arrives by post. Do come collect it, won't you, Prentice." Receiver hits cradle a violent whack, connection breaks, and now Pirate knows where this morning's rocket landed, and why there was no explosion. Incoming mail, indeed. He gazes through sunlight's buttresses, back down the refectory at the others, wallowing in their plenitude of bananas, thick palatals of their hunger lost somewhere in the stretch of morning between them and himself. A hundred miles of it, so suddenly. Solitude, even among the meshes of this war, can when it wishes so take him by the blind gut and touch, as now, possessively. Pirate's again some other side of a window, watching strangers eat breakfast.

BETTY FUSSELL

On Murdering Eels and Laundering Swine

Murder we must. If not cows and pigs and fish, then cabbages and rutabagas. We flay bananas, violate oysters, ravage pomegranates. Our lot is beastly and there's no help for it, for feed we must on creature kinds. Our hands are stained with carrot blood and not all the seas of Noah's Flood will wash them clean, not after God's pact with Noah: "Every moving thing that lives shall be food for you." That's a lot of territory in which to assert our puny manhood and decree that this is fit and this not, this food pure and that dirty. No, all that lives is food for man who, dead, is food for worms. That's the deal.

Some living things are harder to kill than others, even though some things beg to be killed. Snakes, for instance. Their very shape mirrors our throttled circumstances, the narrowness of our confines, the anguish of our passage. The same root, *ango*, generates *anguis* (snake) and anguish (pain). The same root generates *anguilla* (eel), a fish in snake's clothing. Its snaky form makes some eaters queasy and others ravenous, but to eat an eel you must kill him first and quite deliberately, with the zeal of an ax murderer, because he is well armed against us.

I have killed many snakes in the desert when it was their life or mine, but killing an eel in cold blood, on the fourth floor, in a New York City apartment—that's different. The eel and I were already intimate, for I had carried him in my lap in a large plastic bag on the subway from Chinatown, and he had roiled against my belly as if I were pregnant with eels. Watching the bag slither with speed across my kitchen floor, I was afraid to deliver him. I was, in fact, deathly afraid of snakes.

221

My father had kept them in cages in our basement, next to the laundry tub, the newfangled washing machine, and the old-fashioned clothes wringer. Dumping laundry from tub to washer to wringer to basket for hanging on the line, I kept my eye on the snakes. Whether harmless as garters or lethal as rattlers, they were the Serpent *anguiformes*, the One cursed by God to creep without legs or wings on its belly, condemned without mercy to the darkness of a basement with a burnt-out bulb. Their skins, if you touched them, were cold as death and, though dry, wet as an oyster. Because of them I was damned, as my grandfather had read me in the Book of Genesis, "For the imagination of man's heart is evil from his youth." I was young and therefore evil. The logic was impeccable: the snake and I were kin.

Nothing in my basement past, however, had prepared me for murdering an eel. I needed time to think and threw the bag in the freezer overnight. When I opened the bag in the sink next day, he looked stone cold dead. When I turned the water on to remove the slime, he came suddenly to life. I grabbed a Chinese cleaver and tried to grab his thrusting head, but he was all muscle and I was not. With both hands I slammed the cleaver down on what might have been his neck but may have been his shoulders. A mighty whack barely nicked him. I whacked again as, tail thrashing, he tried to worm his way down the minnow-sized drain. "I'm sorry," I apologized with every whack, and I was. But I needn't have been because I had not even scotched the snake, let alone killed him.

I looked for a blunt instrument and found a wooden mallet that I used for pounding meat. I cracked the mallet on his head and the wood split, but nothing else. He was breathing heavily, gulping air that filled a pouch below his jaws. Was he strangling? I didn't want to know. Like Raskolnikov, I wanted him dead. Like Rasputin, he refused to die. I looked to the freezer for respite and held the bag open for him to slither in. He went halfway, then with a quick U-turn wrapped his tail around my arm and began to slither out. Engulfing him with a second bag, I flopped the works onto the ice trays and slammed the freezer door.

I needed time for research and reflection, my brain against his muscle. I consulted books. "To kill eels instantly, without the horrid torture of cutting and skinning them alive, pierce the spinal marrow, close to the back part of the skull, with a sharp-pointed skewer," William Kitchiner advised in the *Cook's Oracle* in 1817. "The humane executioner," he added, "does certain criminals the favour to hang them before he breaks them on the wheel." A kind thought, but what if the criminal refused to hang? Madame Saint-Ange, in *La Cuisine*, advised French housewives to grab the eel's tail in a dishtowel and bash its head violently against a stone or wall. So much for sentimental Brits.

Surely there was some practical, efficient, clean—American—way to kill. The best way to kill an eel, A. J. McClane wrote in his *Encyclopedia of Fish Cookery*, was to put him in a container of coarse salt. I poured two large boxes of coarse kosher salt into a large stockpot, pulled the eel bag from the freezer, and slid the mound of icy coils into the pot. Before they could quiver, I blanketed them with salt and waited. Nothing stirred. Salt, McClane said, also "deslimes" the eel, but my hands and clothes were already covered with an ooze that would not wash off. When I finally inspected my victim, I found the deed was done, his mouth marred by a single drop of blood.

Skinning was yet to come. McClane suggested I attach his head by a string to a nail pounded in a board. I had neither nail nor board. What I wanted was an electric 7¼-inch circular saw with a carbide-tooth blade. What I had was a pair of poultry shears. I pierced his thick hide and cut a jagged circle below his head, then scissored the length of his belly. With one hand I held his head and with the other pulled back the skin with a pair of stout pliers. It was slow work, but the leathery hide finally slipped off the tail like a nylon stocking. Naked, he was malleable as any flesh.

With one clean stroke I severed his head and hacked him into lengths. He was a three-pound meaty boy, thick and fat. He was everything one could ask for in an eel. I put him in a pot and baptized him with white wine and vinegar, vegetables and herbs, and butter whipped to a froth. He was delicious, as fat eels always are, and crowned my murderer's feast with blessing. For the order of eels are in nature born and buried in salt. Enduring a lifetime's banishment to freshwater pastures and the long journey there and back, they return to their cradle in the salt Sargasso Sea to die in a burst of sperm and roe. "It is a covenant of salt forever": God's covenant with Levi matched the one with Noah. The salt that blesses and preserves also deslimes and kills. The eel and I were bound by the same double deal. His life for mine, salt our shared salvation.

A serpent dead, however, did nothing to scotch my deeper anguish. "Shit is a more onerous theological problem than is evil," Milan Kundera wrote in *The Unbearable Lightness of Being*. "Since God gave man freedom, we can, if need be, accept the idea that He is not responsible for man's crimes. The responsibility for shit, however, rests entirely with Him, the Creator of man." If murder is man's crime, shit is not. Shit is God's joke, yet shit we must even as we feed.

What was my relation to the ten pounds of frozen hog's guts, thawing and spreading like drowned Ophelia's hair, in my apartment bathtub? The chitterlings, ten times the length of my own inner tubing, were pastel yellow, white, and pink. They spread like dubious laundry, triggering memories of washing dirty socks and underwear in the bathtubs of innumerable French and Italian hotels that invariably forbade guests to launder. With guts as with underwear, it were better to do as a French cookbook instructs, "Take the stomach and intestines to the nearest stream or river." Women once washed guts as they washed linen, rising at dawn to carry their baskets of offal to the communal gathering place, to laugh and quarrel, a medieval poet said, as they washed "inwards" at the stream.

It is laundry that connects pig's inwards to man's outwards. The ruffles on a shirtfront were once called chitterlings, "exuberant chitterlings," as Washington Irving said, "puffed out at the neck and bosom." Our foppish frills were once the ancients' omens, when offal was deemed awe-ful and the parts most worthy of the gods. A beast's inwards then put men in touch with the stars, the outermost circle of our confinement. But we who see in serpents no more than snakes, in guts no more than garbage, in destiny no more than a gambler's shake—to our narrow and straightened palates, chitterlings are the food of slaves.

I suppose it's the smell that does it, a pervasive stink that clings to hands and hair, slightly sweet, slightly sour, like dank earth turned over, like rotting bodies in a trench, like human shit. It rubs our noses in all we would deny. Washing guts, I found clusters of fat stuck to the inner lining, along with specks of what dignified recipes call "foreign matter." Some guts are thick and rubbery, others thin and limp as wet hankies. Guts are not smooth like plastic tubing, but gathered lengthwise along invisible seams, to puff like parachute silk with gas. They are gathered the way a seamstress gathers cloth for ruffles. To reach the translucent membrane of the casing, I had to strip and strip again the clogging fat until, held to the light, the stretched skin showed leaf patterns, clouds, sea scum, palely mottled and beautiful. Only by laundering the guts of swine did I discover that shit comes wrapped in a layer of clouds trapped in a membrane resilient as nylon. Still, my lustrations were brief. Most of the cleansing had been done for me at the slaughterhouse, before the guts were frozen by the Gwaltney Company, a son of IT&T. The corporate master that sent me hog's guts puts satellites in space, making however inadvertently the cosmic connection of shit and stars.

From Lily of the Valley, Virginia, a slave's granddaughter told me that she cooks chitlins in their own yellow juice with onion and garlic and vinegar, until the guts are tender enough to chew. Chewy they are, rich on the tongue like all rejected vitals—heart, liver, lights, or haslet—all those messy inwards that remind us uneasily of our own. "Cut them chitlins in small lengths, or knot 'em, and cook 'em up with collards or rice in the pot of chitlin gravy, or fry 'em deep in bubblin' fat till they float up crisp and light," she said.

Even crisp and light, a little inwards go a long way. They go a long way as vitals, en route to shitty death. Bre'r hog knows better than I the rhythm that melds eating and shitting in every moving thing that lives, in the dung birth and death of cabbages and swine, men and snakes. "We must pitch our tents in the fields of excrement," cried Crazy Jane, who liked the way my fingers smell, my stove, my bathtub. The smell of chitterlings clings to the air the way the taste of chitterlings sticks to the tongue. It is a lingering power that gives, my Lily of the Valley friend says, satisfaction.

But I am a child of deodorized air and Lysol drains. My pasteurized senses are not ready for the excremental smell of my bathtub. I poured "Fragrant Pine" bubble bath into the water and was ashamed to read the labeled contents: sulfates, chlorides, formaldehydes, succinates, and an in-gredient called "fragrance." I am too sanitized for the fragrance of pig shit. I can turn murder into blessing by symbolic salt, but excrement into sacra-ment is a harder trick to turn. God owes me there. My guts are serpentine as a mess of eels, but the inward darkness of Genesis shakes out as farce. Farce is my Exodus. I know that after a lifetime's wandering through a wilderness of snakes and swine, no amount of murdering, no amount of laundering, will change my promised end as meat and gravy for rutabagas, pudding for worms.

THOMAS WOLFE

His Father's Earth

As the boy stood looking at the circus with his brother, there came to him two images, which had haunted his childhood and the life of every boy who ever lived, but were now for the first time seen together with an instant and magic congruence. And these two images were the images of the circus and his father's earth.

He thought then he had joined a circus and started on the great tour of the nation with it. It was spring: the circus had started in New England and worked westward and then southward as the summer and autumn came on. His nominal duties—for, in his vision, every incident, each face and voice and circumstance were blazing real as life itself—were those of ticket seller, but in this tiny show, everyone did several things: the performers helped put up and take down the tents, load and unload the wagons, and the roustabouts and business people worked wherever they were needed.

The boy sold tickets, but he also posted bills and bartered with tradesmen and farmers in new places for fresh food. He became very shrewd and clever at this work, and loved to do it—some old, sharp, buried talent for shrewd trading, that had come to him from his mountain blood, now aided him. He could get the finest, freshest meats and vegetables at the lowest prices. The circus people were tough and hard, they always had a fierce and ravenous hunger, they would not accept bad food and cooking, they fed stupendously, and they always had the best of everything.

Usually the circus would arrive at a new town very early in the morning, before daybreak. He would go into town immediately: he would go to the markets, or with farmers who had come in for the circus. He felt and saw the purity of first light, he heard the sweet and sudden lutings of first birds, and suddenly he was filled with the earth and morning in new towns, among new men: he walked among the farmers' wagons, and he dealt with them on the spot for the prodigal plenty of their wares—the country melons bedded in sweet hay of wagons, the cool sweet prints of butter wrapped in clean wet cloths, with dew and starlight still on them, the enormous battered cans foaming with fresh milk, the new laid eggs which he bought by the gross and hundred dozens, the tender limy pullets by the score, the rude country wagons laden to the rim with heaped abundancies—with delicate bunches of green scallions, the heavy red ripeness of huge tomatoes, the sweet-leaved lettuces crisp as celery, the fresh podded peas and the succulent young beans, as well as the potatoes spotted with the loamy earth, the powerful winey odor of the apples, the peaches, and the cherries, the juicy corn stacked up in shocks of living green, and the heavy blackened rinds of home-cured hams and bacons.

As the market opened, he would begin to trade and dicker with the butchers for their finest cuts of meat: they would hold great roasts up in their gouted fingers, they would roll up tubs of fresh ground sausage, they would smack with their long palms the flanks of beeves and porks: he would drive back to the circus with a wagon full of meat and vegetables.

At the circus ground the people were already in full activity. He could hear the wonderful timed tattoo of sledges on driven stakes, the shouts of men riding animals down to water, the slow clank and pull of mighty horses, the heavy rumble of the wagons as they rolled down off the circus flat cars. By now the eating table would be erected, and as he arrived, he could see the cooks already busy at their ranges, the long tables set up underneath the canvas with their rows of benches, their tin plates and cups, their strong readiness. There would be the amber indescribable pungency of strong coffee, and the smell of buckwheat batter.

And the circus people would come in for their breakfast: hard and tough, for the most part decent and serious people, the performers, the men and women, the acrobats, the riders, the tumblers, the clowns, the jugglers, the contortionists, and the balancers would come in quietly and eat with a savage and inspired intentness.

The food they ate was as masculine and fragrant as the world they dwelt in: it belonged to the stained world of mellow sun-warmed canvas, the clean and healthful odor of the animals, and the mild sweet lyric nature of the land in which they lived as wanderers, and it was there for the asking with a fabulous and stupefying plenty, golden and embrowned: they ate stacks of buckwheat cakes, smoking hot, soaked in hunks of yellow butter which they carved at will with a wide free gesture from the piled prints on the table, and which they garnished (if they pleased) with ropes of heavy black molasses, or with the lighter, freer maple syrup.

They ate big steaks for breakfast, hot from the pan and lashed with onions, they ate whole melons, crammed with the ripeness of the deep pink meat, rashers of bacon, and great platters of fried eggs, or eggs scrambled with calves' brains, they helped themselves from pyramids of fruit piled up at intervals on the table—plums, peaches, apples, cherries, grapes, oranges, and bananas—they had great pitchers of thick cream to pour on everything, and they washed their hunger down with pint mugs of strong deep-savored coffee.

For their mid-day meal they would eat fiercely, hungrily, with wolfish gusts, mightily, with knit brows and convulsive movements of their corded throats. They would eat great roasts of beef with crackled hides, browned in their juices, rare and tender, hot chunks of delicate pork with hems of fragrant fat, delicate young boiled chickens, only a mouthful for these raven-ous jaws, twelve-pound pot roasts cooked for hours in an iron pot with new carrots, onions, sprouts, and young potatoes, together with every vegetable that the season yielded: huge roasting ears of corn, smoking hot, stacked like cord wood on two-foot platters, tomatoes cut in slabs with wedges of okra and succotash, and raw onion, mashed potatoes whipped to a creamy smother, boats swimming with pure beef gravy, new carrots, turnips, fresh peas cooked in butter, and fat string beans seasoned with the flavor of big chunks of cooking-pork. In addition, they had every fruit that the place and time afforded: hot crusty apple, peach and cherry pies, encrusted with cinna-mon, puddings and cakes of every sort, and blobbering cobblers inches deep.

Thus the circus moved across America, from town to town, from state to state, eating its way from Maine into the great plains of the West, eating its way along the Hudson and the Mississippi rivers, eating its way across the prairies and from the North into the South, eating its way across the flat farm lands of the Pennsylvania Dutch colony, the eastern shore of Maryland and back again across the states of Virginia, North Carolina, Tennessee, and Florida—eating all good things that this enormous, this inevitably bountiful and abundant cornucopia of a continent yielded.

They ate the cod, bass, mackerel, halibut, clams, and oysters of the New England coast, the terrapin of Maryland, the fat beeves, porks, and cereals of the Middle West, and they had, as well, the heavy juicy peaches, watermelons, cantaloupes of Georgia, the fat sweet shad of the Carolina coasts, and the rounded and exotic citrus fruits of the tropics: the oranges, tangerines, bananas, kumquats, lemons, guavas down in Florida, together with a hundred other fruits and meats—the Vermont turkeys, the mountain trout, the bunched heaviness of the Concord grapes, the red winey bulk of the Oregon apples, as well as the clawed, shelled, and crusted dainties, the crabs, the clams, the pink meated lobsters that grope their way along the sea-floors of America.

The boy awoke at morning in three hundred towns with the glimmer of starlight on his face; he was the moon's man; then he saw light quicken in the east, he saw the pale stars drown, he saw the birth of light, he heard the lark's wing, the bird tree, the first liquorous liquefied lutings, the ripe-aired trillings, the plumskinned birdnotes, and he heard the hoof and wheel come down the streets of the nation. He exulted in his work as food-producer for the circus people, and they loved him for it. They said there had never been anyone like him—they banqueted exultantly, with hoarse gulp-ings and with joy, and they loved him.

Slowly, day by day, the circus worked its way across America, through forty states and through a dozen weathers. It was a little world that moved across the enormous loneliness of the earth, a little world that each day began a new life in new cities, and that left nothing to betray where it had been save a litter of beaten papers, the droppings of the camel and the elephant in Illinois, a patch of trampled grass, and a magical memory.

The circus men knew no other earth but this; the earth came to them with the smell of the canvas and the lion's roar. They saw the world behind the lights of the carnival, and everything beyond these lights was phantasmal and unreal to them; it lived for them within the circle of the tent as men and women who sat on benches, as the posts they came to, and sometimes as the enemy.

Their life was filled with the strong joy of food, with the love of traveling, and with danger and hard labor. Always there was the swift vio-lence of change and movement, of putting up and tearing down, and some-times there was the misery of rain and sleet, and mud above the ankles, of wind that shook their flimsy residence, that ripped the tent stakes from their moorings in the earth and lifted out the great center pole as if it were a match. Now they must wrestle with the wind and hold their dwelling to the earth; now they must fight the weariness of mud and push their heavy wagons through the slime; now, cold and wet and wretched, they must sleep on piles of canvas, upon the flat cars in a driving rain, and sometimes they must fight the enemy—the drunk, the savage, the violent enemy, the bloody man, who dwelt in every place. Sometimes it was the city thug, sometimes the mill hands of the South, sometimes the miners in a Pennsylvania town—the circus people cried, "Hey, Rube!" and fought them with fist and foot, with pike and stake, and the boy saw and knew it all.

When the men in a little town barricaded the street against their parade, they charged the barricade with their animals, and once the sheriff tried to stop the elephant by saying: "Now, damn ye, if you stick your God-damned trunk another inch, I'll shoot."

The circus moved across America foot by foot, mile by mile. He came to know the land. It was rooted in his blood and his brain forever—its food, its fruit, its fields and forests, its deserts, and its mountains, its savage lawlessness. He saw the crimes and the violence of the people with pity, with mercy, and with tenderness: he thought of them as if they were children. They smashed their neighbors' brains out with an ax, they disemboweled one another with knives, they were murderous and lost upon this earth they dwelt upon as strangers.

The tongueless blood of the murdered men ran down into the earth, and the earth received it. Upon this enormous and indifferent earth the little trains rattled on over ill-joined rails that loosely bound the sprawling little towns together. Lost and lonely, brief sawings of wood and plaster and cheap brick ugliness, the little towns were scattered like encampments through the wilderness. Only the earth remained, which all these people had barely touched, which all these people dwelt upon but could not possess.

Only the earth remained, the savage and lyrical earth with its rude potency, its thousand vistas, its heights and slopes and levels, with all its violence and delicacy, the terrible fecundity, decay, and growth, its fierce colors, its vital bite and sparkle, its exultancy of space and wandering. And the memory of this earth, the memory of all this universe of sight and sense, was rooted in this boy's heart and brain forever. It fed the hungers of desire and wandering, it breached the walls of his secret and withdrawn spirit. And for every memory of place and continent, of enormous coffee-colored rivers and eight hundred miles of bending wheat, of Atlantic coast and midland prairie, of raw red Piedmont and tropic flatness, there was always the small, fecund, perfect memory of his father's land, the dark side of his soul and his heart's desire, which he had never seen, but which he knew with every atom of his life, the strange phantasmal haunting of man's memory. It was a fertile, nobly swelling land, and it was large enough to live in, walled with fulfilled desire.

Abroad in this ocean of earth and vision he thought of his father's land, of its great red barns and nobly swelling earth, its clear familiarity and its haunting strangeness, and its dark and secret heart, its magnificent, its lovely and tragic beauty. He thought of its smell of harbors and its rumors of the seas, the city, and the ships, its wine-red apples and its brown-red soil, its snug weathered houses, and its lyric unutterable ecstasy.

A wonderful thing happened. One morning he awoke suddenly to find himself staring straight up at the pulsing splendor of the stars. At first he did not know where he was, but he knew instantly, even before he looked about him, that he had visited this place before. The circus train had stopped in the heart of the country, for what reason he did not know. He could hear the languid and intermittent breathing of the engine, the strangeness of men's voices in the dark, the casual stamp of the horses in their cars, and all around him the attentive and vital silence of the earth.

Suddenly he raised himself from the pile of canvas on which he slept. It was the moment just before dawn: against the east, the sky had already begun to whiten with the first faint luminosity of day, the invading tides of light crept up the sky, drowning the stars out as they went. The train had halted by a little river which ran swift and deep next to the tracks, and now he knew that what at first had been the sound of silence was the swift and ceaseless music of the river.

There had been rain the night before, and now the river was filled with the sweet clean rain-drenched smell of earthy deposits. He could see the delicate white glimmer of young birch trees leaning from the banks, and on the other side he saw the winding whiteness of the road. Beyond the road, and bordering it, there was an orchard with a wall of lichened stone: a row of apple trees, gnarled and sweet, spread their squat twisted branches out across the road, and in the faint light he saw that they were dense with blossoms: the cool intoxication of their fragrance overpowered him.

As the wan light grew, the earth and all its contours emerged sharply, and he saw again the spare, gaunt loneliness of the earth at dawn, with all its sweet and sudden cries of spring. He saw the worn and ancient design of lichened rocks, the fertile soil of the baked fields, he saw the kept order, the frugal cleanliness, with its springtime overgrowth, the mild tang of opulent greenery. There was an earth with fences, as big as a man's heart, but not so great as his desire, and after his giant wanderings over the prodigal fecundity of the continent, this earth was like a room he once had lived in. He returned to it as a sailor to a small closed harbor, as a man, spent with the hunger of his wandering, comes home.

Instantly he recognized the scene. He knew that he had come at last into his father's land. It was a magic that he knew but could not speak; he stood upon the lip of time, and all of his life now seemed the mirage of some wizard's spell—the spell of canvas and the circus ring, the spell of the tented world which had possessed him. Here was his home, brought back to him while he slept, like a forgotten dream. Here was the dark side of his soul, his heart's desire, his father's country, the earth his spirit dwelt on as a child. He knew every inch of the landscape, and he knew, past reason, doubt, or argument, that home was not three miles away.

He got up at once and leaped down to the earth; he knew where he would go. Along the track there was the slow swing and dance of the brakemen's lamps, that moving, mournful, and beautiful cloud of light along the rails of the earth, that he had seen so many times. Already the train was in motion; its bell tolled and its heavy trucks rumbled away from him. He began to walk back along the tracks, for less than a mile away, he knew, where the stream boiled over the lip of a dam, there was a bridge. When he reached the bridge, a deeper light had come: the old red brick of the mill emerged sharply and with the tone and temper of deep joy fell sheer into bright shining waters.

He crossed the bridge and turned left along the road: here it moved away from the river, among fields and through dark woods—dark woods bordered with stark poignancy of fir and pine, with the noble spread of maples, shot with the naked whiteness of birch. Here was the woodland maze: the sweet density of the brake and growth. Sharp thrummings, wood-land flitters broke the silence. His steps grew slow, he sat upon a wall, he waited.

Now rose the birdsong in first light, and suddenly he heard each sound the birdsong made. Like a flight of shot the sharp fast skaps of sound arose. With chittering bicker, fast-fluttering skirrs of sound, the palmy honeyed bird-cries came. Smooth drops and nuggets of bright gold they were. Now sang the birdtrees filled with lutings in bright air: the thrums, the lark's wing, and tongue-trilling chirrs arose now. The little nameless cries arose and fell with liquorous liquefied lutings, with lirruping chirp, plumbellied smooth-ness, sweet lucidity.

And now there was the rapid kweet kweet kweet kweet kweet of homing birds and their pwee pwee pwee: others with sharp cricketing stitch, a mosquito buzz with thin metallic tongues, while some with rusty creakings, high shrew's caws, with eerie rasp, with harsh far calls—all birds that are awake in the sweet woodland tangles; and above, there passed the whirr of hidden wings, the strange lost cry of the unknown birds, in full flight now, in which the sweet confusion of their cries was mingled.

Then he got up and went along that road where, he knew, like the prophetic sunrise of a dream, the house of his father's blood and kin lay hidden. At length, he came around a bending in the road, he left the wooded land, he passed by hedges and saw the old white house, set in the shoulder of the hill, worn like care and habit in the earth; clean and cool, it sat below the clean dark shelter of its trees: a twist of morning smoke coiled through its chimney.

Then he turned in to the rutted road that led up to the house, and at this moment the enormous figure of a powerful old man appeared around the corner prophetically bearing a smoked ham in one huge hand. And when the boy saw the old man, a cry of greeting burst from his throat, and the old man answered with a roar of welcome that shook the earth.

Then the old man dropped his ham, and waddled forward to meet the boy: they met half down the road, and the old man crushed him in his hug; they tried to speak but could not; they embraced again and in an instant all the years of wandering, the pain of loneliness and the fierce hungers of desire, were scoured away like a scum of frost from a bright glass.

He was a child again, he was a child that had stood upon the lip and leaf of time and heard the quiet tides that move us to our death, and he knew that the child could not be born again, the book of the days could never be turned back, old errors and confusions never righted. And he wept with sorrow for all that was lost and could never be regained, and with joy for all that had been recovered.

Suddenly he saw his youth as men on hilltops might look at the whole winding course of rivers to the sea, he saw the blind confusions of his wanderings across the earth, the horror of man's little stricken mote of earth against immensity, and he remembered the proud exultancy of his childhood when all the world lay like a coin between his palms, when he could have touched the horned rim of the moon, when heroes and great actions bent before him.

And he wept, not for himself, but out of love and pity for every youth that ever hoped and wandered and was alone. He had become a man, and he had in him unique glory that belongs to men alone, and that makes them great, and from which they shape their mightiest songs and legends. For out of their pain they utter first a cry for wounded self, then, as their vision deepens, widens, the universe of their marvelous sense leaps out and grips the universe; they feel contempt for gods, respect for men alone, and with the indifference of a selfless passion, enact earth out of a lyric cry.

At this moment, also, two young men burst from the house and came running down the road to greet him. They were powerful and heavy young men, already beginning to show signs of that epic and sensual grossness that distinguished their father. Like their father, they recognized the boy instantly, and in a moment he was engulfed in their mighty energies, borne up among them to the house. And they understood all he wanted to say, but could not speak, and they surrounded him with love and lavish heapings of his plate. And the boy knew the strange miracle of return to the dark land of his heart's desire, the father's land which haunts men like a dream they never knew.

Such were the twin images of the circus and his father's land which were to haunt his dreams and waking memory and which now, as he stood there with his brother looking at the circus, fused instantly to a living whole and came to him in a blaze of light.

And in this way, before he had ever set foot upon it, he came for the first time to his father's earth.

JAMES JOYCE

The Dead

Lily, the caretaker's daughter, was literally run off her feet. Hardly had she brought one gentleman into the little pantry behind the office on the ground floor and helped him off with his overcoat than the wheezy hall-door bell clanged again and she had to scamper along the bare hallway to let in another guest. It was well for her she had not to attend to the ladies also. But Miss Kate and Miss Julia had thought of that and had converted the bathroom upstairs into a ladies' dressing-room. Miss Kate and Miss Julia were there, gossiping and laughing and fussing, walking after each other to the head of the stairs, peering down over the banisters and calling down to Lily to ask her who had come.

It was always a great affair, the Misses Morkan's annual dance. Everybody who knew them came to it, members of the family, old friends of the family, the members of Julia's choir, any of Kate's pupils that were grown up enough and even some of Mary Jane's pupils too. Never once had it fallen flat. For years and years it had gone off in splendid style as long as anyone could remember; ever since Kate and Julia, after the death of their brother Pat, had left the house in Stoney Batter and taken Mary Jane, their only niece, to live with them in the dark gaunt house on Usher's Island, the upper part of which they had rented from Mr. Fulham, the cornfactor on the ground floor. That was a good thirty years ago if it was a day. Mary Jane, who was then a little girl in short clothes, was now the main prop of the household for she had the organ in Haddington Road. She had been through the Academy and gave a pupil's concert every year in the upper room of the

Antient Concert Rooms. Many of her pupils belonged to better-class families on the Kingstown and Dalkey line. Old as they were, her aunts also did their share. Julia, though she was quite grey, was still the leading soprano in Adam and Eve's, and Kate, being too feeble to go about much, gave music lessons to beginners on the old square piano in the back room. Lily, the caretaker's daughter, did housemaid's work for them. Though their life was modest they believed in eating well; the best of everything: diamond-bone sirloins, three-shilling tea and the best bottled stout. But Lily seldom made a mistake in the orders so that she got on well with her three mistresses. They were fussy, that was all. But the only thing they would not stand was back answers.

Of course they had good reason to be fussy on such a night. And then it was long after ten o'clock and yet there was no sign of Gabriel and his wife. Besides they were dreadfully afraid that Freddy Malins might turn up screwed. They would not wish for worlds that any of Mary Jane's pupils should see him under the influence; and when he was like that it was sometimes very hard to manage him. Freddy Malins always came late but they wondered what could be keeping Gabriel: and that was what brought them every two minutes to the banisters to ask Lily had Gabriel or Freddy come.

—O, Mr. Conroy, said Lily to Gabriel when she opened the door for him, Miss Kate and Miss Julia thought you were never coming. Good-night, Mrs. Conroy.

—I'll engage they did, said Gabriel, but they forget that my wife here takes three mortal hours to dress herself.

He stood on the mat, scraping the snow from his goloshes, while Lily led his wife to the foot of the stairs and called out:

—Miss Kate, here's Mrs. Conroy.

Kate and Julia came toddling down the dark stairs at once. Both of them kissed Gabriel's wife, said she must be perished alive and asked was Gabriel with her.

—Here I am as right as the mail, Aunt Kate! Go on up. I'll follow, called out Gabriel from the dark.

He continued scraping his feet vigorously while the three women went upstairs, laughing, to the ladies' dressing-room. A light fringe of snow lay like a cape on the shoulders of his overcoat and like toecaps on the toes of his goloshes; and, as the buttons of his overcoat slipped with a squeaking noise through the snow-stiffened frieze, a cold fragrant air from out-of-doors escaped from crevices and folds.

—Is it snowing again, Mr. Conroy? asked Lily.

She had preceded him into the pantry to help him off with his overcoat.

Gabriel smiled at the three syllables she had given his surname and glanced at her. She was a slim, growing girl, pale in complexion and with hay-colored hair. The gas in the pantry made her look still paler. Gabriel had known her when she was a child and used to sit on the lowest step nursing a rag doll.

—Yes, Lily, he answered, and I think we're in for a night of it.

He looked up at the pantry ceiling, which was shaking with the stamping and shuffling of feet on the floor above, listened for a moment to the piano and then glanced at the girl, who was folding his overcoat carefully at the end of a shelf.

—Tell me, Lily, he said in a friendly tone, do you still go to school?

—O no, sir, she answered. I'm done schooling this year and more.

—O, then, said Gabriel gaily, I suppose we'll be going to your wedding one of these fine days with your young man, eh?

The girl glanced back at him over her shoulder and said with great bitterness:

—The men that is now is only all palaver and what they can get out of you.

Gabriel colored as if he felt he had made a mistake and, without looking at her, kicked off his goloshes and flicked actively with his muffler at his patent-leather shoes.

He was a stout tallish young man. The high color of his cheeks pushed upwards even to his forehead where it scattered itself in a few formless patches of pale red; and on his hairless face there scintillated restlessly the polished lenses and the bright gilt rims of the glasses which screened his delicate and restless eyes. His glossy black hair was parted in the middle and brushed in a long curve behind his ears where it curled slightly beneath the groove left by his hat.

When he had flicked lustre into his shoes he stood up and pulled his waistcoat down more tightly on his plump body. Then he took a coin rapidly from his pocket.

—O Lily, he said, thrusting it into her hands, it's Christmas-time, isn't it? Just . . . here's a little. . . .

He walked rapidly towards the door.

—O no, sir! cried the girl, following him. Really, sir, I wouldn't take it.

—Christmas-time! Christmas-time! said Gabriel, almost trotting to the stairs and waving his hand to her in deprecation.

The girl, seeing that he had gained the stairs, called out after him:

—Well, thank you, sir.

He waited outside the drawing-room door until the waltz should finish, listening to the skirts that swept against it and to the shuffling of feet. He was still discomposed by the girl's bitter and sudden retort. It had cast a gloom over him which he tried to dispel by arranging his cuffs and the bows of his tie. Then he took from his waistcoat pocket a little paper and glanced at the headings he had made for his speech. He was undecided about the lines from Robert Browning for he feared they would be above the heads of his hearers. Some quotation that they could recognize from Shakespeare or from the Melodies would be better. The indelicate clacking of the men's heels and the shuffling of their soles reminded him that their grade of culture differed from his. He would only make himself ridiculous by quoting poetry to them which they could not understand. They would think that he was airing his superior education. He would fail with them just as he had failed with the girl in the pantry. He had taken up a wrong tone. His whole speech was a mistake from first to last, an utter failure.

Just then his aunts and his wife came out of the ladies' dressing-room. His aunts were two small plainly dressed old women. Aunt Julia was an inch or so taller. Her hair, drawn low over the tops of her ears, was grey: and grey also, with darker shadows, was her large flaccid face. Though she was stout in build and stood erect her slow eyes and parted lips gave her the appearance of a woman who did not know where she was or where she was going. Aunt Kate was more vivacious. Her face, healthier than her sister's, was all puckers and creases, like a shriveled red apple, and her hair, braided in the same old-fashioned way, had not lost its ripe nut color.

They both kissed Gabriel frankly. He was their favorite nephew, the son of their dead elder sister, Ellen, who had married T. J. Conroy of the Port and Docks.

—Gretta tells me you're not going to take a cab back to Monkstown tonight, Gabriel, said Aunt Kate.

—No, said Gabriel, turning to his wife, we had quite enough of that last year, hadn't we. Don't you remember, Aunt Kate, what a cold Gretta got out of it? Cab windows rattling all the way, and the east wind blowing in after we passed Merrion. Very jolly it was. Gretta caught a dreadful cold.

Aunt Kate frowned severely and nodded her head at every word.

—Quite right, Gabriel, quite right, she said. You can't be too careful.

—But as for Gretta there, said Gabriel, she'd walk home in the snow if she were let.

Mrs. Conroy laughed.

—Don't mind him, Aunt Kate, she said. He's really an awful bother, what with green shades for Tom's eyes at night and making him do the dumb-bells, and forcing Eva to eat the stirabout. The poor child! And she simply hates the sight of it! . . . O, but you'll never guess what he makes me wear now!

She broke out into a peal of laughter and glanced at her husband, whose admiring and happy eyes had been wandering from her dress to her face and hair. The two aunts laughed heartily too, for Gabriel's solicitude was a standing joke with them.

—Goloshes! said Mrs. Conroy. That's the latest. Whenever it's wet underfoot I must put on my goloshes. Tonight even he wanted me to put them on, but I wouldn't. The next thing he'll buy me will be a diving suit.

Gabriel laughed nervously and patted his tie reassuringly while Aunt Kate nearly doubled herself, so heartily did she enjoy the joke. The smile soon faded from Aunt Julia's face and her mirthless eyes were directed towards her nephew's face. After a pause she asked:

—And what are goloshes, Gabriel?

—Goloshes, Julia! exclaimed her sister. Goodness me, don't you know what goloshes are? You wear them over your . . . over your boots, Gretta, isn't it?

—Yes, said Mrs. Conroy. Guttapercha things. We both have a pair now. Gabriel says everyone wears them on the continent.

—O, on the continent, murmured Aunt Julia, nodding her head slowly.

Gabriel knitted his brows and said, as if he were slightly angered:

—It's nothing very wonderful but Gretta thinks it very funny because she says the word reminds her of Christy Minstrels.

—But tell me, Gabriel, said Aunt Kate, with brisk tact. Of course, you've seen about the room. Gretta was saying . . .

—O, the room is all right, replied Gabriel. I've taken one in the Gresham.

—To be sure, said Aunt Kate, by far the best thing to do. And the children, Gretta, you're not anxious about them?

—O, for one night, said Mrs. Conroy. Besides, Bessie will look after them.

—To be sure, said Aunt Kate again. What a comfort it is to have a girl like that, one you can depend on! There's that Lily, I'm sure I don't know what has come over her lately. She's not the girl she was at all.

Gabriel was about to ask his aunt some questions on this point but she broke off suddenly to gaze after her sister who had wandered down the stairs and was craning her neck over the banisters.

—Now, I ask you, she said, almost testily, where is Julia going? Julia! Julia! Where are you going?

Julia, who had gone halfway down one flight, came back and announced blandly:

—Here's Freddy.

At the same moment a clapping of hands and a final flourish of the pianist told that the waltz had ended. The drawing-room door was opened from within and some couples came out. Aunt Kate drew Gabriel aside hurriedly and whispered into his ear:

—Slip down, Gabriel, like a good fellow and see if he's all right, and don't let him up if he's screwed. I'm sure he's screwed. I'm sure he is.

Gabriel went to the stairs and listened over the banisters. He could hear two persons talking in the pantry. Then he recognized Freddy Malins' laugh. He went down the stairs noisily.

—It's such a relief, said Aunt Kate to Mrs. Conroy, that Gabriel is here. I always feel easier in my mind when he's here. . . . Julia, there's Miss Daly and Miss Power will take some refreshment. Thanks for your beautiful waltz, Miss Daly. It made lovely time.

A tall wizen-faced man, with a stiff grizzled moustache and swarthy skin, who was passing out with his partner said:

—And may we have some refreshment, too, Miss Morkan?

—Julia, said Aunt Kate summarily, and here's Mr. Browne and Miss Furlong. Take them in, Julia, with Miss Daly and Miss Power.

—I'm the man for the ladies, said Mr. Browne, pursing his lips until his moustache bristled and smiling in all his wrinkles. You know, Miss Morkan, the reason they are so fond of me is—

He did not finish his sentence, but, seeing that Aunt Kate was out of earshot, at once led the three young ladies into the back room. The middle of the room was occupied by two square tables placed end to end, and on these Aunt Julia and the caretaker were straightening and smoothing a large cloth. On the sideboard were arrayed dishes and plates, and glasses and bundles of knives and forks and spoons. The top of the closed square piano served also as a sideboard for viands and sweets. At a smaller sideboard in one corner two young men were standing, drinking hop-bitters.

Mr. Browne led his charges thither and invited them all, in jest, to some ladies' punch, hot, strong and sweet. As they said they never took anything strong he opened three bottles of lemonade for them. Then he asked one of the young men to move aside, and, taking hold of the decanter, filled out for himself a goodly measure of whisky. The young men eyed him respectfully while he took a trial sip.

—God help me, he said, smiling, it's the doctor's orders.

His wizened face broke into a broader smile, and the three young ladies laughed in musical echo to his pleasantry, swaying their bodies to and fro, with nervous jerks of their shoulders. The boldest said:

—O, now, Mr. Browne, I'm sure the doctor never ordered anything of the kind.

Mr. Browne took another sip of his whisky and said, with sidling mimicry:

—Well, you see, I'm like the famous Mrs. Cassidy, who is reported to have said: *Now, Mary Grimes, if I don't take it, make me take it, for I feel I want it.*

His hot face had leaned forward a little too confidentially and he had assumed a very low Dublin accent so that the young ladies, with one instinct, received his speech in silence. Miss Furlong, who was one of Mary Jane's pupils, asked Miss Daly what was the name of the pretty waltz she had played; and Mr. Browne, seeing that he was ignored, turned promptly to the two young men who were more appreciative.

A red-faced young woman, dressed in pansy, came into the room, excitedly clapping her hands and crying:

—Quadrilles! Quadrilles!

Close on her heels came Aunt Kate, crying:

—Two gentlemen and three ladies, Mary Jane!

—O, here's Mr. Bergin and Mr. Kerrigan, said Mary Jane. Mr. Kerrigan, will you take Miss Power? Miss Furlong, may I get you a partner, Mr. Bergin. O, that'll just do now.

—Three ladies, Mary Jane, said Aunt Kate.

The two young gentlemen asked the ladies if they might have the pleasure, and Mary Jane turned to Miss Daly.

—O, Miss Daly, you're really awfully good, after playing for the last two dances, but really we're so short of ladies tonight.

—I don't mind in the least, Miss Morkan.

—But I've a nice partner for you, Mr. Bartell D'Arcy, the tenor. I'll get him to sing later on. All Dublin is raving about him.

—Lovely voice, lovely voice! said Aunt Kate.

As the piano had twice begun the prelude to the first figure Mary Jane led her recruits quickly from the room. They had hardly gone when Aunt Julia wandered slowly into the room, looking behind her at something.

—What is the matter, Julia? asked Aunt Kate anxiously. Who is it?

Julia, who was carrying in a column of table-napkins, turned to her sister and said, simply, as if the question had surprised her:

—It's only Freddy, Kate, and Gabriel with him.

In fact right behind her Gabriel could be seen piloting Freddy Malins across the landing. The latter, a young man of about forty, was of Gabriel's size and build, with very round shoulders. His face was fleshy and pallid, touched with color only at the thick hanging lobes of his ears and at the wide wings of his nose. He had coarse features, a blunt nose, a convex and receding brow, tumid and protruded lips. His heavy-lidded eyes and the disorder of his scanty hair made him look sleepy. He was laughing heartily in a high key at a story which he had been telling Gabriel on the stairs and at the same time rubbing the knuckles of his left fist backwards and forwards into his left eye.

—Good-evening, Freddy, said Aunt Julia.

Freddy Malins bade the Misses Morkan good-evening in what seemed an offhand fashion by reason of the habitual catch in his voice and then, seeing that Mr. Browne was grinning at him from the sideboard, crossed the room on rather shaky legs and began to repeat in an undertone the story he had just told to Gabriel.

—He's not so bad, is he? said Aunt Kate to Gabriel.

Gabriel's brows were dark but he raised them quickly and answered:

—O no, hardly noticeable.

—Now, isn't he a terrible fellow! she said. And his poor mother made him take the pledge on New Year's Eve. But come on, Gabriel, into the drawing-room.

Before leaving the room with Gabriel she signalled to Mr. Browne by frowning and shaking her forefinger in warning to and fro. Mr. Browne nodded in answer and, when she had gone, said to Freddy Malins:

—Now, then, Teddy, I'm going to fill you out a good glass of lemonade just to buck you up.

Freddy Malins, who was nearing the climax of his story, waved the offer aside impatiently but Mr. Browne, having first called Freddy Malins' attention to a disarray in his dress, filled out and handed him a full glass of lemonade. Freddy Malins' left hand accepted the glass mechanically, his right hand being engaged in the mechanical readjustment of his dress. Mr. Browne, whose face was once more wrinkling with mirth, poured out for himself a glass of whisky while Freddy Malins exploded, before he had well reached the climax of his story, in a kink of high-pitched bronchitic laughter and, setting down his untasted and overflowing glass, began to rub the knuckles of his left fist backwards and forwards into his left eye, repeating words of his last phrase as well as his fit of laughter would allow him.

Gabriel could not listen while Mary Jane was playing her Academy piece, full of runs and difficult passages, to the hushed drawing-room. He liked music but the piece she was playing had no melody for him and he doubted whether it had any melody for the other listeners, though they had begged Mary Jane to play something. Four young men, who had come from the refreshment-room to stand in the doorway at the sound of the piano, had gone away quietly in couples after a few minutes. The only persons who seemed to follow the music were Mary Jane herself, her hands racing along the keyboard or lifted from it at the pauses like those of a priestess in momentary imprecation, and Aunt Kate standing at her elbow to turn the page.

Gabriel's eyes, irritated by the floor, which glittered with beeswax under the heavy chandelier, wandered to the wall above the piano. A picture of the balcony scene in *Romeo and Juliet* hung there and beside it was a picture of the two murdered princes in the Tower which Aunt Julia had worked in red, blue and brown wools when she was a girl. Probably in the school they had gone to as girls that kind of work had been taught, for one year his mother had worked for him as a birthday present a waistcoat of purple tabinet, with little foxes' heads upon it, lined with brown satin and having round mulberry buttons. It was strange that his mother had had no musical talent though Aunt Kate used to call her the brains carrier of the Morkan family. Both she and Julia had always seemed a little proud of their serious and matronly sister. Her photograph stood before the pierglass. She held an open book on her knees and was pointing out something in it to Constantine who, dressed in a man-o'-war suit, lay at her feet. It was she who had chosen the names for her sons for she was very sensible of the dignity of family life. Thanks to her, Constantine was now senior curate in Balbriggan and, thanks to her, Gabriel himself had taken his degree in the Royal University. A shadow passed over his face as he remembered her sullen opposition to his marriage. Some slighting phrases she had used still rankled in his memory; she had once spoken of Gretta as being country cute and that was not true of Gretta at all. It was Gretta who had nursed her during all her last long illness in their house at Monkstown.

He knew that Mary Jane must be near the end of her piece for she was playing again the opening melody with runs of scales after every bar and while he waited for the end the resentment died down in his heart. The piece ended with a trill of octaves in the treble and a final deep octave in the bass. Great applause greeted Mary Jane as, blushing and rolling up her music nervously, she escaped from the room. The most vigorous clapping came from the four young men in the doorway who had gone away to the refreshment-room at the beginning of the piece but had come back when the piano had stopped.

Lancers were arranged. Gabriel found himself partners with Miss Ivors. She was a frank-mannered talkative young lady, with a freckled face and prominent brown eyes. She did not wear a low-cut bodice and the large brooch which was fixed in the front of her collar bore on it an Irish device.

When they had taken their places she said abruptly:

—I have a crow to pluck with you.

—With me? said Gabriel.

She nodded her head gravely.

—What is it? asked Gabriel, smiling at her solemn manner.

—Who is G.C.? answered Miss Ivors, turning her eyes upon him.

Gabriel colored and was about to knit his brows, as if he did not understand, when she said bluntly:

—O, innocent Amy! I have found out that you write for *The Daily Express*. Now, aren't you ashamed of yourself?

—Why should I be ashamed of myself? asked Gabriel, blinking his eyes and trying to smile.

—Well, I'm ashamed of you, said Miss Ivors frankly. To say you'd write for a rag like that. I didn't think you were a West Briton.

A look of perplexity appeared on Gabriel's face. It was true that he wrote a literary column every Wednesday in *The Daily Express*, for which he was paid fifteen shillings. But that did not make him a West Briton surely. The books he received for review were almost more welcome than the paltry cheque. He loved to feel the covers and turn over the pages of newly printed books. Nearly every day when his teaching in the college was ended he used to wander down the quays to the second-hand booksellers, to Hickey's on Bachelor's Walk, to Webb's or Massey's on Aston's Quay, or to O'Clohissey's in the by-street. He did not know how to meet her charge. He wanted to say that literature was above politics. But they were friends of many years' standing and their careers had been parallel, first at the University and then as teachers: he could not risk a grandiose phrase with her. He continued blinking his eyes and trying to smile and murmured lamely that he saw nothing political in writing reviews of books.

When their turn to cross had come he was still perplexed and inattentive. Miss Ivors promptly took his hand in a warm grasp and said in a soft friendly tone:

—Of course, I was only joking. Come, we cross now.

When they were together again she spoke of the University question and Gabriel felt more at ease. A friend of hers had shown her his review of Browning's poems. That was how she had found out the secret: but she liked the review immensely. Then she said suddenly:

—O, Mr. Conroy, will you come for an excursion to the Aran Isles this summer? We're going to stay there a whole month. It will be splendid out in the Atlantic. You ought to come. Mr. Clancy is coming, and Mr. Kilkelly and Kathleen Kearney. It would be splendid for Gretta too if she'd come. She's from Connacht, isn't she?

—Her people are, said Gabriel shortly.

—But you will come, won't you? said Miss Ivors, laying her warm hand eagerly on his arm.

—The fact is, said Gabriel, I have already arranged to go—

—Go where? asked Miss Ivors.

—Well, you know, every year I go for a cycling tour with some fellows and so—

—But where? asked Miss Ivors.

—Well, we usually go to France or Belgium or perhaps Germany, said Gabriel awkwardly.

—And why do you go to France and Belgium, said Miss Ivors, instead of visiting your own land?

—Well, said Gabriel, it's partly to keep in touch with the languages and partly for a change.

—And haven't you your own language to keep in touch with—Irish? asked Miss Ivors.

—Well, said Gabriel, if it comes to that, you know, Irish is not my language.

Their neighbors had turned to listen to the cross-examination. Gabriel glanced right and left nervously and tried to keep his good humor under the ordeal which was making a blush invade his forehead.

—And haven't you your own land to visit, continued Miss Ivors, that you know nothing of, your own people, and your own country?

—O, to tell you the truth, retorted Gabriel suddenly, I'm sick of my own country, sick of it!

—Why? asked Miss Ivors.

Gabriel did not answer for his retort had heated him.

—Why? repeated Miss Ivors.

They had to go visiting together and, as he had not answered her, Miss Ivors said warmly:

—Of course, you've no answer.

Gabriel tried to cover his agitation by taking part in the dance with great energy. He avoided her eyes for he had seen a sour expression on her face. But when they met in the long chain he was surprised to feel his hand firmly pressed. She looked at him from under her brows for a moment quizzically until he smiled. Then, just as the chain was about to start again, she stood on tiptoe and whispered into his ear:

—West Briton!

When the lancers were over Gabriel went away to a remote corner of the room where Freddy Malins' mother was sitting. She was a stout feeble old woman with white hair. Her voice had a catch in it like her son's and she stuttered slightly. She had been told that Freddy had come and that he was nearly all right. Gabriel asked her whether she had had a good crossing. She lived with her married daughter in Glasgow and came to Dublin on a visit once a year. She answered placidly that she had had a beautiful crossing and that the captain had been most attentive to her. She spoke also of the beautiful house her daughter kept in Glasgow, and of all the nice friends they had there. While her tongue rambled on Gabriel tried to banish from his mind all memory of the unpleasant incident with Miss Ivors. Of course the girl or woman, or whatever she was, was an enthusiast but there was a time for all things. Perhaps he ought not to have answered her like that. But she had no right to call him a West Briton before people, even in joke. She had tried to make him ridiculous before people, heckling him and staring at him with her rabbit's eyes.

He saw his wife making her way towards him through the waltzing couples. When she reached him she said into his ear:

—Gabriel, Aunt Kate wants to know won't you carve the goose as usual. Miss Daly will carve the ham and I'll do the pudding.

—All right, said Gabriel.

—She's sending in the younger ones first as soon as this waltz is over so that we'll have the table to ourselves.

—Were you dancing? asked Gabriel.

—Of course I was. Didn't you see me? What words had you with Molly Ivors?

—No words. Why? Did she say so?

—Something like that. I'm trying to get that Mr. D'Arcy to sing. He's full of conceit, I think.

—There were no words, said Gabriel moodily, only she wanted me to go for a trip to the west of Ireland and I said I wouldn't.

His wife clasped her hands excitedly and gave a little jump.

—O, do go, Gabriel, she cried. I'd love to see Galway again.

—You can go if you like, said Gabriel coldly.

She looked at him for a moment, then turned to Mrs. Malins and said:

—There's a nice husband for you, Mrs. Malins.

While she was threading her way back across the room Mrs. Malins, without advertising to the interruption, went on to tell Gabriel what beautiful places there were in Scotland and beautiful scenery. Her son-in-law brought them every year to the lakes and they used to go fishing. Her son-in-law was a splendid fisher. One day he caught a fish, a beautiful big big fish, and the man in the hotel boiled it for their dinner.

Gabriel hardly heard what she said. Now that supper was coming near he began to think again about his speech and about the quotation. When he saw Freddy Malins coming across the room to visit his mother Gabriel left the chair free for him and retired into the embrasure of the window. The room had already cleared and from the back room came the clatter of plates and knives. Those who still remained in the drawing-room seemed tired of dancing and were conversing quietly in little groups. Gabriel's warm trembling fingers tapped the cold pane of the window. How cool it must be outside! How pleasant it would be to walk out alone, first along by the river and then through the park! The snow would be lying on the branches of the trees and forming a bright cap on the top of the Wellington Monument. How much more pleasant it would be there than at the supper-table!

He ran over the headings of his speech: Irish hospitality, sad memories, the Three Graces, Paris, the quotation from Browning. He repeated to himself a phrase he had written in his review: *One feels that one is listening to a thought-tormented music.* Miss Ivors had praised the review. Was she sincere? Had she really any life of her own behind all her propagandism? There had never been any ill-feeling between them until that night. It unnerved him to think that she would be at the supper-table, looking up at him while he spoke with her critical quizzing eyes. Perhaps she would not be sorry to see him fail in his speech. An idea came into his mind and gave him courage. He would say, alluding to Aunt Kate and Aunt Julia: *Ladies and Gentlemen, the generation which is now on the wane among us may have had its faults but for my part I think it had certain qualities of hospitality, of humor, of humanity, which the new and very serious and hypereducated generation that is growing up around us seems to me to lack.* Very good: that was one for Miss Ivors. What did he care that his aunts were only two ignorant old women?

A murmur in the room attracted his attention. Mr. Browne was advancing from the door, gallantly escorting Aunt Julia, who leaned upon his arm, smiling and hanging her head. An irregular musketry of applause escorted her also as far as the piano and then, as Mary Jane seated herself on the stool, and Aunt Julia, no longer smiling, half turned so as to pitch her voice fairly into the room, gradually ceased. Gabriel recognized the prelude. It was that of an old song of Aunt Julia's—*Arrayed for the Bridal.* Her voice, strong and clear in tone, attacked with great spirit the runs which embellish the air and though she sang very rapidly she did not miss even the smallest of the grace notes. To follow the voice, without looking at the singer's face, was to feel and share the excitement of swift and secure flight. Gabriel applauded loudly with all the others at the close of the song and loud applause was borne in from the invisible supper-table. It sounded so genuine that a little color struggled into Aunt Julia's face as she bent to replace in the music-stand the old leather-bound songbook that had her initials on the cover. Freddy Malins, who had listened with his head perched sideways to hear her better, was still applauding when everyone else had ceased and talking animatedly to his mother who nodded her head gravely and slowly in acquiescence. At last, when he could clap no more, he stood up suddenly and hurried across the room to Aunt Julia whose hand he seized and held in both his hands, shaking it when words failed him or the catch in his voice proved too much for him.

—I was just telling my mother, he said, I never heard you sing so well, never. No, I never heard your voice so good as it is tonight. Now! Would you believe that now? That's the truth. Upon my word and honor that's the truth. I never heard your voice sound so fresh and so . . . so clear and fresh, never.

Aunt Julia smiled broadly and murmured something about compliments as she released her hand from his grasp. Mr. Browne extended his open hand towards her and said to those who were near him in the manner of a showman introducing a prodigy to an audience:

—Miss Julia Morkan, my latest discovery!

He was laughing very heartily at this himself when Freddy Malins turned to him and said:

—Well, Browne, if you're serious you might make a worse discovery. All I can say is I never heard her sing half so well as long as I am coming here. And that's the honest truth.

—Neither did I, said Mr. Browne. I think her voice has greatly improved.

Aunt Julia shrugged her shoulders and said with meek pride:

—Thirty years ago I hadn't a bad voice as voices go.

—I often told Julia, said Aunt Kate emphatically, that she was simply thrown away in that choir. But she never would be said by me.

She turned as if to appeal to the good sense of the others against a refractory child while Aunt Julia gazed in front of her, a vague smile of reminiscence playing on her face.

—No, continued Aunt Kate, she wouldn't be said or led by anyone, slaving there in that choir night and day, night and day. Six o'clock on Christmas morning! And all for what?

—Well, isn't it for the honor of God, Aunt Kate? asked Mary Jane, twisting round on the piano-stool and smiling.

Aunt Kate turned fiercely on her niece and said:

—I know all about the honor of God, Mary Jane, but I think it's not at all honorable for the pope to turn out the women out of the choirs that have slaved there all their lives and put little whipper-snappers of boys over their heads. I suppose it is for the good of the Church if the pope does it. But it's not just, Mary Jane, and it's not right.

She had worked herself into a passion and would have continued in defense of her sister for it was a sore subject with her but Mary Jane, seeing that all the dancers had come back, intervened pacifically:

—Now, Aunt Kate, you're giving scandal to Mr. Browne who is of the other persuasion.

Aunt Kate turned to Mr. Browne, who was grinning at this allusion to his religion, and said hastily:

—O, I don't question the pope's being right. I'm only a stupid old woman and I wouldn't presume to do such a thing. But there's such a thing as common everyday politeness and gratitude. And if I were in Julia's place I'd tell that Father Healy straight up to his face . . .

—And besides, Aunt Kate, said Mary Jane, we really are all hungry and when we are hungry we are all very quarrelsome.

—And when we are thirsty we are also quarrelsome, added Mr. Browne.

—So that we had better go to supper, said Mary Jane, and finish the discussion afterwards.

On the landing outside the drawing-room Gabriel found his wife and Mary Jane trying to persuade Miss Ivors to stay for supper. But Miss Ivors, who had put on her hat and was buttoning her cloak, would not stay. She did not feel in the least hungry and she had already overstayed her time.

—But only for ten minutes, Molly, said Mrs. Conroy. That won't delay you.

—To take a pick itself, said Mary Jane, after all your dancing.

—I really couldn't, said Miss Ivors.

—I am afraid you didn't enjoy yourself at all, said Mary Jane hopelessly.

—Ever so much, I assure you, said Miss Ivors, but you really must let me run off now.

—But how can you get home? asked Mrs. Conroy.

—O, it's only two steps up the quay.

Gabriel hesitated a moment and said:

—If you will allow me, Miss Ivors, I'll see you home if you really are obliged to go.

But Miss Ivors broke away from them.

—I won't hear of it, she cried. For goodness sake go in to your suppers and don't mind me. I'm quite well able to take care of myself.

—Well, you're the comical girl, Molly, said Mrs. Conroy frankly.

—*Beannacht libh*, cried Miss Ivors, with a laugh, as she ran down the staircase.

Mary Jane gazed after her, a moody puzzled expression on her face, while Mrs. Conroy leaned over the banisters to listen for the hall-door. Gabriel asked himself was he the cause of her abrupt departure. But she did not seem to be in ill humor: she had gone away laughing. He stared blankly down the staircase.

At that moment Aunt Kate came toddling out of the supper-room, almost wringing her hands in despair.

—Where is Gabriel? she cried. Where on earth is Gabriel? There's everyone waiting in there, stage to let, and nobody to carve the goose!

—Here I am, Aunt Kate! cried Gabriel, with sudden animation, ready to carve a flock of geese, if necessary.

A fat brown goose lay at one end of the table and at the other end, on a bed of creased paper strewn with sprigs of parsley, lay a great ham, stripped of its outer skin and peppered over with crust crumbs, a neat paper frill round its shin and beside this was a round of spiced beef. Between these rival ends ran parallel lines of side-dishes: two little minsters of jelly, red and yellow; a shallow dish full of blocks of blancmange and red jam, a large green leaf-shaped dish with a stalk-shaped handle, on which lay bunches of purple raisins and peeled almonds, a companion dish on which lay a solid rectangle of Smyrna figs, a dish of custard topped with grated nutmeg, a small bowl full of chocolates and sweets wrapped in gold and silver papers and a glass vase in which stood some tall celery stalks. In the center of the table there stood, as sentries to a fruit-stand which upheld a pyramid of oranges and American apples, two squat old-fashioned decanters of cut glass, one containing port and the other dark sherry. On the closed square piano a pudding in a huge yellow dish lay in waiting and behind it were three squads of bottles of stout and ale and minerals, drawn up according to the colors of their uniforms, the first two black, with brown and red labels, the third and smallest squad white, with transverse green sashes.

Gabriel took his seat boldly at the head of the table and, having looked to the edge of the carver, plunged his fork firmly into the goose. He felt quite at ease now for he was an expert carver and liked nothing better than to find himself at the head of a well-laden table.

—Miss Furlong, what shall I send you? he asked. A wing or a slice of the breast?

—Just a small slice of the breast.

—Miss Higgins, what for you?

—O, anything at all, Mr. Conroy.

While Gabriel and Miss Daly exchanged plates of goose and plates of ham and spiced beef Lily went from guest to guest with a dish of hot floury potatoes wrapped in a white napkin. This was Mary Jane's idea and she had also suggested apple sauce for the goose but Aunt Kate had said that plain roast goose without apple sauce had always been good enough for her and she hoped she might never eat worse. Mary Jane waited on her pupils and saw that they got the best slices and Aunt Kate and Aunt Julia opened and carried across from the piano bottles of stout and ale for the gentlemen and bottles of minerals for the ladies. There was a great deal of confusion and laughter and noise, the noise of orders and counter-orders, of knives and forks, of corks and glass-stoppers. Gabriel began to carve second helpings as soon as he had finished the first round without serving himself. Everyone protested loudly so that he compromised by taking a long draught of stout for he had found the carving hot work. Mary Jane settled down quietly to her supper but Aunt Kate and Aunt Julia were still toddling round the table, walking on each other's heels, getting in each other's way and giving each other unheeded orders. Mr. Browne begged of them to sit down and eat their suppers and so did Gabriel but they said there was time enough so that, at last, Freddy Malins stood up and, capturing Aunt Kate, plumped her down on her chair amid general laughter.

When everyone had been well served Gabriel said, smiling:

—Now, if anyone wants a little more of what vulgar people call stuffing let him or her speak.

A chorus of voices invited him to begin his own supper and Lily came forward with three potatoes which she had reserved for him.

—Very well, said Gabriel amiably, as he took another preparatory draught, kindly forget my existence, ladies and gentlemen, for a few minutes.

He set to his supper and took no part in the conversation with which the table covered Lily's removal of the plates. The subject of talk was the opera company which was then at the Theatre Royal. Mr. Bartell D'Arcy, the tenor, a dark-complexioned young man with a smart moustache, praised very highly the leading contralto of the company but Miss Furlong thought she had a rather vulgar style of production. Freddy Malins said there was a negro chieftain singing in the second part of the Gaiety pantomime who had one of the finest tenor voices he had ever heard.

—Have you heard him? he asked Mr. Bartell D'Arcy across the table.

—No, answered Mr. Bartell D'Arcy carelessly.

—Because, Freddy Malins explained, now I'd be curious to hear your opinion of him. I think he has a grand voice.

—It takes Teddy to find out the really good things, said Mr. Browne familiarly to the table.

—And why couldn't he have a voice too? asked Freddy Malins sharply. Is it because he's only a black?

Nobody answered this question and Mary Jane led the table back to the legitimate opera. One of her pupils had given her a pass for *Mignon*. Of course it was very fine, she said, but it made her think of poor Georgina Burns. Mr. Browne could go back farther still, to the old Italian companies that used to come to Dublin—Tietjens, Ilma de Murzka, Campanini, the great Trebelli, Giuglini, Ravelli, Aramburo. Those were the days, he said, when there was something like singing to be heard in Dublin. He told too of how the top gallery of the old Royal used to be packed night after night, of how one night an Italian tenor had sung five encores to *Let Me Like a Soldier Fall*, introducing a high C every time, and of how the gallery boys would sometimes in their enthusiasm unyoke the horses from the carriage of some great *prima donna* and pull her themselves through the streets to her hotel. Why did they never play the grand old operas now, he asked, *Dinorah*, *Lucrezia Borgia?* Because they could not get the voices to sing them: that was why.

—O, well, said Mr. Bartell D'Arcy, I presume there are as good singers today as there were then.

—Where are they? asked Mr. Browne defiantly.

—In London, Paris, Milan, said Mr. Bartell D'Arcy warmly. I suppose Caruso, for example, is quite as good, if not better than any of the men you have mentioned.

—Maybe so, said Mr. Browne. But I may tell you I doubt it strongly.

—Oh, I'd give anything to hear Caruso sing, said Mary Jane.

—For me, said Aunt Kate, who had been picking a bone, there was only one tenor. To please me, I mean. But I suppose none of you ever heard of him.

—Who was he, Miss Morkan? asked Mr. Bartell D'Arcy politely.

—His name, said Aunt Kate, was Parkinson. I heard him when he was in his prime and I think he had then the purest tenor voice that was ever put into a man's throat.

—Strange, said Mr. Bartell D'Arcy. I never even heard of him.

—Yes, yes, Miss Morkan is right, said Mr. Browne. I remember hearing of old Parkinson but he's too far back for me.

—A beautiful pure sweet mellow English tenor, said Aunt Kate with enthusiasm.

Gabriel having finished, the huge pudding was transferred to the table. The clatter of forks and spoons began again. Gabriel's wife served out spoonfuls of the pudding and passed the plates down the table. Midway down they were held up by Mary Jane, who replenished them with raspberry or orange jelly or with blancmange and jam. The pudding was of Aunt Julia's making and she received praises for it from all quarters. She herself said that it was not quite brown enough.

—Well, I hope, Miss Morkan, said Mr. Browne, that I'm brown enough for you because, you know, I'm all brown.

All the gentlemen, except Gabriel, ate some of the pudding out of compliment to Aunt Julia. As Gabriel never ate sweets the celery had been left for him. Freddy Malins also took a stalk of celery and ate it with his pudding. He had been told that celery was a capital thing for the blood and he was just then under doctor's care. Mrs. Malins, who had been silent all through the supper, said that her son was going down to Mount Melleray in a week or so. The table then spoke of Mount Melleray, how bracing the air was down there, how hospitable the monks were and how they never asked for a penny-piece from their guests.

—And do you mean to say, asked Mr. Browne incredulously, that a chap can go down there and put up there as if it were a hotel and live on the fat of the land and then come away without paying a farthing?

—O, most people give some donation to the monastery when they leave, said Mary Jane.

—I wish we had an institution like that in our Church, said Mr. Browne candidly.

He was astonished to hear that the monks never spoke, got up at two in the morning and slept in their coffins. He asked what they did it for.

—That's the rule of the order, said Aunt Kate firmly.

—Yes, but why? asked Mr. Browne.

Aunt Kate repeated that it was the rule, that was all. Mr. Browne still seemed not to understand. Freddy Malins explained to him, as best he could, that the monks were trying to make up for the sins committed by all the sinners in the outside world. The explanation was not very clear for Mr. Browne grinned and said:

—I like that idea very much but wouldn't a comfortable spring bed do them as well as a coffin?

—The coffin, said Mary Jane, is to remind them of their last end.

As the subject had grown lugubrious it was buried in a silence of the table during which Mrs. Malins could be heard saying to her neighbor in an indistinct undertone:

—They are very good men, the monks, very pious men.

The raisins and almonds and figs and apples and oranges and choco-lates and sweets were now passed about the table and Aunt Julia invited all the guests to have either port or sherry. At first Mr. Bartell D'Arcy refused to take either but one of his neighbors nudged him and whispered something to him upon which he allowed his glass to be filled. Gradually as the last glasses were being filled the conversation ceased. A pause followed, broken only by the noise of the wine and by unsettlings of chairs. The Misses Morkan, all three, looked down at the tablecloth. Someone coughed once or twice and then a few gentlemen patted the table gently as a signal for silence. The silence came and Gabriel pushed back his chair and stood up.

The patting at once grew louder in encouragement and then ceased altogether. Gabriel leaned his ten trembling fingers on the tablecloth and smiled nervously at the company. Meeting a row of upturned faces he raised his eyes to the chandelier. The piano was playing a waltz tune and he could hear the skirts sweeping against the drawing-room door. People, perhaps, were standing in the snow on the quay outside, gazing up at the lighted windows and listening to the waltz music. The air was pure there. In the distance lay the park where the trees were weighted with snow. The Welling-ton Monument wore a gleaming cap of snow that flashed westward over the white field of Fifteen Acres.

He began:

—Ladies and Gentlemen.

—It has fallen to my lot this evening, as in years past, to perform a very pleasing task but a task for which I am afraid my poor powers as a speaker are all too inadequate.

—No, no! said Mr. Browne.

—But, however that may be, I can only ask you tonight to take the will for the deed and to lend me your attention for a few moments while I endeavor to express to you in words what my feelings are on this occasion.

—Ladies and Gentlemen. It is not the first time that we have gathered together under this hospitable roof, around this hospitable board. It is not the first time that we have been the recipients—or perhaps, I had better say, the victims—of the hospitality of certain good ladies.

He made a circle in the air with his arm and paused. Everyone laughed or smiled at Aunt Kate and Aunt Julia and Mary Jane who all turned crimson with pleasure. Gabriel went on more boldly:

—I feel more strongly with every recurring year that our country has no tradition which does it so much honor and which it should guard so jealously as that of its hospitality. It is a tradition that is unique as far as my experience goes (and I have visited not a few places abroad) among the modern nations. Some would say, perhaps, that with us it is rather a failing than anything to be boasted of. But granted even that, it is, to my mind, a princely failing, and one that I trust will long be cultivated among us. Of one thing, at least, I am sure. As long as this one roof shelters the good ladies aforesaid—and I wish from my heart it may do so for many and many a long year to come—the tradition of genuine warm-hearted courteous Irish hospitality, which our forefathers have handed down to us and which we in turn must hand down to our descendants, is still alive among us.

A hearty murmur of assent ran round the table. It shot through Gabriel's mind that Miss Ivors was not there and that she had gone away discourteously: and he said with confidence in himself:

—Ladies and Gentlemen.

—A new generation is growing up in our midst, a generation actuated by new ideas and new principles. It is serious and enthusiastic for these new ideas and its enthusiasm, even when it is misdirected, is, I believe, in the main sincere. But we are living in a sceptical and, if I may use the phrase, a thought-tormented age: and sometimes I fear that this new generation, educated or hypereducated as it is, will lack those qualities of humanity, of hospitality, of kindly humor which belonged to an older day. Listening tonight to the names of all those great singers of the past it seemed to me, I must confess, that we were living in a less spacious age. Those days might, without exaggeration, be called spacious days: and if they are gone beyond recall let us hope, at least, that in gatherings such as this we shall still speak of them with pride and affection, still cherish in our hearts the memory of those dead and gone great ones whose fame the world will not willingly let die.

—Hear, hear! said Mr. Browne loudly.

—But yet, continued Gabriel, his voice falling into a softer inflection, there are always in gatherings such as this sadder thoughts that will recur to our minds: thoughts of the past, of youth, of changes, of absent faces that we miss here tonight. Our path through life is strewn with many such sad memories: and were we to brood upon them always we could not find the heart to go on bravely with our work among the living. We have all of us living duties and living affections which claim, and rightly claim, our strenuous endeavors.

—Therefore, I will not linger on the past. I will not let any gloomy moralizing intrude upon us here tonight. Here we are gathered together for a brief moment from the bustle and rush of our everyday routine. We are met here as friends, in the spirit of good-fellowship, as colleagues, also to a certain extent, in the true spirit of *camaraderie*, and as the guests of—what shall I call them?—the Three Graces of the Dublin musical world.

The table burst into applause and laughter at this sally. Aunt Julia vainly asked each of her neighbors in turn to tell her what Gabriel had said.

—He says we are the Three Graces, Aunt Julia, said Mary Jane.

Aunt Julia did not understand but she looked up, smiling, at Gabriel, who continued in the same vein:

—Ladies and Gentlemen.

—I will not attempt to play tonight the part that Paris played on another occasion. I will not attempt to choose between them. The task would be an invidious one and one beyond my poor powers. For when I view them in turn, whether it be our chief hostess herself, whose good heart, whose too good heart, has become a byword with all who know her, or her sister, who seems to be gifted with perennial youth and whose singing must have been a surprise and a revelation to us all tonight, or, last but not least, when I consider our youngest hostess, talented, cheerful, hard-working and the best of nieces, I confess, Ladies and Gentlemen, that I do not know to which of them I should award the prize.

Gabriel glanced down at his aunts and, seeing the large smile on Aunt Julia's face and the tears which had risen to Aunt Kate's eyes, hastened to his close. He raised his glass of port gallantly, while every member of the company fingered a glass expectantly, and said loudly:

—Let us toast them all three together. Let us drink to their health, wealth, long life, happiness and prosperity and may they long continue to hold the proud and self-won position which they hold in their profession and the position of honor and affection which they hold in our hearts.

All the guests stood up, glass in hand, and, turning towards the three seated ladies, sang in unison, with Mr. Browne as leader:

> *For they are jolly gay fellows,*
> *For they are jolly gay fellows,*
> *For they are jolly gay fellows,*
> *Which nobody can deny.*

Aunt Kate was making frank use of her handkerchief and even Aunt Julia seemed moved. Freddy Malins beat time with his pudding-fork and the singers turned towards one another, as if in melodious conference, while they sang, with emphasis:

Unless he tells a lie,
Unless he tells a lie.

Then, turning once more towards their hostesses, they sang:

For they are jolly gay fellows,
For they are jolly gay fellows,
For they are jolly gay fellows,
Which nobody can deny.

The acclamation which followed was taken up beyond the door of the supper-room by many of the other guests and renewed time after time, Freddy Malins acting as officer with his fork on high.

The piercing morning air came into the hall where they were standing so that Aunt Kate said:

—Close the door, somebody. Mrs. Malins will get her death of cold.

—Browne is out there, Aunt Kate, said Mary Jane.

—Browne is everywhere, said Aunt Kate, lowering her voice.

Mary Jane laughed at her tone.

—Really, she said archly, he is very attentive.

—He has been laid on here like the gas, said Aunt Kate in the same tone, all during the Christmas.

She laughed herself this time good-humoredly and then added quickly:

—But tell him to come in, Mary Jane, and close the door. I hope to goodness he didn't hear me.

At that moment the hall-door was opened and Mr. Browne came in from the doorstep, laughing as if his heart would break. He was dressed in a long green overcoat with mock astrakhan cuffs and collar and wore on his head an oval fur cap. He pointed down the snow-covered quay from where the sound of shrill prolonged whistling was borne in.

—Teddy will have all the cabs in Dublin out, he said.

Gabriel advanced from the little pantry behind the office, struggling into his overcoat and, looking round the hall, said:

—Gretta not down yet?

—She's getting on her things, Gabriel, said Aunt Kate.

—Who's playing up there? asked Gabriel.

—Nobody. They're all gone.

—O no, Aunt Kate, said Mary Jane. Bartell D'Arcy and Miss O'Callaghan aren't gone yet.

—Someone is strumming at the piano, anyhow, said Gabriel.

Mary Jane glanced at Gabriel and Mr. Browne and said with a shiver:

—It makes me feel cold to look at you two gentlemen muffled up like that. I wouldn't like to face your journey home at this hour.

—I'd like nothing better this minute, said Mr. Browne stoutly, than a rattling fine walk in the country or a fast drive with a good spanking goer between the shafts.

—We used to have a very good horse and trap at home, said Aunt Julia sadly.

—The never-to-be-forgotten Johnny, said Mary Jane, laughing.

Aunt Kate and Gabriel laughed too.

—Why, what was wonderful about Johnny? asked Mr. Browne.

—The late lamented Patrick Morkan, our grandfather, that is, explained Gabriel, commonly known in his later years as the old gentleman, was a glue-boiler.

—O, now, Gabriel, said Aunt Kate, laughing, he had a starch mill.

—Well, glue or starch, said Gabriel, the old gentleman had a horse by the name of Johnny. And Johnny used to work in the old gentleman's mill, walking round and round in order to drive the mill. That was all very well; but now comes the tragic part about Johnny. One fine day the old gentleman thought he'd like to drive out with the quality to a military review in the park.

—The Lord have mercy on his soul, said Aunt Kate compassionately.

—Amen, said Gabriel. So the old gentleman, as I said, harnessed Johnny and put on his very best tall hat and his very best stock collar and drove out in grand style from his ancestral mansion somewhere near Back Lane, I think.

Everyone laughed, even Mrs. Malins, at Gabriel's manner and Aunt Kate said:

—O now, Gabriel, he didn't live in Back Lane, really. Only the mill was there.

—Out from the mansion of his forefathers, continued Gabriel, he drove with Johnny. And everything went on beautifully until Johnny came in sight of King Billy's statue: and whether he fell in love with the horse King Billy sits on or whether he thought he was back again in the mill, anyhow he began to walk round the statue.

Gabriel paced in a circle round the hall in his goloshes amid the laughter of the others.

—Round and round he went, said Gabriel, and the old gentleman, who was a very pompous old gentleman, was highly indignant. *Go on, sir! What do you mean, sir? Johnny! Johnny! Most extraordinary conduct! Can't understand the horse!*

The peals of laughter which followed Gabriel's imitation of the incident were interrupted by a resounding knock at the hall-door. Mary Jane ran to open it and let in Freddy Malins. Freddy Malins, with his hat well back on his head and his shoulders humped with cold, was puffing and steaming after his exertions.

—I could only get one cab, he said.

—O, we'll find another along the quay, said Gabriel.

—Yes, said Aunt Kate. Better not keep Mrs. Malins standing in the draught.

Mrs. Malins was helped down the front steps by her son and Mr. Browne and, after many maneuvers, hoisted into the cab. Freddy Malins clambered in after her and spent a long time settling her on the seat, Mr. Browne helping him with advice. At last she was settled comfortably and Freddy Malins invited Mr. Browne into the cab. There was a good deal of confused talk, and then Mr. Browne got into the cab. The cabman settled his rug over his knees, and bent down for the address. The confusion grew greater and the cabman was directed differently by Freddy Malins and Mr. Browne, each of whom had his head out through a window of the cab. The difficulty was to know where to drop Mr. Browne along the route and Aunt Kate, Aunt Julia and Mary Jane helped the discussion from the doorstep with cross-directions and contradictions and abundance of laughter. As for Freddy Malins he was speechless with laughter. He popped his head in and out of the window every moment, to the great danger of his hat, and told his mother how the discussion was progressing till at last Mr. Browne shouted to the bewildered cabman above the din of everybody's laughter:

—Do you know Trinity College?

—Yes, sir, said the cabman.

—Well, drive bang up against Trinity College gates, said Mr. Browne, and then we'll tell you where to go. You understand now?

—Yes, sir, said the cabman.

—Make like a bird for Trinity College.

—Right, sir, cried the cabman.

The horse was whipped up and the cab rattled off along the quay amid a chorus of laughter and adieus.

Gabriel had not gone to the door with the others. He was in a dark part of the hall gazing up the staircase. A woman was standing near the top of the first flight, in the shadow also. He could not see her face but he could see the terracotta and salmonpink panels of her skirt which the shadow made appear black and white. It was his wife. She was leaning on the banisters, listening to something. Gabriel was surprised at her stillness and strained his ear to listen also. But he could hear little save the noise of laughter and dispute on the front steps, a few chords struck on the piano and a few notes of a man's voice singing.

He stood still in the gloom of the hall, trying to catch the air that the voice was singing and gazing up at his wife. There was grace and mystery in her attitude as if she were a symbol of something. He asked himself what is a woman standing on the stairs in the shadow, listening to distant music, a symbol of. If he were a painter he would paint her in that attitude. Her blue felt hat would show off the bronze of her hair against the darkness and the dark panels of her skirt would show off the light ones. *Distant Music* he would call the picture if he were a painter.

The hall-door was closed; and Aunt Kate, Aunt Julia and Mary Jane came down the hall, still laughing.

—Well, isn't Freddy terrible? said Mary Jane. He's really terrible.

Gabriel said nothing but pointed up the stairs towards where his wife was standing. Now that the hall-door was closed the voice and the piano could be heard more clearly. Gabriel held up his hand for them to be silent. The song seemed to be in the old Irish tonality and the singer seemed uncertain both of his words and of his voice. The voice, made plaintive by distance and by the singer's hoarseness, faintly illuminated the cadence of the air with words expressing grief:

> O, *the rain falls on my heavy locks*
> *And the dew wets my skin,*
> *My babe lies cold* . . .

—O, exclaimed Mary Jane. It's Bartell D'Arcy singing and he wouldn't sing all the night. O, I'll get him to sing a song before he goes.

—O do, Mary Jane, said Aunt Kate.

Mary Jane brushed past the others and ran to the staircase but before she reached it the singing stopped and the piano was closed abruptly.

—O, what a pity! she cried. Is he coming down, Gretta?

Gabriel heard his wife answer yes and saw her come down towards them. A few steps behind her were Mr. Bartell D'Arcy and Miss O'Callaghan.

—O, Mr. D'Arcy, cried Mary Jane, it's downright mean of you to break off like that when we were all in raptures listening to you.

—I have been at him all the evening, said Miss O'Callaghan, and Mrs. Conroy too and he told us he had a dreadful cold and couldn't sing.

—O, Mr. D'Arcy, said Aunt Kate, now that was a great fib to tell.

—Can't you see that I'm as hoarse as a crow? said Mr. D'Arcy roughly.

He went into the pantry hastily and put on his overcoat. The others, taken aback by his rude speech, could find nothing to say. Aunt Kate wrinkled her brows and made signs to the others to drop the subject. Mr. D'Arcy stood swathing his neck carefully and frowning.

—It's the weather, said Aunt Julia, after a pause.

—Yes, everybody has colds, said Aunt Kate readily, everybody.

—They say, said Mary Jane, we haven't had snow like it for thirty years; and I read this morning in the newspapers that the snow is general all over Ireland.

—I love the look of snow, said Aunt Julia sadly.

—So do I, said Miss O'Callaghan. I think Christmas is never really Christmas unless we have the snow on the ground.

—But poor Mr. D'Arcy doesn't like the snow, said Aunt Kate, smiling.

Mr. D'Arcy came from the pantry, full swathed and buttoned, and in a repentant tone told them the history of his cold. Everyone gave him advice and said it was a great pity and urged him to be very careful of his throat in the night air. Gabriel watched his wife who did not join in the conversation. She was standing right under the dusty fanlight and the flame of the gas lit up the rich bronze of her hair which he had seen her drying at the fire a few days before. She was in the same attitude and seemed unaware of the talk about her. At last she turned towards them and Gabriel saw that there was color on her cheeks and that her eyes were shining. A sudden tide of joy went leaping out of his heart.

—Mr. D'Arcy, she said, what is the name of that song you were singing?

—It's called *The Lass of Aughrim*, said Mr. D'Arcy, but I couldn't remember it properly. Why? Do you know it?

—*The Lass of Aughrim*, she repeated. I couldn't think of the name.

—It's a very nice air, said Mary Jane. I'm sorry you were not in voice tonight.

—Now, Mary Jane, said Aunt Kate, don't annoy Mr. D'Arcy. I won't have him annoyed.

Seeing that all were ready to start she shepherded them to the door where good-night was said:

—Well, good-night, Aunt Kate, and thanks for the pleasant evening.

—Good-night, Gabriel. Good-night, Gretta!

—Good-night, Aunt Kate, and thanks ever so much. Good-night, Aunt Julia.

—O, good-night, Gretta, I didn't see you.

—Good-night, Mr. D'Arcy. Good-night, Miss O'Callaghan.

—Good-night, Miss Morkan.

—Good-night, again.

—Good-night, all. Safe home.

—Good-night. Good-night.

The morning was still dark. A dull yellow light brooded over the houses and the river; and the sky seemed to be descending. It was slushy underfoot; and only streaks and patches of snow lay on the roofs, on the parapets of the quay and on the area railings. The lamps were still burning redly in the murky air and, across the river, the palace of the Four Courts stood out menacingly against the heavy sky.

She was walking on before him with Mr. Bartell D'Arcy, her shoes in a brown parcel tucked under one arm and her hands holding her skirt up from the slush. She had no longer any grace of attitude but Gabriel's eyes were still bright with happiness. The blood went bounding along his veins; and the thoughts went rioting through his brain, proud, joyful, tender, valorous.

She was walking on before him so lightly and so erect that he longed to run after her noiselessly, catch her by the shoulders and say something foolish and affectionate into her ear. She seemed to him so frail that he longed to defend her against something and then to be alone with her. Moments of their secret life together burst like stars upon his memory. A heliotrope envelope was lying beside his breakfast-cup and he was caressing it with his hand. Birds were twittering in the ivy and the sunny web of the curtain was shimmering along the floor: he could not eat for happiness. They were standing on the crowded platform and he was placing a ticket inside the warm palm of her glove. He was standing with her in the cold, looking in through a grated window at a man making bottles in a roaring furnace. It was very cold. Her face, fragrant in the cold air, was quite close to his; and suddenly she called out to the man at the furnace:

—Is the fire hot, sir?

But the man could not hear her with the noise of the furnace. It was just as well. He might have answered rudely.

A wave of yet more tender joy escaped from his heart and went coursing in warm flood along his arteries. Like the tender fires of stars moments of their life together, that no one knew of or would ever know of, broke upon and illumined his memory. He longed to recall to her those moments, to make her forget the years of their dull existence together and remember only their moments of ecstasy. For the years, he felt, had not quenched his soul or hers. Their children, his writing, her household cares had not quenched all their souls' tender fire. In one letter that he had written to her then he had said: *Why is it that words like these seem to me so dull and cold? Is it because there is no word tender enough to be your name?*

Like distant music these words that he had written years before were borne towards him from the past. He longed to be alone with her. When the others had gone away, when he and she were in their room in the hotel, then they would be alone together. He would call her softly:

—Gretta!

Perhaps she would not hear at once: she would be undressing. Then something in his voice would strike her. She would turn and look at him. . . .

At the corner of Winetavern Street they met a cab. He was glad of its rattling noise as it saved him from conversation. She was looking out of the window and seemed tired. The others spoke only a few words, pointing out some building or street. The horse galloped along wearily under the murky morning sky, dragging his old rattling box after his heels, and Gabriel was again in a cab with her, galloping to catch the boat, galloping to their honeymoon.

As the cab drove across O'Connell Bridge Miss O'Callaghan said:

—They say you never cross O'Connell Bridge without seeing a white horse.

—I see a white man this time, said Gabriel.

—Where? asked Mr. Bartell D'Arcy.

Gabriel pointed to the statue, on which lay patches of snow. Then he nodded familiarly to it and waved his hand.

—Good-night, Dan, he said gaily.

When the cab drew up before the hotel Gabriel jumped out and, in spite of Mr. Bartell D'Arcy's protest, paid the driver. He gave the man a shilling over his fare. The man saluted and said:

—A prosperous New Year to you, sir.

—The same to you, said Gabriel cordially.

She leaned for a moment on his arm in getting out of the cab and while standing at the curbstone, bidding the others good-night. She leaned lightly on his arm, as lightly as when she had danced with him a few hours before. He had felt proud and happy then, happy that she was his, proud of her grace and wifely carriage. But now, after the kindling again of so many memories, the first touch of her body, musical and strange and perfumed, sent through him a keen pang of lust. Under cover of her silence he pressed her arm closely to his side; and, as they stood at the hotel door, he felt that they had escaped from their lives and duties, escaped from home and friends and run away together with wild and radiant hearts to a new adventure.

An old man was dozing in a great hooded chair in the hall. He lit a candle in the office and went before them to the stairs. They followed him in silence, their feet falling in soft thuds on the thickly carpeted stairs. She mounted the stairs behind the porter, her head bowed in the ascent, her frail shoulders curved as with a burden, her skirt girt tightly about her. He could have flung his arms about her hips and held her still for his arms were trembling with desire to seize her and only the stress of his nails against the palms of his hands held the wild impulse of his body in check. The porter halted on the stairs to settle his guttering candle. They halted too on the steps below him. In the silence Gabriel could hear the falling of the molten wax into the tray and the thumping of his own heart against his ribs.

The porter led them along a corridor and opened a door. Then he set his unstable candle down on a toilet-table and asked at what hour they were to be called in the morning.

—Eight, said Gabriel.

The porter pointed to the tap of the electric-light and began a muttered apology but Gabriel cut him short.

—We don't want any light. We have light enough from the street. And I say, he added, pointing to the candle, you might remove that handsome article, like a good man.

The porter took up his candle again, but slowly for he was surprised by such a novel idea. Then he mumbled good-night and went out. Gabriel shot the lock to.

A ghostly light from the street lamp lay in a long shaft from one window to the door. Gabriel threw his overcoat and hat on a couch and crossed the room towards the window. He looked down into the street in order that his emotion might calm a little. Then he turned and leaned against a chest of drawers with his back to the light. She had taken off her hat and cloak and was standing before a large swinging mirror, unhooking her waist. Gabriel paused for a few moments, watching her, and then said:

—Gretta!

She turned away from the mirror slowly and walked along the shaft of light towards him. Her face looked so serious and weary that the words would not pass Gabriel's lips. No, it was not the moment yet.

—You looked tired, he said.

—I am a little, she answered.

—You don't feel ill or weak?

—No, tired: that's all.

She went on to the window and stood there, looking out. Gabriel waited again and then, fearing that diffidence was about to conquer him, he said abruptly:

—By the way, Gretta!

—What is it?

—You know that poor fellow Malins? he said quickly.

—Yes. What about him?

—Well, poor fellow, he's a decent sort of chap after all, continued Gabriel in a false voice. He gave me back that sovereign I lent him and I didn't expect it really. It's a pity he wouldn't keep away from that Browne, because he's not a bad fellow at heart.

He was trembling now with annoyance. Why did she seem so abstracted? He did not know how he could begin. Was she annoyed, too, about something? If she would only turn to him or come to him of her own accord! To take her as she was would be brutal. No, he must see some ardor in her eyes first. He longed to be master of her strange mood.

—When did you lend him the pound? she asked, after a pause.

Gabriel strove to restrain himself from breaking out into brutal language about the sottish Malins and his pound. He longed to cry to her from his soul, to crush her body against his, to overmaster her. But he said:

—O, at Christmas, when he opened that little Christmas-card shop in Henry Street.

He was in such a fever of rage and desire that he did not hear her come from the window. She stood before him for an instant, looking at him strangely. Then, suddenly raising herself on tiptoe and resting her hands lightly on his shoulders, she kissed him.

—You are a very generous person, Gabriel, she said.

Gabriel, trembling with delight at her sudden kiss and at the quaintness of her phrase, put his hands on her hair and began smoothing it back, scarcely touching it with his fingers. The washing had made it fine and brilliant. His heart was brimming over with happiness. Just when he was wishing for it she had come to him of her own accord. Perhaps her thoughts had been running with his. Perhaps she had felt the impetuous desire that was in him and then the yielding mood had come upon her. Now that she had fallen to him so easily he wondered why he had been so diffident.

He stood, holding her head between his hands. Then, slipping one arm swiftly about her body and drawing her towards him, he said softly:

—Gretta dear, what are you thinking about?

She did not answer nor yield wholly to his arm. He said again, softly:

—Tell me what it is, Gretta. I think I know what is the matter. Do I know?

She did not answer at once. Then she said in an outburst of tears:

—O, I am thinking about that song, *The Lass of Aughrim*.

She broke loose from him and ran to the bed and, throwing her arms across the bed-rail, hid her face. Gabriel stood stock-still for a moment in astonishment and then followed her. As he passed in the way of the cheval-glass he caught sight of himself in full length, his broad, well-filled shirt-front, the face whose expression always puzzled him when he saw it in a mirror and his glimmering gilt-rimmed eyeglasses. He halted a few paces from her and said:

—What about the song? Why does that make you cry?

She raised her head from her arms and dried her eyes with the back of her hand like a child. A kinder note than he had intended went into his voice.

—Why, Gretta? he asked.

—I am thinking about a person long ago who used to sing that song.

—And who was the person long ago? asked Gabriel, smiling.

—It was a person I used to know in Galway when I was living with my grandmother, she said.

The smile passed away from Gabriel's face. A dull anger began to gather again at the back of his mind and the dull fires of his lust began to glow angrily in his veins.

—Someone you were in love with? he asked ironically.

—It was a young boy I used to know, she answered, named Michael Furey. He used to sing that song, *The Lass of Aughrim*. He was very delicate.

Gabriel was silent. He did not wish her to think that he was interested in this delicate boy.

—I can see him so plainly, she said after a moment. Such eyes as he had: big dark eyes! And such an expression in them—an expression!

—O then, you were in love with him? said Gabriel.

—I used to go out walking with him, she said, when I was in Galway.

A thought flew across Gabriel's mind.

—Perhaps that was why you wanted to go to Galway with that Ivors girl? he said coldly.

She looked at him and asked in surprise:

—What for?

Her eyes made Gabriel feel awkward. He shrugged his shoulders and said:

—How do I know? To see him perhaps.

She looked away from him along the shaft of light towards the window in silence.

—He is dead, she said at length. He died when he was only seventeen. Isn't it a terrible thing to die so young as that?

—What was he? asked Gabriel, still ironically.

—He was in the gasworks, she said.

Gabriel felt humiliated by the failure of his irony and by the evocation of this figure from the dead, a boy in the gasworks. While he had been full of memories of their secret life together, full of tenderness and joy and desire, she had been comparing him in her mind with another. A shameful consciousness of his own person assailed him. He saw himself as a ludicrous figure, acting as a pennyboy for his aunts, a nervous well-meaning sentimentalist, orating to vulgarians and idealizing his own clownish lusts, the pitiable fatuous fellow he had caught a glimpse of in the mirror. Instinctively he turned his back more to the light lest she might see the shame that burned upon his forehead.

He tried to keep up his tone of cold interrogation but his voice when he spoke was humble and indifferent.

—I suppose you were in love with this Michael Furey, Gretta, he said.

—I was great with him at that time, she said.

Her voice was veiled and sad. Gabriel, feeling now how vain it would be to try to lead her whither he had purposed, caressed one of her hands and said, also sadly:

—And what did he die of so young, Gretta? Consumption, was it?

—I think he died for me, she answered.

A vague terror seized Gabriel at this answer as if, at that hour when he had hoped to triumph, some impalpable and vindictive being was coming against him, gathering forces against him in its vague world. But he shook himself free of it with an effort of reason and continued to caress her hand. He did not question her again for he felt that she would tell him of herself. Her hand was warm and moist: it did not respond to his touch but he continued to caress it just as he had caressed her first letter to him that spring morning.

—It was in the winter, she said, about the beginning of the winter when I was going to leave my grandmother's and come up here to the convent. And he was ill at the time in his lodgings in Galway and wouldn't be let out and his people in Oughterard were written to. He was in decline, they said, or something like that. I never knew rightly.

She paused for a moment and sighed.

—Poor fellow, she said. He was very fond of me and he was such a gentle boy. We used to go out together, walking, you know, Gabriel, like the way they do in the country. He was going to study singing only for his health. He had a very good voice, poor Michael Furey.

—Well; and then? asked Gabriel.

—And then when it came to the time for me to leave Galway and come up to the convent he was much worse and I wouldn't be let see him so I wrote a letter saying I was going up to Dublin and would be back in the summer and hoping he would be better then.

She paused for a moment to get her voice under control and then went on:

—Then the night before I left I was in my grandmother's house in Nuns' Island, packing up, and I heard gravel thrown up against the window. The window was so wet I couldn't see so I ran downstairs as I was and slipped out the back into the garden and there was the poor fellow at the end of the garden, shivering.

—And did you not tell him to go back? asked Gabriel.

—I implored him to go home at once and told him he would get his death in the rain. But he said he did not want to live. I can see his eyes as well as well! He was standing at the end of the wall where there was a tree.

—And did he go home? asked Gabriel.

—Yes, he went home. And when I was only a week in the convent he died and he was buried in Oughterard where his people came from. O, the day I heard that, that he was dead!

She stopped, choking with sobs, and, overcome by emotion, flung herself face downward on the bed, sobbing in the quilt. Gabriel held her hand for a moment longer, irresolutely, and then, shy of intruding on her grief, let it fall gently and walked quietly to the window.

She was fast asleep.

Gabriel, leaning on his elbow, looked for a few moments unresentfully on her tangled hair and half-open mouth, listening to her deep-drawn breath. So she had had that romance in her life: a man had died for her sake. It hardly pained him now to think how poor a part he, her husband, had played in her life. He watched her while she slept as though he and she had never lived together as man and wife. His curious eyes rested long upon her face and on her hair: and, as he thought of what she must have been then, in that time of her first girlish beauty, a strange friendly pity for her entered his soul. He did not like to say even to himself that her face was no longer beautiful but he knew that it was no longer the face for which Michael Furey had braved death.

Perhaps she had not told him all the story. His eyes moved to the chair over which she had thrown some of her clothes. A petticoat string dangled to the floor. One boot stood upright, its limp upper fallen down: the fellow of it lay upon its side. He wondered at his riot of emotions of an hour before. From what had it proceeded? From his aunt's supper, from his own foolish speech, from the wine and dancing, the merry-making when saying good-night in the hall, the pleasure of the walk along the river in the snow. Poor Aunt Julia! She, too, would soon be a shade with the shade of Patrick Morkan and his horse. He had caught that haggard look upon her face for a moment when she was singing *Arrayed for the Bridal*. Soon, perhaps, he would be sitting in that same drawing-room, dressed in black, his silk hat on his knees. The blinds would be drawn down and Aunt Kate would be sitting beside him, crying and blowing her nose and telling him how Julia had died. He would cast about in his mind for some words that might console her, and would find only lame and useless ones. Yes, yes: that would happen very soon.

The air of the room chilled his shoulders. He stretched himself cautiously along under the sheets and lay down beside his wife. One by one they were all becoming shades. Better pass boldly into that other world, in the full glory of some passion, than fade and wither dismally with age. He thought of how she who lay beside him had locked in her heart for so many years that image of her lover's eyes when he had told her that he did not wish to live.

Generous tears filled Gabriel's eyes. He had never felt like that himself towards any woman but he knew that such a feeling must be love. The tears gathered more thickly in his eyes and in the partial darkness he imagined he saw the form of a young man standing under a dripping tree. Other forms were near. His soul had approached that region where dwell the vast hosts of the dead. He was conscious of, but could not apprehend, their wayward and flickering existence. His own identity was fading out into a grey impalpable world: the solid world itself which these dead had one time reared and lived in was dissolving and dwindling.

A few light taps upon the pane made him turn to the window. It had begun to snow again. He watched sleepily the flakes, silver and dark, falling obliquely against the lamplight. The time had come for him to set out on his journey westward. Yes, the newspapers were right: snow was general all over Ireland. It was falling on every part of the dark central plain, on the treeless hills, falling softly upon the Bog of Allen and, farther westward, softly falling into the dark mutinous Shannon waves. It was falling, too, upon every part of the lonely churchyard on the hill where Michael Furey lay buried. It lay thickly drifted on the crooked crosses and headstones, on the spears of the little gate, on the barren thorns. His soul swooned slowly as he heard the snow falling faintly through the universe and faintly falling, like the descent of their last end, upon all the living and the dead.

Acknowledgments

ACKNOWLEDGMENTS

"Define This Word" by M. F. K. Fisher from *The Art of Eating* is reprinted with the permission of Macmillan Publishing Company. Copyright © 1936 by M. F. K. Fisher, renewed by Mary Kennedy Freide.

"The Continental Angle" by Zelda Fitzgerald. Reprinted with permission of Charles Scribner's Sons, an imprint of Macmillan Publishing Company. From *Zelda Fitzgerald: The Collected Writings*, edited by Matthew J. Bruccoli. Copyright © 1932 by the F.-R. Publishing Corporation; renewal copyright © 1959 by Frances Scott Fitzgerald Lanahan. Originally appeared in *The New Yorker*.

"On Murdering Eels and Laundering Swine" by Betty Fussell from *Antaeus: Not for Bread Alone*. Copyright © 1992 by Antaeus. Reprinted by permission of Betty Fussell.

Excerpt from *The Wind in the Willows* by Kenneth Grahame, first published in 1908.

"Madame Vache" by William Hamilton, copyright © 1989. Reprinted by permission of William Hamilton.

"Bird Hunting" by Jim Harrison, copyright © 1991. Reprinted by permission of Jim Harrison.

"Hunger Was Good Discipline" by Ernest Hemingway is reprinted by permission of Charles Scribner's Sons, an imprint of Macmillan Publishing Company, from *A Moveable Feast*, copyright © 1964 by Mary Hemingway; renewal copyright © 1992 by John Hemingway, Patrick Hemingway, and Gregory Hemingway.

"All You Can Eat" by Robin Hemley from *All You Can Eat*, copyright © 1988. Reprinted by permission of Atlantic Monthly Press.

"The Announcement" from *Fling and Other Stories* by John Hersey. Copyright © 1990 by John Hersey. Reprinted by permission of Alfred A. Knopf, Inc.

"A Feeder in France" by Jay Jacobs from *A Glutton for Punishment: Confessions of a Mercenary Eater*, copyright © 1990 by Jay Jacobs. Reprinted with permission of Atlantic Monthly Press.

"The Dead" from *Dubliners* by James Joyce. Copyright © 1916 by B. W. Heubsch. Definitive text copyright © 1967 by the Estate of James Joyce. Used by permission of Viking Penguin, a division of Penguin Books USA Inc.

ACKNOWLEDGMENTS

"A Good Appetite" by A. J. Liebling from *Between Meals: An Appetite for Paris* is reprinted by permission of Russell and Volkening as agents for the author. Copyright © 1962 by A. J. Liebling, © copyright renewed 1990 by Norma Liebling Stonehill.

"The Three Fat Women of Antibes" by W. Somerset Maugham from *The Complete Short Stories of W. Somerset Maugham*. Reprinted by permission of A. P. Watt Ltd. on behalf of The Royal Literary Fund.

Excerpt from "January" from *A Year in Provence* by Peter Mayle, copyright © 1990 by Peter Mayle. Reprinted with permission of Alfred A. Knopf, Inc.

"The Evils of Spain" from *Complete Collected Stories* by V. S. Pritchett. Copyright © 1990 by V. S. Pritchett. Reprinted by permission of Random House, Inc.

Excerpt from *Gravity's Rainbow* by Thomas Pynchon. Copyright © 1973 by Thomas Pynchon. Used by permission of Viking Penguin, a division of Penguin Books USA Inc.

"Short Friday," from *Short Friday and Other Stories* by Isaac Bashevis Singer, copyright © 1964 by Isaac Bashevis Singer. Translated by Joseph Singer and Roger Klein. Copyright © renewed 1992 by Alma Singer. Reprinted by permission of Farrar, Straus and Giroux, Inc.

"I Took *Die Kur*" from *Villas at Table* by James Villas. Copyright © 1988 by James Villas. Reprinted by permission of HarperCollins Publishers Inc.

"His Father's Earth" by Thomas Wolfe from *The Complete Short Stories of Thomas Wolfe*. Copyright © 1937, 1938, 1939 by Maxwell Perkins, Executor. Renewal 1967, by Paul Gitlin, Administrator, C.T.A.

"Smorgasbord" by Tobias Wolff, copyright © 1987 by Tobias Wolff. Reprinted by permission of Tobias Wolff. First appeared in *Esquire*.

Excerpt from *To the Lighthouse* by Virginia Woolf, copyright © 1927 by Harcourt Brace and Company and renewed 1954 by Leonard Woolf, reprinted by permission of Harcourt Brace and Company and Hogarth Press.

The Repentant Thief
Taverna